The Shutout in Major League Baseball

ALSO BY WARREN N. WILBERT
AND FROM McFARLAND

*The Arrival of the American League: Ban Johnson and the
1901 Challenge to National League Monopoly* (2007)

*What Makes an Elite Pitcher? Young, Mathewson, Johnson,
Alexander, Grove, Spahn, Seaver, Clemens, and Maddux* (2003)

A Cunning Kind of Play: The Cubs-Giants Rivalry, 1876–1932 (2002)

*The Best of Baseball: The 20th Century's
Greatest Players Ranked by Position* (2001)

Rookies Rated: Baseball's Finest Freshman Seasons (2000)

BY WARREN N. WILBERT AND WILLIAM C. HAGEMAN

*The 1917 White Sox: Their World
Championship Season* (McFarland, 2004)

The Shutout in Major League Baseball
A History

Warren N. Wilbert

McFarland & Company, Inc., Publishers
Jefferson, North Carolina, and London

LIBRARY OF CONGRESS CATALOGUING-IN-PUBLICATION DATA

Wilbert, Warren N.
    The shutout in Major League baseball : a history / Warren N. Wilbert.
      p.   cm.
    Includes bibliographical references and index.

    ISBN 978-0-7864-6851-5
    softcover : acid free paper ∞

    1. Baseball—United States—History. 2. Shutouts (Sports)—United States—History. I. Title.
    GV873.W545 2013
    796.357'22—dc23   2013002279

BRITISH LIBRARY CATALOGUING DATA ARE AVAILABLE

© 2013 Warren N. Wilbert. All rights reserved

No part of this book may be reproduced or transmitted in any form or by any means, electronic or mechanical, including photocopying or recording, or by any information storage and retrieval system, without permission in writing from the publisher.

Front cover design by David K. Landis (Shake It Loose Graphics)

Manufactured in the United States of America

McFarland & Company, Inc., Publishers
  Box 611, Jefferson, North Carolina 28640
    www.mcfarlandpub.com

To the Nebraska State High School Champions
of 1957 and to Ethan Warren Hale

Acknowledgments

The supporting cast is spare — but brilliant! Among those who stepped up and cleared the bases, there were several folks who patiently and skillfully worked with me to clean up the numbers, the manuscript and a number of places where what was said could, and should have been much better said. Their work was a substantial part of whatever success *The Shutout in Major League Baseball* might encounter. Chief among these were veteran baseball historians Bill Deane and Walt Wilson, who, as always, were ready and able to protect the record books from mistakes I'm so prone to make.

Ed Reed, sports editor of the Fort Myers *News-Press*, gave generously of his time and resources at the *News-Press* to help review the perfect game played at Palms Park between the Boston Red Sox and the Toronto Blue Jays, carried in their March 15, 2000, issue.

Dave Smith, Retrosheet's Generalisimo, was, as per usual, not only prompt, but creative with his answers to my inquiries. Once the numbers have been checked and verified by Smith & Co., historians know that their assertions go into print with authority and accuracy.

Two Texans helped immeasurably. One of them, Joe Stanka, took the time, after talking with me about it, to share his likeness in his NPB livery, helping dress up that section considerably. The other, Larry Dierker, spent quite a bit of time via email and conversations, discussing his career and his "assignment," that of writing the Foreword to this book, and he did so in a generous spirit of helpfulness.

Thanks to all of these fine people the book finally came together. There is, however, one more note of thanks due to two very special people in my life, daughters Ellen and Karen. Always encouraging and always there, especially when needed, they are special blessings to an old baseball warrior.

God go with all of you!

Table of Contents

Acknowledgments — vi
Prologue — 1
Introduction — 5

1. May 4, 1871: 2–0 ... With More to Come — 11
2. A Shutout in the Making — 20
3. The Nineteenth Century Shutout Story — 30
4. Grubby Baseballs and Shutout Artistry — 39
5. From the 1920s to the 1940s — 46
6. There's a War Going On ... and After — 51
7. The Shutout During an Era of Transition: 1961–1984 — 61
8. The Modern Era: 1985–2010 — 73
9. Shutouts in Other Leagues and Venues — 84
10. Zeroes in the Ballbag — 111
11. The No-No — 130
12. Perfection — 151
13. With One Swat — 158
14. Shutout Summitry — 179

Appendix A: The First One — 187
Appendix B: From 50' to 60'6" — 191
Appendix C: Crushed and Chicagoed — 192
Selected Bibliography — 195
Name Index — 199

Prologue

America's bicentennial year, 1976, was one long gala celebration. It was a time to celebrate just about anything and everything Americana dating back to its 1776 roots, and that necessarily included the national pastime, baseball. Shortly after the glitter of the July 4 parades, concerts and colorful fireworks, on July 9, to be exact, Larry Dierker and his Houston teammates staged a bici celebration of their own with a no-hit conquest of the Montreal Expos, 6–0. Now that's the way to throw a shutout!

Dick Peebles, who covered the game for the *Houston Chronicle,* summed up the evening's festive occasion this way:

> In winning his eighth game of the season against as many losses, Dierker threw mostly fastballs, mixing in an occasional slider. In the late innings he smelled a no-hit game. Dierker was really throwing smoke. His fast ball was rising and he challenged every hitter that came to the plate.
>
> Dierker finished with eight strikeouts, two of them in the ninth inning as the crowd was standing and cheering his every move. The Astros exploded in one loud roar when Mike Jorgensen grounded to first baseman Bob Watson for the final out.

For ballplayers, and for most fans rooting for the home team, for that matter, it doesn't get much better. It may happen but once in a career, but when it does—look out! Let the party begin!

In this book, "the party" is a celebration of one of baseball's premier events, the shutout, which also includes no-hit and perfect games. As I got to thinking about it, I thought I might ask Larry Dierker to share some of his experiences, insights and feelings about what it takes to put together a shutout (to say nothing of a no-hit ball game!). The former Astro's pitcher, and later manager, responded graciously and in midseason form. The following, by Larry himself, is what he shared.

> To begin with, if you want to pitch a shutout you have to get through the first inning. That's the first and biggest stumbling block. You have to face the top of the lineup and you'd better be ready. If a guy like Lou Brock or Rickey Henderson gets on to start the game [Ed. Today we would say a player like Ichiro

Suzuki], you can lose it right there. Or if a three or four hitter hits one out, it's over.

I usually felt like I could finish it after the seventh inning unless I had thrown a ton of pitches or if it was extremely hot and humid. At that stage of the game, I knew what pitches were working and I was less likely to make a mistake and throw the ball over the middle of the plate.

To prepare for the first inning, I spent the last five minutes of my warm-up imagining I was facing the other team's lineup. I would mix my pitches up and move them around in the strike zone. Then I had my eight pitches on the game mound to get ready. Often the game mound was a little steeper, or it would be flatter than the bullpen mound.

On a windy day the wind affected the movement of my pitches a little differently than it did in the bullpen. I felt that those preliminary pitches were important so that I could get situated before the first hitter stepped in. Once the game started I could usually use the warm-up pitches between innings just to stay loose. If the game kept on moving right along I really didn't have to bear down, but if I had to sit on the bench a long time during a rally, I warmed up for the next frame just like I warmed up for the very first one. Later, when I was managing, I reminded our pitcher to bear down on his warm-ups if he had to sit for 15 or more minutes whether he had a shutout going or not.

A couple of impressive shutouts I witnessed during my career were the 24-inning game with the Mets and Kerry Wood's 20-strikeout game at Wrigley Field. Tom Seaver started the 24-inning game for the Mets and Don Wilson started for us. In bonus frames, after great pitching by Seaver and Wilson, the pitching got even better. Jim Ray had perhaps his best day in the majors, striking out 11 in seven innings of relief pitching. Ron Swoboda struck out five times in ten at-bats, and Tommie Agee four times in ten. Both went 0-for-10. And we won the game when Norm Miller scored from third with two out in the bottom of the 24th on a grounder Bob Aspromonte hit right at shortstop Al Weis. It went right through his legs. We might still be playing!

I had pitched the day before and when it got past 20 innings I went back to the clubhouse to get ready to pitch if necessary. The Mets used eight pitchers that night and we used five.

The game at Wrigley*: Talk about overpowering! Wood's fastball was riding [Ed. had movement as it came to the plate] and we were lucky to pop it up. His breaking stuff was even nastier and he was throwing it even though he was behind in the count! The only hit we got was a bouncer between third and short. Ricky Gutierrez hit it and Kevin Orie should have caught it, but he didn't. It could have been the greatest game ever pitched.

On September 13, 1969, the Atlanta Braves beat us in a 13-inning game that was, in my opinion, the best shutout game I ever pitched aside from the no-hit game in 1976. I was shooting for my 20th win, trying to beat Phil Niekro. I had great stuff and great control. I did walk a few batters [4] but not because I was wild. I just didn't want to give them anything to hit. Despite the fact that I knew I had a no-hitter going into the ninth inning and my 20th win in the

---

On May 6, 1998, Kerry Wood defeated the Houston Astros, 2–0, striking out 20 batters to tie the single game strikeout record. He struck out the heart of the Houston batting order three times each. Larry Dierker was the manager of the Astros at the time.— W.N.W.

offing, my focus was on winning the game. It was the only year in my 12 at Houston when we had a chance to win the Division. That was paramount. With two out in the bottom of the ninth I threw Felix Milan a slider and he chopped it into the hole at short. Denis Menke tried to make a running throw because he didn't have time to plant himself solidly and throw. It was a close play, but it was scored as a hit. After that I gave up a hit in the 10th, 11th and 12th, but no runs. John Mayberry batted for me in the 13th and walked, and we scored twice. I was thrilled. I was going to win my 20th with a 12-inning shutout and we were going to close to within a game of first place. But it wasn't to be. We wound up losing in Atlanta's half of the 13th as they scored three times to win, 3–2. But I did get another chance at a no-hitter.

In 1976 the no-hitter finally happened. Into the eighth and ninth innings of that game I threw nothing but four-seam fastballs and we won it, 6–0. After the game, I was asked when I first realized I had a no-hitter going and I truthfully replied, "Right after the first inning. I remember walking to the dugout, trying to remember the last time I had gotten through the first inning unscathed!"

The no-hitter I pitched against the Expos in 1976 was a thrilling moment in my career. But there were 24 shutouts more in my resume and at least one more where I pitched more than nine innings without giving up a run but didn't get a decision. And I remember that there were a few good ones around, like Mike Cuellar and Claude Osteen and Gaylord Perry, who threw a few shutouts of their own — and lost a few just like I did. But Warren Wilbert has searched the shutout archives and organized them into a fascinating journey that I'm sure you'll enjoy. Get ready to enjoy the trip!

Introduction

Shutout. By definition, a game in which a team prevents its opponent from scoring. In major league baseball that happens approximately ten times for every 100 games played — a shutout is rare enough to cause baseball fans to sit up and take notice. And within the framework of this artistic achievement there are degrees of perfection that mark the event as sheer drama as the game nears its ninth inning climax and the final out.

The epitome of this extraordinary accomplishment, the perfect game, is rarer still, gracing the pages of baseball history with heroic exploits of peerless fielding, incredible pitching and the combined efforts of a team that turns its talent into a work of baseball artistry.

On March 14, 2000, it was my good fortune to attend a perfect game at Fort Myers, the Spring Training base of the Boston Red Sox. It was one of those days just meant for a ball game, with fair skies and the warmth of a Florida sun. There were some 7,000 old timers and grandkids on hand to take in a ball game, featuring the Toronto Blue Jays and the home-standing Red Sox. Pedro Martinez was slated to start for the Bosox against the Jays' Nerio Rodriguez, and the two of them

Larry Dierker.

proceeded through the first three innings without giving up a run, Martinez shutting down nine straight, and Rodriguez almost as effective, allowing only a scratch hit and one free pass in his three-inning stint.

I can remember remarking to the fellow sitting next to me that I was looking for a little more bombast from the likes of Nomar Garciaparra and his Boston teammates, but that I could settle for some good pitching at the start of the game. He ventured that Pedro was tough at any time, and that this youngster Rodriguez looked like he was ready to head north.

So we settled in to see what the next pitchers could do. Martinez was followed by Fernando De La Cruz, who notched two more perfect innings, while his teammates nicked Toronto pitching for a couple of markers. After Dan Smith's perfect inning, the sixth, the stands began to buzz in anticipation of a possible no-no. Wouldn't that be something special — and at a Spring Training game at that?!

Two popouts and a groundout later, Boston had a 3–0 lead and the perfect game, furthered by Rheal Cormier, became a stronger possibility. Through seven, Toronto had nary a hit nor run — not even a base on balls — to show for its efforts.

By this time the crowd was edging forward with each pitch, abuzz in "great expectations." It isn't every day that a no-hitter comes along, much less a perfect game, and to see that happen during a Spring Training game was, well, next to unbelievable. The City of Palms Park fans, many of them far more knowledgeable about things baseball than the pros at ESPN might expect, were ready for more! There was electricity in the air.

Rich Garces took to the hill to see what he could do about stretching Boston's no-hitter another inning. Toronto found his slants as mystifying as his predecessors', retiring meekly on a groundout, a strikeout and a nice play on a fly ball. By this time the Carmines had a 5–0 lead and the outcome of the game was no longer in any doubt. But the perfecto?

That was left in the hands of relief specialist Rod Beck, who, by virtue of two K's and a pop fly, subdued Toronto yet again. The stands exploded with cheers for the rarity Beck closed out. Six Bosox hurlers had forged an 11–K masterpiece that included but three groundouts along with 13 fly balls for the 27 consecutive outs necessary to call the game Perfect! As Nomar Garciaparra, whose three-run blast had put his ball club in front to stay, remarked after the game, "The fans who came out got their money's worth, that's for sure!"

The Fort Myers *News-Press* coverage of the game featured a full spread with this headline: Red Sox Already Perfect, So Why Play the Season? The article noted that there had been a Spring Training no-hit game in 1996, but that there was no prior record of a perfect game. So the rarity was officially recorded as the first of its kind, if not in all of Spring Training history, at least at City of Palms Park.

One of the interesting observations in the article was made by Boston manager Jimy Williams, who commented that he didn't remember ever having personally seen a perfect game. Coming from a baseball coach and manager who was in his 35th season of professional baseball, that is quite a statement, and attests to the rarity of the perfect game!

True, perfect games are thrown in regular season play, authored by stars of the distant past like Cy Young and Addie Joss, and more recently by Randy Johnson and Roy Halladay, and some 14 others including Don Larsen, who crafted the only no-hit and perfect game masterpiece in World Series history. They met the requirements for retiring 27 consecutive hitters. Though there have been games in which more than one pitcher has been used to toss a no-hitter, pitchers receive credit for no-hit and perfect games only if they go the route.

Shutouts of the more common "garden variety" seem a bit pedestrian after talking about perfect games, but they are among baseball's more choice accomplishments, and their relative rarity, at around ten per 100 games played, has been noted by sports writers like John Kuenster in the July 1, 2005, issue of *Baseball Digest* as "jewels" in the pitching trade.

That makes them worthy of closer scrutiny, and it brings us to the focal point of this book: the history and development of the shutout. It might be best to begin rather close to the beginning, which would be the 1860s. During those years the conventions, courtesies and regulations that governed baseball were vastly different from those we're accustomed to today. The breakthrough of national baseball popularity coincided with the Civil War years, and in the late 1860s the game began to turn away from its amateur status to professionalized play, emphasizing skilled performance and winning teams. Originally, games had been played in the genteel atmosphere of friendly club settings, among fraternal teams more concerned about gentlemanly behavior and hospitality in vying with one another than in winning games, or winning at all costs. Runs were scored by the dozens as pitchers made it their business to accommodate rather than retire the hitter, giving hitters—strikers as they were called—every chance to drive the ball into a generously bounded playing field. To be held scoreless in a game was practically unheard of, and the first such event, which occurred on November 8, 1860, became a major sports headline in the nation's newspapers. Multi-talented Jim Creighton, who stood head and shoulders above ball players of his day, authored that stunner in a victory that was forged on an autumnal, all-victorious tour of Eastern city teams by the Brooklyn Excelsiors.

To the great dismay of many baseball pioneers, the customs and conventions of those more simplistic days soon faded under the relentless competitive spirit of a new baseball age that featured "reimbursement for services rendered," better known these days as pay for play. To be sure, paying baseball players, even then, was not uncommon. But the phenomenon changed everything. Profoundly. Teams were banded into leagues; skillful, if not artistic, pitching became important; and winning ball games became *le principal*. So it was that by 1871 the first league of professional baseball banded nine teams together, all of whom paid every player on their teams. That league became known as the National Association of Professional Base Ball Players (referred to throughout this book as the NA). The NA established a whip flag as the championship trophy for the most successful team in the league. And, inevitably, the dynamics and conduct of the game took on a demanding style of play that players and sports-minded aficionados supported enthusiastically, much to the chagrin of the "Old Guard."

Because the shutout was a rarity throughout amateur and professional baseball, it was an event that drew special attention. As the first games of the NA dawned there weren't many who expected the outcome of what was to become pro ball's inaugural contest, complete with local dignitaries and a new grandstand at its ballpark, to result in a low-scoring, shutout game.

Bobby Mathews, winner of 297 major league games.

The NA opener, played in Fort Wayne, Indiana, a small northwestern hamlet situated at the summit of the St. Joe, St. Mary and Maumee Rivers, was exactly that, a taut, lean baseball affair resulting in the now-historic Mathews blanking at the expense of the Cleveland professionals.

On a cloudy, dank and foreboding day in May 1871, the Fort Wayne Kekiongas hosted the Cleveland Forest Citys, defeating them 2 to 0, in a well-played game won by the mighty Baltimorian, little Bobby Mathews, a stripling possessed of a wicked breaking ball that baffled Cleveland hitters, putting Fort Wayne into the record books as the first professional baseball team to register a shutout in league play.

Fantastico! The game must have amazed even its competitors. Cleveland's "Uncle Al" Pratt pitched creditably, allowing but two Fort Wayners to cross the plate in a briskly played game that ended just a few moments before the heavens unloaded torrential rains, sending the good burghers of Fort Wayne, population 17,718, scurrying for cover.

The news made its way eastward, where the Boston and Philadelphia teams were idled by a day-long rain that postponed their league's inaugural, thus enabling the Cleveland and Fort Wayne teams to share the honor of playing the NA's first game. One can only imagine what went through the minds of baseball enthusiasts in those long-established baseball capitals of the Eastern Seaboard, denied the honor they must have felt should have been theirs. But Mother Nature ordained otherwise, finally nodding their way in June of that eventful first year, when both New York and Boston inflicted shutouts (there were four during the NA's first season of play) on visiting teams.

From Bobby Mathews, a youthful 20 at the time of his famous shutout, to Madison Bumgarner, equally youthful (21), and the San Francisco Giants who twice blanked the Texas Rangers in the 2010 World Series, major league teams have shut out their opponents in about 10 percent of the total number of games played in major league baseball. That's not minuscule, but it is surely significant, significant enough to cause raised eyebrows, especially in this modern era when most players with a bat in their hands are home run threats.

In order to get at the ins and outs of shutout play, we've put together a resource base consisting of every last shutout thrown from the beginning of professional baseball to the 2010 World Series, and from which are drawn the stories and significant moments that make up this very special part of baseball lore. The story line travels over some 140 seasons. That's a lot of ball games. Between regular season, post-season, All-Star games and games played in other leagues beside America's major leagues, there are enough of these engaging contests to keep the hot stove league busy for years to come!

It should be noted at the outset that there is a difference between a shutout credited to a pitcher and a *shutout game.* The shutout game, lasting from five to as many extra innings as needed to complete the contest, a tie notwithstanding, differs from the pitcher's shutout in that the starting pitcher must pitch every inning in the contest, that is, a complete game, to be credited with a shutout. Across the years of major league play the number of individual pitchers' shutouts has steadily dwindled under the influence of ever more scientific approaches to the pitching (and relief pitching) art. The season that completes this review, 2010, for example, totaled 127 shutout games in the American League. However, there were but 21 pitchers among the league's 14 teams who threw shutouts, and three teams, Baltimore, New York and Texas, went the entire season without a pitcher recording a shutout. Dare we remind one and all that there was a time when it was *de rigueur* to have a pitcher on nearly every team's pitching staff in the league who posted anywhere from five to ten and more, and sometimes more than one on the same staff who threw that many shutouts in a single season?

Please note that the emphasis in this book, the shutout, does not preclude discussions, stories and special events highlighting pitchers whose skill and artistry brought shutouts and perfect games into prominence as a notably exceptional part of the game.

Note also, if you will, that there are more than a few no-hit games in which the losing team scored at least one run; these are *not* included in this review. While acknowledging that the pitchers, from Bobby Mathews to Roy Halladay, the first major league pitcher to throw a no-hitter in a post-season playoff game, are, inevitably, pivotal variables in these shutout episodes, it is well to note that there is much more to the shutout story.

I hope that you can someday share (perhaps you already have) my good fortune and experience a shutout — or perhaps a no-hitter or even a perfect game — and get the feel of a rare baseball "happening"! But if that hasn't been your lot, perhaps this gathering of shutout gems will ease the pain of missing something big under The Big Tent!

1

May 4, 1871: 2–0 ... With More to Come

Only a decade removed from the opening salvos of the Civil War, the National Association (NA), America's first professional baseball league, inaugurated play on May 4, 1871, at Fort Wayne, Indiana. On the following two days games were played, in Washington on the fifth and in Rockford, Illinois, on the sixth. Chicago's home opener, which drew an estimated 5,000 fans on May 8, featured the Cleveland Forest Citys, who had opened Fort Wayne's season, and would journey from Chicago to Rockford to complete their first western swing of the season. Those openers were as auspicious as the times and circumstances would permit, replete with parades, opening ceremonies, grandstands dressed up in bunting, and flags waving in springtime warmth.

As previously noted, the league's opening encounter produced professional baseball's very first shutout. That in and of itself was sensational, to say nothing of the opening of a fully professional league of baseball teams. However, the NA made its beginning amid skepticism, misgivings and some hostility, most sporting people believing that a professional band of baseball warriors, trooping from city to city, would soon make a bad situation among baseball's amateurs—who were wary of the professionals already in their ranks—worse yet. Many believed that, given the times and the lingering enchantment with a gentleman's game played in the bucolic setting of a town's park or nearby field, the amateurs' game was the only way to restore order and to preserve the grand old pastime's integrity. The pioneering professionals thought otherwise.

Note the use of that term professional. The newly formed professional teams and some of the leagues of the nineteenth century, especially the NA, were simply not considered major league as we use the term in the modern era of baseball. Although the record books include the NA's five-year statistics along with its history, there is an aversion among baseball historians and researchers to label the caliber of its play as "major league."

The view from this corner is that the state of the art existing during the years of the NA *was,* in modern parlance, *what it was,* just as the state of the art during modern times *is what it is.* That is why this account starts out as it does with the shutout record of the National Association.

As long as tickets are sold and the best players and leagues available are competing for championships, the upper tier of the professional game might just as well be recognized as major league. It is interesting to note that the record books include the NA in their reviews alongside several other major leagues, tacitly implying that it was the first major league.

You, dear reader, will have to make up your mind about this baseball conundrum. There is no lack of baseball literature covering the NA and nineteenth-century major league history. That will surely help you come to your own, and personally satisfying conclusion. But we have digressed long enough. On to the shutout story and the pitching art as it evolved in the NA.

A summary review of the five years of NA baseball follows, including some of its essential league statistics. The WH/9 column in the table below lists walks and hits per nine innings, and LFA designates *league* fielding average among other numbers that tell us something about the quantity and, further, about the quality of play as it affects the shutout.

To make a comparison with the modern era, the National League's 2005 season numbers have been added.

	Tms	*Gms*	*SHO*	*SHO%*	*CG*	*WH/9*	*LFA*
1871	9	127	4	3.15	231	14.0	.833
1872	11	183	11	6.01	327	13.0	.837
1873	9	199	8	4.02	362	13.2	.830
1874	8	232	15	6.47	439	11.8	.827
1875	13	345	51	14.78	621	10.3	.849
NL2005	16	1297	148	11.41	104	12.8	.983

The numbers for the years 1871 and 1875 that fairly jump from this table are 4 and 51. They illustrate the sharp rise in shutout categories during the five-season history of the NA. Whereas in 1871 there were but four shutouts thrown in the league's 127 games, there were 51 out of 345 games by the 13 teams in 1875. Those 1875 figures represent a 14.8 shutout percentage, approximating major league statistics during its halcyon shutout eras.

The table's last two columns give an indication: (WH/9) of the pitcher's ability to limit the opposing team's scoring opportunities by the number of baserunners per nine innings he allowed (the lower the number, the fewer chances to score); and (LFA) an indication of the support pitchers received because of increasingly more defensive play. You will note that there is an enormous difference between the NA's fielding average (around the .840

mark), and the .983 registered by the National League in 2005. That factors out to far fewer errors, considerably fewer scoring opportunities, and significantly higher, more capable defensive play. Skills, equipment, facilities, playing fields, strategies, training and coaching have undergone improvement and refinement through the years, of course, and the grand old game has evolved into a highly scientific chess match, especially with regard to pitching. All of that plays a significant role in preventing a team's opponent from scoring.

The previous table tells its own singular story. The following NA pitching log tells us more about the shutout story between 1871 and 1875. Winning and losing pitchers are recorded; no score is given for losing teams since all games are shutouts.

Designations for the 25 teams in the 1871–75 NA follow:

BaltC	Baltimore Canaries	NY	New York Mutuals
BaltM	Baltimore Marylands	PhlA	Phil. Athletics
Bos	Boston Red Stockings	PhlC	Phil. Centennials
BrkA	Brooklyn Atlantics	PhilP	Phil. Pearls
BrkE	Brooklyn Eckfords	PhilW	Phil. White Stockings
Chi	Chicago White Stockings	Rock	Rockford Forest Citys
Clv	Cleveland Forest Citys	StLB	St. Louis Browns
Eliz	Elizabeth (NJ) Resolutes	StLR	St. Louis Reds
FtW	Fort Wayne (IN) Kekiongas	Troy	Troy Haymakers
Hart	Hartford Dark Blues	WashB	Washington Blue Legs
Keo	Keokuk (IA) Westerns	WashN	Washington Nationals
Mans	Middletown Mansfields	WashO	Washington Olympics
NH	New Haven Elm Citys		

NA 1871

Games Played: 127
Shutouts: 4
Shutout % of Games Played: 3.15

Date/At	Tm/Score/WP	Tm/LP
5/4 at FtW	FtW 2, Mathews	Clv, Pratt

This was the first of Bobby Mathews' 297 professional victories.

6/21 at Bos	Bos 21, Spalding	FtW, Mathews

(See special chapter on shutouts won by 18–0 scores and more.)

6/28 at NY	NY 13, Wolters	FtW, Mathews
8/3 at Rock	Rock 4, Fisher	FtW, Mathews

NA 1872

Games Played: 183
Shutouts: 11
Shutout % of Games Played: 6.01

Date/At	Tm/Score/WP	Tm/LP
4/18 at WashO	BaltC 16, Fisher (7 inn. game)	WashO, Brainard
4/26 at Troy	Troy 10, Zettlein	Mans, Bentley
4/29 at NY	NY 12, Cummings	Mans, Bentley

Candy Cummings won 33 of the 34 New York Mutuals victories in 1872.

5/9 at BrkA	Bos 20, Spalding	BrkE, McDermott
6/6 at Bos	Bos 7, Spalding	BaltC, Mathews
6/8 at Phl	PhlA 19, McBride	NY, Cummings
7/1 at Bos	Bos 17, Spalding	Clv, Pratt
7/13 at NY	NY 8, Cummings	PhlA, McBride

The Athletics managed only five hits as Cummings avenged a 19–0 shellacking a month earlier in Philadelphia, defeating ten-year veteran and Philadelphia favorite Dick McBride.

7/23 at Mans	Troy 7, Zettlein	Mans, Bentley
9/14 at NY	NY 7, Cummings	BrkA, Britt
10/5 at Bos	Bos 10, Spalding	PhlA, McBride

Al Spalding, who had won 19 of Boston's 20, 1871 victories, won 22 of his first 23 games in 1872, finishing with a 38–8 record.

NA 1873

Games Played: 199
Shutouts: 8
Shutout % of Games Played: 4.02

Date/At	Tm/Score/WP	Tm/LP
5/17 at PhlA	PhlA 12, McBride	NY, Mathews
6/2 at BrkE	Bos 5, Spalding	BrkE, Britt
6/14 at Bos	PhlA 3, McBride	Bos, Spalding
6/27 at BaltM	BaltC 20, Cummings	BaltM, Stratton
6/28 at Brk	BrkE 10, Britt	Eliz, Campbell
8/16 at Phl	PhlA 14, McBride	WashB, Stearns

Dick McBride, who was the Philadelphia Athletics' manager, led the NA in shutouts during the 1873 season with three.

9/2 at NY	NY 9, Mathews	WashB, Greason
10/10 at NY	NY 7, Mathews	BaltC, Brainard

Bobby Mathews shut down the Canaries on two hits in this 7–0 shutout, the day after Baltimore had exploded for 29 runs on 32 hits in a 29–4 rout of Brooklyn's Atlantics.

NA 1874

Games Played: 232
Shutouts: 15
Shutout % of Games Played: 6.47

1. May 4, 1871: 2–0 ... With More to Come   15

Date/At	Tm/Score/WP	Tm/LP
4/22 at BaltC	Phl 13, Cummings	BaltC, Brainard
5/8 at Bos	Bos 14, Spalding	BaltC, Brainard
5/13 at Chi	Chi 4, Zettlein	PhlA, McBride

More than 4,000 fans turned out to see the first professional game played in Chicago since the disastrous Great Fire of 1871. Though the Athletics got to George Zettlein for 8 hits and 16 base-runners, Zettlein was tough enough in the tight spots to prevail for the White Stockings.

5/29 at Bos	Bos 8, Spalding	PhlP, Cummings
5/30 at NY	NY 2, Mathews	BrkA, Bond

Ten thousand fans crammed the stands at Union Park in New York to watch the Mutuals edge the Brooklyn Atlantics, 2–0. Atlantics first baseman Herman Dehlman had 21 putouts as the Mutes constantly grounded Tommy Bond's breaking pitches into the dirt outs.

6/1 at PhlP	PhlP 10, Cummings	BrkA, Bond
6/4 at Phl	PhlP 2, Cummings	NY, Mathews
7/9 at Hart	NY 14, Mathews	Hart, Fisher
8/29 at Chi	Chi 4, Zettlein	BaltM, Manning
8/31 at NY	NY 4, Mathews	BrkA, Bond
9/1 at Hart	NY 14, Mathews	Hart, Fisher
9/14 at Bos	Chi 10, Zettlein	Bos, Spalding
10/1 at Bos	Bos 29, Spalding	BrkA, Bond

This was the highest shutout score in the history of professional baseball. A combination of 30 Brooklyn errors, 26 Boston hits and Al Spalding's five-hit pitching produced the most lopsided blanking ever.

10/6 at NY	NY 3, Mathews	PhlA, McBride
10/20 at Brk	BrkA 5, Bond	NY, Mathews

Eighteen-year-old Tommy Bond came within one out of throwing professional baseball's first no-hitter but had to settle, finally, for a two-hit shutout victory.

NA 1875

Games Played: 345
Shutouts: 51
Shutout % of Games Played: 14.78

The 1875 chronology of shutouts is presented by teams listed in order of their finish at season's end, and does not include teams without shutouts during 1875: New Haven, Washington, Philadelphia Centennials, Brooklyn Atlantics, and Keokuk.

Date/At	Tm/Score/WP	Tm/LP
4/19 at Bos	Bos 6, Spalding	NH, Nichols

Season opener (1,200 attendance) at Boston, the second shutout opener in NA history, and the first of 71 league victories in a 71–8 record, with an .899 winning percentage, highest championship record in baseball history.

5/1 at Wash	Bos 24, Spalding	Wash, Stearns

5/17 at Bos	Bos 12, Spalding	PhlA, McBride
5/24 at Phl	Bos 5, Spalding	PhlC, Bechtel
6/17 at Bos	Bos 11, Spalding	Hart, Bond
7/5 at Hart	Bos 7, Spalding	Hart, Bond
7/17 at Bos	Bos 6, Spalding	Chi, Zettlein
9/3 at PhlA	Bos 16, Spalding	PhlA, McBride
9/25 at Hart	Bos 6, Spalding	Hart, Bond

Al Spalding, Boston's ace throughout the NA's history, was an incredible 54–5 winner in 1875, including 16 shutouts and a composite 156–41, .792 winning percentage record during his five-season NA career.

5/8 at Hart	Hart 16, Cummings	WashN, Stearns
5/17 at BrkA	Hart 5, Cummings	BrkA, Clinton
5/21 at NY	Hart 1, Cummings	NY, Mathews

Candy Cummings was a 35-game winner in 1875. Hartford, with a second-place, 54–28 record, picked up another 19 wins from teenager Tommy Bond. (All other major league 1–0 games are listed in the Gems chapter.)

6/11 at NH	Hart, 12, Cummings	NH, Luff
6/14 at Nart	Hart 10, Cummings	NH, Ryan
6/26 at StLB	Hart 9, Bond	StLB, Blong
7/14 at Hart	Hart 8, Bond	PhlP, Fisher
8/6 at BrkA	Hart 13, Bond	BrkA, Clinton
8/10 at Hart	Hart 7, Bond	NY, Mathews

Jim Holdsworth's leadoff single in the first inning was the only hit given up by Tommy Bond in this game. It was the first one-hitter on record.

8/20 at BrkA	Hart 2, Bond	BrkA, Cassidy
9/13 at StLR	Hart 3, Bond	StLB, Bradley
10/4 at NH	Hart 18, Cummings	NH, Nichols
10/18 at Hart	Hart 5, Cummings	StLB, Bradley

It was left to Candy Cummings to throw the last shutout in the National Association's history, defeating George Bradley on October 18 at Hartford.

5/3 at Wash	PhlA 21, McBride	WashN, Stearns
5/11 at BrkA	PhlA 5, McBride	BrkA, Clinton
6/9 at PhlA	PhlA 23, McBride	BrkA, Cassidy
7/22 at PhlA	PhlA 9, McBride	NY, Mathews
8/27 at Chi	PhlA 5, McBride	Chi, Devlin
10/2 at PhlA	PhlA 14, McBride	NY, Mathews
5/6 at StLB	StLB 10, Bradley	Chi, Zettlein
5/29 at StLB	StLB 6, Bradley	StLR, Blong

5,000 attended this contest, a four-hit shutout at the Grand Avenue Grounds, later known as Sportsman Park. Winner George Bradley won 33 of the St. Louis Brown Stockings' 39 1875 victories.

6/21 at StLB	StLB 2, Bradley	PhlP, Fisher
7/23 at NH	StLB, 6, Bradley	NH, Nichols
9/11 at StLB	StLB, 6, Bradley	Hart, Bond
5/5 at BrkA	PhlP 8, Fisher	BrkA, Cassidy

5/10 at NH	PhlP 13, Fisher	NH, Nichols
7/28 at PhlP	PhlP 4, Borden	Chi, Golden

In his second major league start, 21-year-old-rookie Joe Borden whipped the dangerous White Stockings, 4–0, in the first no-hitter recorded in pro ball's history. He authored another significant first in 1876, opening the National League's inaugural season with a 6–5 win for Boston in its debut game at Philadelphia before 3,000 on April 22 in the nation's centennial year.

8/9 at StLR	PhlP 16, Borden	StLR, Galvin
9/23 at Chi	PhlP 5, Zettlein	Chi, Devlin
5/22 at NY	NY 4, Mathews	BrkA, Clinton

Diminutive Bobby Mathews faced only 28 batters in one-hitting the Mutuals' crosstown rival Brooklyn Atlantics. He would go on to win 21 of New York's 30 victories in 1876. His career record in the NA was 131–112.

8/13 at NH	NY 4, Mathews	NH, Nichols
5/27 at Chi	Chi 15, Zettlein	StLR, Blong
6/3 at Chi	Chi 8, Zettlein	NY, Mathews

This two-hitter was one of seven shutouts "The Charmer," handsome George Zettlein, threw in 1875. He was a five-year NA veteran who tossed 12 shutouts in the league's five seasons, including a 1–0 masterpiece against the St. Louis Reds on May 11 of the 1875 season, the lowest scoring game in professional baseball history to that point.

6/7 at Chi	Chi 14, Zettlein	NY, Mathews
6/8 at Chi	Chi 2, Zettlein	Bos, Spalding
8/5 at PhlP	Chi 2, Golden	PhlP, Borden
6/27 at StLR	StLR 3, Blong	WashN, Parks
7/3 at StLR	StLR 8, Morgan	WashN, Parks

From the first shutout thrown on May 4, 1871, to the last in the NA on October 18, 1875, when two famous pitchers of the game's earliest years, Candy Cummings and George Bradley, dueled in a 4–0 Hartford conquest of the St. Louis Brown Stockings, National Association teams became the first to venture into the rarified atmosphere of low-hit and no-hit games, one of baseball's supreme achievements.

During its first season, there were, *in toto*, but 19 NA hurlers. They pitched from a six-foot-square box at ground level some 45 feet from the batter at home plate. The plate was a 12-inch square of stone or marble. This quaint arrangement (compared to the venues and measurements of modern times) set the stage for the confrontation between hitters like Cap Anson, Ross Barnes and Joe Start, and the Al Spaldings and Dick McBrides of that pioneering era, when pitchers were restricted to delivering the ball with a stiffened wrist and an underhand motion. The task was even more challenging because batters called for high or low pitches to suit their hitting preferences. Small wonder that games were often nothing more than scoring bouts with teams tallying as many as 25 to 35 runs. But those stout-hearted hurlers did find ways and means on occasion to stifle the howitzers of earlier days, posting some of the exceptional outings recorded in the shutout log above.

Among the more accomplished of the NA pitchers were several who made the transition from the NA to the newly organized National League, which, under team-oriented auspices, rather than the player-dominated organization the National Association had been, debuted in 1876, picking up professional ball where the NA left off without losing a step. Most notable among these hurlers were Bobby Mathews, who logged ten seasons (with 10 shutouts) in the National League and the American Association, Tommy Bond, with seven seasons in the NL (35 shutouts), and George Bradley, whose service included eight seasons divided among National League, Union Association and American Association League teams (28 shutouts and the first no-hitter in NL history on July 15 of its very first season). The list must also include Al Spalding, whose electrifying 47–12 record (eight shutouts) paced the NL's first champions, the Chicago White Stockings. Admitted to the Hall of Fame in 1939 as a Pioneer, he might well have been enshrined as a player had he not cut short his pitching career to enter the sports equipment and publishing business. His baseball numbers had been nothing short of phenomenal.

By the time the National League had finished its first season, almost a half-century of amateur and professional baseball had gone by, and whatever doubts there had been about its place in American culture, or as an enterprise doomed by professionalism, were put to rest, never to be questioned again. Benjamin Rader, in his *Baseball: A History of America's Game* (Rader 1994, 35), summed up the background and framework for the shutouts, low-hit and no-hit games gathered in this review accordingly:

Al Spalding, who threw the first National League shutout, against Louisville on April 25, 1876.

> During the 1870s and 1880s the professional teams fully established their ascendancy over all of baseball. The Cincinnati Reds and dozens

of other clubs soon proved that full-time salaried players could nearly always outperform those players who held down other jobs during the playing season. Seizing mainly on urban rivalries, an assortment of civic boosters, small-time entrepreneurs, and politicians organized hundreds of professional and semi-professional teams.

Beyond organizational and cultural considerations, there were still other factors that affected the way the game was played and shutouts were thrown. Among the most important of these were the layout of the playing field and the rules that governed the game. For modern fans it is nearly impossible to imagine what a game was like in which pitchers were stationed only 45 feet from home plate and catchers were often positioned some 15 to 25 feet behind the batter. The 45-foot distance was increased first to 57 feet under rules crafted by the Players League for 1890, and then to its present distance at 60'6" in 1893. Each time these changes were made there were adjustments and dramatic changes in the performance of pitchers and hitters. Those and other changes, such as reducing the strike zone and lowering the pitching mound from 15" to 10" in 1969 made the game more attractive to spectators (hitters even more so), but each one had implications and consequences for pitchers, hitters and the record book.

In order to examine what these and other changes meant to nineteenth century hurlers and those who followed in their footsteps, we look next at some of the variables involved in putting together this unique event called the shutout.

2

A Shutout in the Making

Since professional baseball's first shutout in 1871 there have been 198,721 games played during regular season play in seven professional leagues, and 21,074 of them resulted in shutouts. That figures to 10.61 percent of the time. The numbers for the National League since its founding in 1876 are approximately similar, roughly 11 out of 100 games.

The American League averages around 10 percent, spanning the 110 seasons that it has been in existence. Those statistics have established the shutout's relative rarity among major league games. To bring these numbers up to the very recent past, the stats look like this:

Year	NLGP	NLSHO	NLSHO%	ALGP	ALSHO	ALSHO%
2001	1296	138	10.65	1133	89	7.86
2002	1294	153	11.82	1132	122	10.78
2003	1295	150	11.58	1135	109	9.60
2004	1295	136	10.50	1133	115	10.15
2005	1297	148	11.41	1134	113	9.96
2006	1295	136	10.50	1134	124	10.94
2007	1297	128	9.87	1134	115	10.14
2008	1294	143	11.05	1134	128	11.29
2009	1295	150	11.58	1135	123	10.84
2010	1296	202	15.59	1134	127	11.20

Whatever the numbers, and however stated, this scoreless event is something to behold, and when one considers the number of variables working together to bring it to a successful conclusion, there is even more of a sense of wonderment over the accomplishment. Following are a number of those variables at work.

The Rules of the Game

Baseball's rules, like those of other sports, provide the framework within which the game is played. The rule book is one of the more significant variables affecting the team's chances of scoring a shutout victory. Among baseball's rules, the distance from the pitcher's box to home plate ranks as one of the most significant. (See Appendix A for an interesting discussion about these distances.) In 1892 the 12-team National League resolved to move the pitcher's box from its 50' distance, to 60' 6" for the 1893 season. There were immediate consequences. In 1892 the NL recorded 92 shutouts, posting a league ERA of 3.28. The 1893 results were 43 shutouts and a 4.66 ERA.

In 1968, dubbed the "Year of the Pitcher" the MLB Rules Committee met in San Francisco and introduced three far-reaching changes for the 1969 season: (a) the pitcher's mound would be lowered from 15" to 10"; (b) the strike zone was redefined to its present height between the armpits and the top of the batter's knee; and (c) they enacted a stricter enforcement of the ban on foreign substances used by pitchers, enabling the umpires to eject pitchers in violation of the ruling. Again, there were immediate results in 1969:

II-3 League/Yr	Tms	GP	RUNS	HR	ERA	SHO
AL 1968	10	812	5532	1104	2.98	154
AL 1969	12	973	7960	1649	3.62	134
NL 1968	10	813	5577	891	2.99	185
NL 1969	12	973	7890	1470	3.60	166

Note these changes from 1968 to 1969: In the American League home runs increased by an average of 110 per team in 1968 to 137 in 1969 while the league ERA average went from 2.98 to 3.69, an increase of two-thirds of a run in 1969. In the NL, teams averaged about 560 runs per season in 1968, upping that number to around 660 in 1969. The NL's home run totals were up and the ERA significantly higher, as in the AL. The scheme of things as far as baseball's moguls were concerned was to enhance the offense, and one glance at these and other stats shows that their expectations were met. Beyond expectation.

Many of the rules and rule changes over the years have been intended to increase scoring or to place limitations on what a batter could do (using bats within limitations of length, circumference or composition). Restrictions were also legislated for pitchers, such as banning the use of substances or defacing the ball in one way or another that have an effect on the ball's movement toward the plate, or the distance a ball will travel when it is hit.

The nineteenth century was rife with rule changes, for example: legalizing the overhand pitch; changing the number of balls it would take to put a batter on base; and refining balk rules. But the one rule that surpassed all others in its effect on the game's outcome as well as the probability of the pitcher's throwing a shutout, was the ban on foreign substances in 1920 with the outlawing of the spitball, emory ball and other means of doctoring the ball. That ruling, combined with the use of a new ball put in play after having been marred, lost in the stands or dirtied in play, made for a new hitter's era, but simultaneously made for new pitching challenges in the pitcher's attempt to retire the hitter. The statistics of the post-deadball era, as with every era since, underscore the offensive upswing baseball has experienced since the 1920s. Exceptions have been rather rare, at least rare enough to have been labeled "The Year of the Pitcher!"

For the fan, there's nothing quite like a booming home run to spice up a game. That special sound of wood against cowhide that everyone in the stands recognizes as an extra-base crack of thunder has its special appeal — but not to the fellow out there on the mound. One such blast may ruin his game, his shutout, his no-no. Consequently, the rule book as it applies to hitter and pitcher is a very significant variable at work with every pitch thrown.

Team Defense

Many a shutout has been saved by a brilliant play afield, and many a shutout has been lost because a fielder threw to the wrong base or simply botched a play on an easy ground ball. More often than not the defense determines the fate of a shutout in the making. One such example of a more spectacular variety will help bring the defensive component into sharp focus.

Without Sandy Amoros, the Brooklyn Dodgers might not have won the 1955 World Series. Ahead by two runs in the sixth inning of the winner-takes-all seventh game of that fabled Series, Yogi Berra came to bat with two on and none out. Johnny Podres was in trouble. The Yanks had the makings of a rally with Berra, as dangerous a World Series competitor as ever lived, at bat. Walt Alston, the Dodgers skipper, didn't make a move in the dugout. He had already made his move by inserting journeyman utility player Sandy Amoros into the Dodgers outfield at the beginning of the sixth frame for defensive purposes to play Yankee Stadium's hazardous left field. Sure enough, Berra slashed a Podres breaking ball toward the line in left field that caught Amoros somewhat out of position, having been moved more toward left-center to play the hard-hitting Berra. Amoros then made one of the greatest defensive plays in World Series history, racing to the foul line to spear Berra's fly ball, extending his glove-hand as far as he could to make an incredible catch. But the play was not yet over.

The left-handed Amoros wheeled and threw to cutoff man Pee Wee Reese in short left field who, in turn, relayed Amoros' throw to Gil Hodges, doubling off Gil McDougald. A potential run-scoring, extra-base blow had been turned

2. A Shutout in the Making   23

into a doubled-up gem, and Podres soon got the third out to end the Yankees' threat. And, incidentally, the final score showed the series champion Dodgers with two and the Yankees zero. It was a magnificent shutout.

Catching the ball! That baseball fundamental, so spectacularly executed, was the first step in this extraordinary sequence. Throwing to cutoff man Reese followed, and the completion of the play, an accurate throw to the outstretched Hodges, finished the twin killing. Each of the fundamentals had to be executed to perfection to make that play work. And because the play was made, Podres' shutout remained intact.

Great defensive teams get that way by virtue of execution. It begins with seemingly endless drills in Spring Training, and the primary purpose of those drills is catching the ball, whether it be a ground ball, a line drive or a pop fly. Over and over, again and again, fielders are drilled in these most basic of fundamentals. Those drills, piling one repetition atop another, touching as many variations and possibilities as possible, do not end with Spring Training. They are part and parcel of baseball life all season long.

Although the quality of a team's defense is hard to measure, some of the statistics that are most frequently used at least give us an indication of a defense that is more efficient and hence more effective. Statistics like fielding average and ERA, often ridiculed as simplistic and probably unreliable in distinguishing between good and great defensive ball clubs, nonetheless point unmistakably in the right direction with respect to making some judgments as to whether team A is better at picking up the ball and throwing out potential base runners than team B.

In the following table an example, the 1959 American League championship team, Chicago's White Sox, is presented. First, the appropriate numbers:

WH/9	E	FA	SHO	OAV	ERA
12.3/?	130	.979/.977	13	.242/.253	3.29/3.86

KP: Wynn, Shaw, Staley, Lollar, Fox, Aparicio, Landis.

The Legend and comments follow:

WH/9/L: walks and hits per nine innings, and the league's average behind the slash mark.
E: errors committed during the 1959 season.
FA/L: The White Sox team fielding average followed by the league average.
SHO: Shutouts logged during the 1959 season.
OAV/L: Opponents' team batting average and league batting average.
ERA/L: Pitching staff Earned Run Average followed by league ERA.
KP: Key Players on defense (includes top pitchers and catcher(s), infielders and outfielders).

In the WH/9 column interested readers will be able to determine just how much better the White Sox were (almost one walk and hit less than the league average). They were .02 percentage points better than league-average fielding teams (further, they committed 130 errors against a league average 139). Opponents hit for a batting average of .242 (OAV/L) while the league averaged .253, and as for ERA, the Pale Hose posted a staff average of 3.29 against the league's 3.86.

The better defensive teams have fewer WH/9, higher fielding averages, lower OAV and lower ERA's. Some of the best fielding teams in the game's history follow below:

Tm/Yr	WH/9/LG	E	FA/L	SHO	OAV	ERA
Hart/1875	8.4/10.3	438	.881/.849	13	.228/.254	1.57/2.23
KP: Cummings, Bond, Allison, Burdock, Ferguson, York, Remsen						
Balt/1894	15.2/15.8	454	.923/.927	1	.299/.309	5.00/5.33
KP: McMahon, Gleason, W. Robinson, Brouthers, Jennings, McGraw, Keeler						
PhlAL/1911	12.5/12/6	225	.964/.963	13	.264/.273	3.01/3.34
KP: Coombs, Plank, Bender, I. Thomas, Collins, Baker, D. Murphy						
PitNL/1912	11.8/12.7	169	.972/.960	18	.251/.272	2.85/3.40
KP: Hendrix, Camnitz, G. Gibson, A. McCarthy, Wagner, Carey						
Wash/1932	13.0/13.6	125	.979/.969	10	.271/.277	4.16/4.48
KP: Crowder, Weaver, Marberry, Spencer, Cronin, Myers, Bluege, Manush						
Balt/1969	10.5/12.1	101	.984/.978	20	.223/.246	2.83/3.62
KP: Cuellar, McNally, Palmer, Hendricks, Belanger, B. Robinson, F. Robinson						
Cinc/1975	12.0/12.4	102	.984/.976	8	.257/.257	3.37/3.62
KP: Nolan, Billingham, P. Borbon, Bench, Morgan, Concepcion, Geronimo						
StL/1985	11.2/12.0	108	.983/.983	20	.246/.252	3.10/3.59
KP: Tudor, Andujar, Forsch, O. Smith, Herr, Coleman, McGee, Van Slyke						
NYNL/1999	12.6/13.3	68	.989/.980	7	.252/.268	4.27/4.56
KP: Leiter, Hershiser, Benitez, Piazza, Ordonez, Ventura, Henderson						
Bos/2007	11.8/13.	81	.986/.984	13	.247/.271	3.87/4.50
KP: Matsuzaka, Beckett, Schilling, Papelbon, Youkilis, Pedroia, Crisp, Drew						

These teams put the brakes on their opponents' scoring potential with superior fielding, digging balls out of the dirt, running down potential extra-base hits, throwing to the right bases—accurately—and playing the hitters (and their tendencies) according to the pitch count. Put all of that together with an offense sufficient to score when it counts, and it's more likely that a shutout is on the way. If the defense is as good as those in the table above, it's likely that a pennant is on the way. That proved to be the case for six of the ten teams above.

The Battery

Catcher and Pitcher. A team within the team. This unit is the single most significant factor in the likelihood of a shutout. While some might insist that the most important component in a shutout is the pitcher alone, or that perhaps the role of the defense is understated and worthy of prime consideration in this regard, it is the author's opinion that the two players who initiate every play of the game ultimately hold its fate in their own hands.

A listing of baseball's exceptional batteries would include among its very best: Buck Ewing and Amos Rusie; Christy Mathewson and Roger Bresnahan; Yogi Berra and Whitey Ford; Dwight Gooden and Gary Carter; and Mickey Cochrane and Lefty Grove. These few scratch the tip of the iceberg, but through them, we are able to get an insight into the characteristics that make for superior achievement.

Using the Cochrane-Grove battery as an example, it is interesting to note, even before getting into things like mechanics, mental toughness, or strategy, that these two fellows were intensely competitive. Their fire and mettle was a driving force behind everything they did. How the long-suffering Connie Mack, who brought both to Philadelphia the same year, 1925, and then was faced with the more-than-challenging task of managing them, survived their hot-headed incandescence is beyond imagination. You have no doubt heard of the odd couple. This was the *Tres Sui Generis* that was nonetheless the heart and soul of those 1929–31 Philadelphia A's champions, one of the most accomplished baseball aggregations in baseball history.

The website Baseball Page (thebaseballpage.com/players/Cochrane/p.2 of 3), in its biographical write-up of Cochrane, describes him this way, touching both on his personality and considerable ability:

> Equally important was the receiver's (Cochrane's) ability to handle the A's pitching staff, which included the temperamental Lefty Grove. Perhaps Cochrane understood Grove better than most since he shared the lefthander's volatile disposition, competitive nature, and strong distaste for losing. Outfielder Doc Cramer, who played with both men on the A's, discussed the fierce temper of his former teammates when he said, "Lose a one-to-nothing game, and you didn't want to get into the clubhouse with Grove and Cochrane. You'd be ducking stools and gloves and bats and whatever would fly."

It is left to your imagination (and conjure the worst) to picture in your mind what happened in the heat of a 1931 summer day in St. Louis after Lefty and Mickey lost to the Browns, 1–0, breaking Grove's 16-game winning streak. It was a shutout, all right, but it didn't bring with it the W for Grove most might have expected. It wasn't the first 1–0 game Grove ever lost, but it was no doubt the most galling of them all. That it prevented him from establishing a new record for most consecutive wins by an American League pitcher was probably the least of the matter. The bitter fact of the matter was that he not only lost—to the lowly Browns, puddling along some 35 games behind the front-running A's, which no doubt made the loss all the more provoking—but it came about because, according to Grove, Al Simmons wasn't there to play left field. Jimmy Moore was inserted in the lineup to play left field, batting fourth in Simmons' place.

All went well—for two innings. Then it happened. In the third inning Oscar Melillo smashed a line drive to left field with Fred Schulte aboard. Poor Jimmy somehow managed to play the sinking drive into a two-bagger that scored Schulte, simultaneously lighting the fires of Grove's wrath. There was no way to cool off the seething Grove. How he managed to get through the rest of the game without blowing up Sportsman's Park is one of 1931's greater mysteries, but there was indeed an aftermath.

The visiting locker room took Grove's searing heat in one of his more lengthy and vehement tirades. Not even Cochrane could do anything with him. And Connie Mack? Well, the wise old saint simply let the storm blow itself out, as he had done not a few times before.

Unfortunately, the Browns' Dick Coffman, who turned in a magnificent effort, was lost in the shuffle of the latest Grove escapade. His three-hit masterpiece, though gleefully heralded in both St. Louis newspapers the next day, simply went down as a victory, a momentary blip in Philadelphia's march to the pennant. Just two weeks before he had one-hit the White Sox, which gave notice that he was "in the zone." Coffman that summer joined Grove, Lefty Burke of the Senators and Wes Ferrell of the Indians as authors of some of the best low-hit games of the season, the latter two

Quite possibly the greatest southpaw ever: Lefty Grove (Brace photograph).

having thrown no-hitters. It was one of the finer pitching efforts of the year, and a shutout rarity (there were only 49 thrown that season in the American League for a 7.92 percentage of all games played), and one of but seven 1–0 games in the American League in 1931.

The catalogue of catcher responsibilities is crammed with more things to master than the rest of the team combined. Some of those responsibilities include: calling pitches; setting a target; blocking home plate (one of baseball's more brutal plays); moving out to the mound to participate in discussions about which pitches to throw, changing signals, or just calming the pitcher in stressful situations; knowing what pitches to call in certain situations with certain hitters, discussing with both skipper and hurler the batting order they will face, as well as dealing with special circumstances, for example, dangerous base stealers; knowing the strengths, weaknesses and idiosyncracies of each pitcher on the staff; and adjusting to how the umpire behind the plate calls a game. And that by no means exhausts the list. To say that it is also expected of the catcher to contribute to the team's offensive efforts seems a little much to tack on to all the rest, but it should be added that weak-hitting catchers then, as now, were not really in demand.

For the best of this genre Mickey Cochrane comes close to topping a list that would include the catchers mentioned above, plus Lance Parrish, Ivan "Pudge" Rodriguez, Roy Campanella, Johnny Bench, Bill Dickey, "Gabby" Hartnett, Jim Sundberg, Jerry Grote, Carlton Fisk, Jim Hegan, and Ray Schalk — among still others. All of these catchers were great athletes, strong-armed, team leaders and great in the clubhouse.

The other half of the battery, more conspicuous by position on the field of play than any other player, is the pitcher, the fellow whose every pitch, base on balls, wild pitch, win, shutout, strikeout, and award is counted and recorded with infinite, meticulous care. If there is going to be a shutout, much less a no-hit game, this chap with his pitching bag of tricks will be in the middle of it. While it isn't necessary to have the exceptional, white-hot intensity of a Grove, an Early Wynn or a Bob Gibson, the great ones are competitors to the marrow of their bones. That's where shutout victories start, are put together and ultimately completed. Perseverance, focus, and knowledge are equally important, adding to the mental and emotional makeup necessary to work through the tight spots that are a part of most supreme accomplishments.

The best of the lot are usually the ones who "live on the black," consistently throwing strikes grazing the last of the 17 inches (plus a few more outside that edge) that make up the width of the pentagonal surface of home plate. Greg Maddux, with impeccable control, was just such an excellent example. Hitting the far edge of the strike zone, combined with his ever-

"The Professor," aka "Mad Dog," Greg Maddux (Brace photograph).

increasing knowledge of each hitter he faced, brought his practiced skills and studied approach to a fine art and 355 victories. "The Professor," as he will forever be known in baseball lore, also had another mental dimension going for him in his Hall of Fame, 23-year career: he pitched with consummate smarts, mixing spots, speeds and pitches. Over the course of a career studded with league-leading marks, he hurled 35 shutouts, leading the NL five times.

Doug Myers and Mark Gola, in their 2000 Mountain Lion treatise, titled *The Louisville Slugger Complete Book of Pitching* (Meyers and Gola, 2000, 221), assert that

> Greg Maddux will drive batters nuts by working them differently each time he faces them in a ball game. As a result, he actually gets tougher to hit as the game goes along, and if you don't get to him in the first inning you might not get to him at all.

In 1998 Maddux was involved in seven of Atlanta's 23 shutouts, credited with five of them himself. On August 6 he shut down Cincinnati on three hits, all singles. Two double plays backed up his masterful pitching, as he faced but 29 batters, striking out six and walking nary a Red. On a great day at the workplace even for Mr. Maddux, the Atlanta ace was on his A-game, keeping hitters off-balance while bedeviling them with his assortment of pitches and arm angles. The game went into the record books as a 5–0 shutout, a sterling exhibition of what it takes to put a string of nine goose eggs on the board.

    If you want to see a shutout some nice summer day, or evening, your chances will improve appreciably if you pick a ball game featuring a pitcher with super control who knows what he's doing on the mound and can throw a fast one that looks like an aspirin tablet. Add to that a tough-minded, rifle-armed catcher, a sturdy defense behind the Randy Johnson or Nolan Ryan you've picked, and sit back as the innings roll by while your team gets a run or two and those other guys go down 1–2–3. Ought to be a shutout, something like 3 or 4 to zip.

3

The Nineteenth Century Shutout Story

During the last two seasons of the National Association it became increasingly evident that its troubling arrangements with teams and players, and serious financial complications, among still other vexing problems, would surely cause its demise. The end came long before the final game was played, a Boston conquest of Hartford on October 30, 1875. Long before, William Hulbert, with the assistance of Al Spalding, who had agreed to do his pitching for Chicago in 1876, charted the course for a league of teams that would dominate contractual, administrative and playing arrangements, in short, everything to do with its off-the-field and playing field affairs.

Hulbert wasted no time in chartering the new league, making certain that all involved would follow the president's directives out of a central office located in his own Chicago, and operate through individual franchise officials who would enforce a new constitution that enabled teams, rather than individual players and stars, to run the show. Having seen how "revolvers," that is, players who left one team for another, which regularly caused one team to gain advantage over another by offering a star player more money, had raised havoc with their illegal moves (equally to blame were team officials who offered contracts knowing that these players were already under binding agreements), Hulbert was determined to prevent that from happening again. Though there were a host of other things that needed change, contractual agreements became a much more reliable and settling influence throughout the newly minted National League.

With teams in eight cities, each of them except Hartford a larger metropolitan center, the National League was better situated for financial stability than its predecessor, the NA. The first venture into the new league's 1876 schedule occurred on April 22, before some 3,000 fans in the nation's Centennial City, Philadelphia. Five months and 260 games later, Chicago, a juggernaut that bullied its way to a championship with 52 wins out of 66 games, wound up its season on September 27, defeating Hartford, 16–10. That day two old NA hands did the pitching, Al Spalding, who won his 47th game, and Candy Cummings, who that season won 16 and lost 8 behind second-place Hartford's Tommy Bond (31–13).

Spalding, with 19 of Boston's 20 wins in the National Association's 1871 maiden season, saw to it that his Chicago White Stockings would start out the same way his old league began its inaugural season, with a shutout. As a matter of fact, Spalding started with the first two shutouts in NL history. David Nemec, respected nineteenth century baseball historian, detailed those first NL moments in his *Great Encyclopedia of 19th-Century Major League Baseball* (Nemec, 1997) in an insert "p. 86" captioned "The 'Chicago' King":

> In 1876 a shutout was still a rarity and was called a "Chicago," dating from a humiliating 9–0 loss suffered by the original Chicago White Stockings in 1870. Chicago's Al Spalding began the 1876 season with two straight shutouts against Louisville but the "Chicago" king that year turned out not to be Spalding. Though he logged eight shutouts to break a major league record he and two other hurlers— George Zettlein and Candy Cummings— had set a year earlier in the final NA season, his total was exactly doubled by George Bradley of St. Louis. Bradley's 16 shutouts in 1876 are still a major league record, though the mark has since been tied by Pete Alexander. Oddly, Bradley's first "Chicago" victim of the season was none other than Chicago, which succumbed 1–0 on May 5. His 16th and final shutout came in his 53rd start of the season, against the New York Mutuals on September 5 at Brooklyn's Union Grounds.

At least for Chicago, then, its National League history got off to an impressive start. The White Stockings' attendance numbers and their financial ledgers were the best in the league, the only franchise showing a decent profit at the end of the year. That bothersome fact clearly indicated the need for the league's improvement in every phase of the game, from its caliber of professional play to its front office. In the end, what proved to be one of the most influential factors in saving the game from itself was an almost irrational love affair with the national pastime by fans who endured the antics and rowdy behavior of their heroes, less than major league accommodations, rules tinkering that literally changed the game from season to season, and a continuing warfare between owners and players. Despite the many shortcomings and the constant outcries against "hippodroming" (that is, fixing games), fans kept on making their way through the turnstiles in enough numbers to pay their heroes to play and to keep franchises afloat. Through that late nineteenth century maelstrom of constant unrest and no little chaos, the game did manage to improve and did survive the threat of extinction at the hands of other leagues and other ambitious people who wanted a cut of major league prestige and its financial largess.

As for the many games within *the* game, one of which, the shutout, is of primary interest here, it was during the late 1800s that National League play paved the way to the establishment of the many records that would be of great interest to baseball aficionados. Team records that bear on defense and shutouts during the National League's early years follow.

Legend:
RA: Number of relief appearances made by pitchers
DP: Double Plays
TmE: Team Errors committed
(Number in parentheses behind year designates
number of teams in the league.)

Year	GP	CG	RA	SO	DP	TmE	FA	ERA	SHO	SHO%
1876(8)	260	472	50	589	274	3123	.866	2.31	47	18.1
1877(6)	180	326	35	726	210	1857	.884	2.81	20	11.1
1878(6)	184	352	17	1081	233	1778	.893	2.30	25	13.6
1879(8)	321	609	34	1843	384	3126	.892	2.50	45	14.0
1880(8)	340	608	76	1989	411	2949	.901	2.37	52	15.3
1881(8)	336	631	42	1784	490	2781	.905	2.77	52	15.5
1882(8)	338	642	34	2156	451	3031	.897	2.88	41	12.1
1883(8)	395	717	76	2877	521	3782	.891	3.13	38	9.6
1884(8)	456	863	53	4335	545	3952	.899	2.98	70	15.4
1885(8)	442	863	28	3335	573	3536	.908	2.82	72	16.2
1886(8)	492	933	51	4321	583	3457	.916	3.29	46	9.3
1887(8)	508	969	52	2840	696	3674	.915	4.05	34	6.7
1888(8)	542	1045	40	4000	673	3589	.921	2.83	91	17.0
1889(8)	531	948	124	3508	773	3465	.923	4.02	41	7.7
1890(8)	539	982	99	3707	792	3253	.928	3.56	54	10.0
1891(8)	552	948	164	3641	763	3383	.928	3.34	51	9.2
1892(12)	918	1623	223	5978	1339	5579	.928	3.28	90	9.8
1893(12)	785	1294	293	3342	1268	4581	.931	4.66	43	5.5
1894(12)	798	1299	333	3333	1298	4853	.927	5.33	31	3.9
1895(12)	797	1287	329	3623	1202	4619	.930	4.77	46	5.8
1896(12)	792	1306	301	3523	1238	4081	.938	4.36	58	7.3
1897(12)	807	1362	269	3734	1102	4029	.939	4.30	51	6.3
1898(12)	920	1609	246	4247	1354	4387	.942	3.60	89	9.7
1899(12)	921	1593	270	3867	1395	4458	.942	3.85	90	9.8
1900(8)	568	934	221	2697	834	2757	.942	3.69	68	12.0

Comparison Season, 2000:
Am. Lg.(14) 1132 107 5710 14033 2280 1568 .982 4.91 92 8.1

These numbers show some unmistakable trends. During the 25-season span before the American League appeared, the National League gradually hiked the quality of its overall play from a pitching and defensive standpoint. Players adjusted and then readjusted to a constant parade of rule changes and new regulations between 1876 and 1900. There were marked improvements in playing equipment, notably gloves and mitts, and groundskeeping, that vastly increased the fielders' potential for successfully picking up grounders in the league's infields and outfields. Except for teams weak in pitching and defensive personnel, those trends were also obvious in leagues like the American Association (1882–1891) and the Players League (1890). While those ancient ball diamonds were primitive by modern standards, they nonetheless gradually began to appear like those we've become accustomed to in the recent past.

In 1880 National League teams committed almost 370 errors on average, and this brought with it huge consequences for the number of shutouts they logged. By 1898 the average number of errors was 365 per team. But to show just how far that was removed from these latter years, in 2000 the average number of errors per team was 112, a figure that cut the margin in half over the course of a century.

In the 1888 season the NL reached a high-water mark with 91 shutouts. There were 90 in both 1892 and 1899. Curiously, the 2000 AL mark was still in the 90s range, a figure that was largely due to the specialists in the bullpens around the league. These hurlers were summoned in the game's late innings at the first sign of trouble, or when a starting hurler's pitch count exceeded 100. By bringing relievers into the game as specialists who were signed exclusively for bullpen duty managers and coaches sought to nip rallies in the bud. It was a benchmark change in professional baseball that significantly altered the game. That measure, and its studied refinement over the years, will come up again in the discussion of pitching's evolution, especially between 1980 and 2010.

We have already noted that the most significant rule change in the closing years of the nineteenth century was moving the pitcher's box to 60'6" from its pre–1893 distance of 50'. A glance at the table above illustrates a dramatic rise in the Earned Run Averages (from 3.28 in 1892, to 4.66 in 1893 and up to 5.33 in 1894), a telltale indication that pitchers had their problems with the new distance as the hitters had additional time to gauge the speed and rotation of oncoming pitches. That would inevitably produce lustier offense. At the same time shutouts nose-dived from 90 in 1892 to 43 in 1893, dropping more than half in one season. Heavy lumber asserted itself. It was a change that owners wanted — and they got it.

To bring the fledgling National League into sharp focus we turn to a review of four selected seasons among the last 25 of the nineteenth century as seen through its teams and star pitchers: 1876, 1884, 1893 — a season that featured the change from a 50' distance to 60'6" between the pitcher's box and home plate, and in a league composed of 12 teams— and 1900, by which time the NL had returned to its original eight-team format and began to look forward, however apprehensively, to the challenge of yet another new league. (Except for the American League, founded in 1901, other leagues are reviewed in the chapter on the American Association [AA], Union Association [UA], Players League [PL], Federal League [FL], Negro Leagues and, briefly, professional baseball in Japan.)

Many of the stars who played on NA teams in 1875, its last season, appeared in National League lineups in 1876. A number of the better pitchers, Cummings and Bonds (Hartford), Bradley (St. Louis), and Mathews (New York) stayed with their 1875 teams for the 1876 season. Other pitchers, principally Spalding (Boston to Chicago), Devlin (Chicago to Louisville), Zettlein (Chicago to Philadelphia) and McBride (Philadelphia to Boston) cast their lots with new franchises as the NL began play. Al Spalding, Ross Barnes, "Deacon" White, and Cal McVey, each a star in his own right, made the move from Boston to Chicago, splitting up Boston's NA powerhouse, and at the same time bringing to Chicago the kind of talent that would spur the White Stockings to their phenomenal 52–14 record, establishing NL records, for example, a team batting average of .337 and Ross Barnes' league-leading .426 batting average, that stand to this day. In 1876 the top five pitchers in the league stacked up this way:

	W-L (%)	IP	ERA	SO	SHO
Spalding	47–12 (.783)	528⅔	1.75	39	8
Bradley	45–19 (.703)	573	1.23	103	16*
Bond	31–13 (.705)	408	1.68	88	6
Cummings	16–8 (.667)	216	1.67	26	5
Devlin	30–35 (.462)	622	1.56	122	5

*One of those shutouts was the NL's first no-hitter, July 15, 2–0 over Hartford.

The shutout story for 1876 was written largely by George Bradley, who never again put together numbers like he did in the NL's first season. His 45 wins included a record-setting 16 whitewashings, doubling the efforts of Al Spalding. Pete Alexander's 16 in 1916 tied that mark, which has never been exceeded.

In a three-game series against Hartford on July 11, 13 and 15, Bradley pinned three consecutive shutout losses on Hartford's Tommy Bond, culminating in a tight, 2–0 victory on the 15th that entered the National League record books as its first no-hitter. His complete shutout record for that season follows:

May 5 at StL	1–0 over Chicago (Spalding), one of the NL's three 1–0 games in 1876
May 9 at StL	5–0 (Louisville, Devlin LP)
May 11 at StL	3–0 (Louisville, Devlin)
May 13 at StL	11–0 (Cincinnati, Pierson)
May 25, at NY	2–0 (New York, Mathews)
June 1 at Phl	17–0 (Philadelphia, Zettlein)
June 22 at StL	5–0 (Philadelphia, Knight)
June 29 at StL	8–0 (New York, Mathews)
July 11 at StL	2–0 (Hartford, Bond)
July 13, at StL	3–0 (Hartford, Bond)
July 15, at StL	2–0 (Hartford, Bond)
July 29 at StL	7–0 (Louisville, Devlin)

August 3 at Cinc   10–0 (Cincinnati, Dean)
August 8 at Louv   3–0 (Louisville, Devlin)
August 17 at StL   3–0 (Chicago, Spalding)
September 5 at NY   9–0 (New York, Mathews)

By comparison, Al Spalding's eight shutout wins appears quite modest. Yet, to fashion as many as eight in a single season would become, years hence, a singular achievement. Tommy Bond with six, and Jimmy Devlin and Candy Cummings with five, followed the two kingpins among NL pitchers.

The next year of our four-season review, 1884, was the most remarkable season in nineteenth century baseball, as it showcased three leagues sporting 33 teams playing in 24 different cities. It was a strong indicator of the rapid growth of the national pastime, and of the rabid interest of American fandom. Not every team made it to the end of the season, but the Union Association, for example, still drew in excess of 400,000 of the two million-plus who made their way through major league turnstiles.

In what was becoming an annual event, there were several significant rule changes, one of which, the overhand delivery, was an acknowledgment of its widespread practice in the professional ranks. That change brought out a number of cannonball hurlers who reared back and let their fastballs fly, and at the same time it complicated matters for the hitter, giving him less time to gauge the flight and movement of the missiles unleashed by the Radbourns, Galvins and One Arm Dailys of major league baseball.

By 1884, a scant eight seasons after the 1876 NL season, there were new baseball parks as well as new stars to capture the imagination of sports fans. Among them were a number of pitchers who were building Hall of Fame careers, and a number of others close on their heels. Some of these future immortals and others, along with some of their 1884 numbers, follow:

George Bradley set the pace with 16 shutouts in one season (1876), equaled only by Pete Alexander in 1916.

	W-L, W%	IP	ERA	GS/CG	SHO	SO
Old Hoss Radbourn	59–12 (.831)	678.2	1.38	73/73	11	441

(Prov, NL) During 18-game winning streak he beat Buffinton 1–0 twice

Pud Galvin	46–22 (.676)	636.1	1.99	72/71	12	369

(Buf, NL) 18–0 over Detroit on August 4 was worst ML no-hit drubbing

Charlie Buffinton	48–16 (.750)	587	2.15	67/63	8	417

(Bos, NL) 1884 was his best year in a 233-victory career

Mickey Welch	39–21 (.650)	557.1	2.50	65/62	4	345

(NY, NL) On Aug. 28 he struck out first 9 Cleveland batters for record

Guy Hecker, Louisville AA, with 52 wins in 1884; Tony Mullane, 36 wins with Toledo, AA; Bobby Mathews, 30 victories with the Philadelphia Athletics, AA: Jim McCormick, 21–3 with seven shutouts for Cincinnati of the UA; and Hugh Daily, the one-handed wonder who pitched for Chicago and posted a record 19 strikeouts in a 5–0 shutout at Boston in a Union Association game, were among other pitchers who distinguished themselves in 1884.

As the twentieth century dawned the National League had restored its professional baseball hegemony, though with trimmed sails, having reduced its numbers to eight from the bulky 12-team arrangement between the 1892 and 1899 seasons. The NL had withstood the "intrusion" of three leagues between 1881 and 1891. And it didn't take long before the question they were most likely asking — what next? — was answered. Before turning to the new century, with its advent of the brash and well-heeled American League, a look at the 1900 NL season:

In 1900 the National League was the only big-league show in town, and it was trimmed to an eight-team league that had thrown the evils of syndication overboard and, in the process, tightened up league rosters to a fine edge that produced a most competitive race for championship laurels. Larry Lajoie, Elmer Flick,

Old Hoss Radbourn, who, during an incredible 1884 season, won 59 games, with 11 shutouts and an 18-game winning streak.

Hans Wagner and a new set of pitching wizards such as Iron Man Joe McGinnity, Cy Young and Rube Waddell, all of whom wound up with a Cooperstown address, were in the midst of some of baseball's most noteworthy careers. Among still others was a young Tennessean by the name of Frank Hahn, a lefty, who did his pitching for the Cincinnati Reds. They called him Noodles. Relying on a sizzling heater, the 21-year-old southpaw led the NL in strikeouts with 132 and in shutouts, with four. One of those shutouts came on July 12 at Cincinnati's League Park, where he no-hit the Phillies, 4–0. It was the first no-hit game of the twentieth century. Just three days later he followed up with a nine-hit, 9–0 whitewashing in the last game of the St. Louis series. Later that summer, on August 26, he put the screws on the Pirates, besting Deacon Phillippe in a taut, 1–0 duel.

Sixty-eight of the NL's 569 games in 1900 (11.95 percent) resulted in shutouts. Some of the better blankings are detailed, following:

> June 11–13: The last-place Giants, with the second-worst staff ERA in the NL, put all their eggs in one basket over a three-day span, when they posted three consecutive shutouts: the first by Win Mercer over "Coldwater Jim" Hughey on June 11; the second, a 4–0 Bill Carrick victory over Nixey Callahan of the Chicago Orphans; and the third, a 5–0 kayo of Chicago (Emerson "Pink" Hawley over Clark Griffith).
> June 19: In the summer's best pitching due, the Chicago Orphans squeaked home the winning run in the 13th inning to vanquish the Pirates, 1–0. Two future Hall of Famers faced each other, Pittsburgh's Rube Waddell and Clark Griffith of the winning Chicago nine.
> June 25: St. Louis' Jack Powell bested Ted Breitenstein, Cincinnati moundsman, 2–0.
> July 5 and 6: Not since June 17 and 18 of the fabled 1884 season had there been back to back one-hitters. However, the pennant-winning Brooklyn club put an end to that with belated pitching fireworks ignited by Jerry Nops, who hurled his only shutout of the season at the Flatbush home grounds, Washington Park, downing rookie Doc Newton and his Reds compadres, 2–0. Nops gave up but a single safe blow, and was followed the very next day by another one-hit effort, this time by Frank Kitson. Cincinnati's Archie Stimmel took the loss.
> October 14: In the last game of the 1900 season, played at Sportsman Park, St. Louis, the Cardinals hosted the Cincinnati Reds. The contest produced the 68th shutout of the season, St. Louis prevailing by a 7–0 count. The diminutive veteran, Willie Sudhoff, did the honors for St. Louis, beating Cincinnati's Ed Scott, a 17-game winner that summer.

Between May 4, 1871, and October 14, 1900, 20,827 major league games were played in four different leagues. Of at least some significance to the shutout subject of this book, both were opening and closing dates on which only one game was played, and both were shutouts. The latter of these two brought an end to an era, and though it actually ended in the twentieth century, that era was the very essence of nineteenth century baseball.

It would be amiss to leave the nineteenth century behind without mention of the top shutout hurlers of those formative years in baseball history. The list (* indicates Hall of Fame player):

Name/Yrs	Shutouts	Career Wins	Shutout (% of Wins)
Pud Galvin,* 1875–92	57	365	15.6
Tommy Bond, 1874–1884	42	234	17.9
Mickey Welch,* 1880–92	41	307	13.4
Tim Keefe,* 1880–93	39	342	11.4
John Clarkson,* 1882–94	37	328	11.3
Will White, 1877–86	36	229	15.7
Hoss Radbourn,* 1881–91	35	309	11.3
Jim McCormick, 1878–87	33	265	12.5

4

Grubby Baseballs and Shutout Artistry

Featuring much the same lineups day-in-day-out, season after season, the Deadball Era, aptly named and defined rather crisply by the years 1901 to 1919, was noted for the hit-and-run, grubby baseballs, stolen bases, "inside baseball" à la the Giants and the Cubs, and, not least, pitchers who usually finished what they started. It comes as no surprise, then, that among the top 20 shutout hurlers in baseball history, nine of them, all Hall of Famers, were Deadball Era pitchers. That's just about half. The list includes:

Walter Johnson	110 (career ML SHO record)
Pete Alexander	90 (career NL SHO record)
Christy Mathewson	79
Cy Young*	76
Eddie Plank	69
Ed Walsh	57
Mordecai Brown	55
Rube Waddell	50
Vic Willis	50

*Cy Young threw 44 of his 76 shutouts between 1901 and 1911, his last year, in a career that began in 1890.

An additional 20 pitchers fashioned between 32 and 46. That listing includes luminaries like Joe McGinnity (32), Eddie Cicotte (35), Ed Reulbach (40), Chief Bender (40), and Addie Joss (45). All of these, and more, headed up a glistening array of shutout masters. During an era that emphasized base-to-base, one-run strategies, the game's offensive productivity was throttled not only by exceptional pitching, but by a deliberate design that produced a plethora of 2–1, 3–2 and shutout games. It is fair to say that the prevailing mindset, accompanied by a ball that was doctored and dead, created both consequences. The net result of those 19 seasons was a hatful of shutout records, many of which stand to this very day. The team records that follow include the American (A), National (N) and Federal (F) Leagues. Major league records appear in boldface. The columns indicate the total number of shutouts per team during the years 1901–19 and the average number of per year. High designates the year in which a given team logged its most shutouts.

Team/Yrs	SHO	AVE	HIGH/YR
BaltA/2	7	3.5	4/1901
BaltF/2	20	10.0	15/1914
BosA/19	290	15.3	26/1918
BosN/19	239	12.6	23/1916
BrkF/2	21	10.5	11/1914
BrkN/19	264	13.9	22/1906, 1916
BufF/2	29	14.5	15/1914
ChiA/19	340	17.9	**32**/1906
ChiF/2	38	19.0	21/1915
ChiN/19	362	19.1	**32**/1907, 1909
CincN/19	228	12.0	23/1919
ClvA/19	267	14.1	27/1906
DetA/19	224	11.8	20/1917
IndyF/1	15	15.0	15/1914
KanCityF/2	26	13.0	16/1915
MilA/1	3	3.0	3/1901
NewarkF/1	16	16.0	16/1915
NYA/17	195	11.5	19/1905
NYN/19	304	16.0	25/1908
PhlA/19	290	15.3	27/1907, 1909
PhlN/19	295	15.5	25/1916
PitF/2	25	12.5	16/1915
PitN/19	311	16.4	27/1906
StLA/18	214	11.9	21/1909
StLF/2	33	16.5	24/1915
StLN/19	163	8.6	19/1907
WashA/19	262	13.8	25/1913

On the wrong side of the team shutout ledger stand the St. Louis Cardinals and the Washington Senators, who hold the record for absorbing the most shutout losses in a single season. St. Louis, with 33, holds the major league record set in 1908.

The major league record of 33 SHO losses was set by the Cardinals on September 29, 1908, in the first game of a doubleheader. Pittsburgh won that game by a 7–0 margin that put an exclamation mark on the St. Louis defeat, as Pirates hurler Howie Camnitz came within a hair's breadth of throwing a no-hitter — except for a ninth-inning single by Cardinals shortstop Champ Osteen.

Among the more noteworthy shutout games in an era dotted with so many superlative shutout games, these are the best:

4. Grubby Baseballs and Shutout Artistry

May 15, 1901: Rookies Christy Mathewson and Watty Lee were both victorious. Mathewson's Giants defeated Chicago and Jack Taylor, 6–0, moving New York into first place. It was Matty's third straight shutout win. In the American League the Boston Americans were set down by Washington, 4–0, in Boston by Lee, the Senators' ace, winner of 16 games that year and author of two of Washington's eight shutouts in the AL's debut season.

July 15, 1901: Legendary Christy Mathewson, hurling the fifth shutout of his rookie year and a no-hit gem as well, defeated St. Louis at Sportsman's Park as the Giants tallied twice off Willie Sudhoff in the first stanza for more than enough runs in their 5–0 victory. It was the first major league no-hitter of the Deadball Era. There were 40 more of the shutout variety. The last was engineered by Ray Caldwell, who won a 3–0 no-hitter on September 10, 1919, as Cleveland beat New York at the Polo Grounds. (Four years later, in the 1905 World Series Mathewson would accomplish the remarkable feat of shutting out the opposing team, the Philadelphia Athletics, each of the three times he took the mound.)

October, 1906: On the first two days in October the Chicago White Sox defeated the St. Louis Browns. Both victories were shutouts, a 1–0 gem by Nick Altrock in the first game followed by a Frank Owen 4–0 whitewashing on October 2.

On October 4 in Pittsburgh Jack Pfiester won his 20th game with a 4–0 victory for the Cubs' record-setting 116th win. That set the stage for the famed 1906 World Series between Chicago's "Hitless Wonders" and the mighty Cubs in which two of the six games were shutouts.

September 7, 1907: Not quite yet the Big Train, rookie Walter Johnson shut down the Boston Red Sox,

Baseball Immortal Christy Mathewson (Brace photograph).

1–0. It was the first of an incredible 110 career shutouts and the first among 38 career 1–0 victories, also a record. He followed the Red Sox win just five days later with a 2–0 win over New York. (In 1908, a still-young Johnson tossed three shutouts in four days, including an off day on Sunday because of the prevailing blue laws.)

1908: In a season crammed to the hilt with extraordinary wonders, several of them are noteworthy shutouts:

June 30. Cy Young, at 41, no-hit New York at Highlanders Park to become the oldest no-hit winner, 8–0, until Nolan Ryan, at 44, threw his last no-hitters in 1990 and 1991.

July 17. "Three Finger" Brown outdueled Christy Mathewson, 1–0, winning on an inside-the-park home run by Joe Tinker at Chicago in the fifth inning.

September 26. In Brooklyn at Washington Park Ed Reulbach became the only pitcher in baseball history to throw two shutouts in one day, besting Brooklyn by 5–0 and 3–0 scores. With a 24–7 record that season, the Cubs hurler led the NL in winning percentage at .774. It was his third straight title.

October 2: Addie Joss out-pitched Ed Walsh, though not by much, with a perfect game at League Park in Cleveland, defeating the White Sox in a 1–0 thriller that tightened up the AL pennant race.

October 7: "Wild Bill" Donovan, Detroit ace, clinched the pennant for Detroit with a 7–0 conquest of the White Sox, whose Doc White was the losing pitcher, giving up big blows to the Tigers' Cobb, Crawford and Matty McIntyre.

October 14: In World Series Game 5, which turned out to be the finale, Cubs pitcher Orvie Overall silenced Detroit bats for a 2–0 victory over the Tigers [Dave Anderson's delightful account of the 1908 season, *More Than Merkle* (University of Nebraska Press, 2000), is aptly subtitled *A History of the Best and Most Exciting Baseball Season in Human History*].

The winningest pitcher in baseball history, Cy Young.

September 22, 1911: Cy Young posted the 511th victory of his peerless career, a record that will stand through the ages. It also happened to be his 76th career shutout, a 1–0 victory that beat the Pirates at Pittsburgh. The box score:

Boston Rustlers	AB	R	H	PO	A		Pittsburgh	AB	R	H	PO	A
Sweeney, 2b	4	0	1	5	5		Byrne, 3b	4	0	1	0	2
Donlin, cf	4	0	1	0	1		Carey, cf	3	0	2	4	0
Jackson, lf	4	0	1	2	0		Campbell, lf	4	0	1	3	0
Kirke, 1b	4	1	1	11	0		Wagner, 1b	4	0	1	6	0
Miller, rf	3	0	0	2	0		Wilson, rf	4	0	0	2	0
Bridwell, ss	3	0	1	1	5		McKe'nie, 2b	4	0	2	3	4
McDonald, 3b	3	0	0	1	1		McCarthy, ss	4	0	0	3	1
Rariden, c	3	0	1	5	3		Simon, c	3	0	1	6	2
C. Young, p	3	0	0	0	1		Clarke, ph	1	0	1	0	0
Adams, p	3	0	0	0	0							
Leach, ph	1	0	0	0	0							
Totals	31	1	6	27	16		Totals	35	0	9	27	9

```
BOS   000   000   100   1 6 3
PIT   000   000   000   0 9 1
```

E: Jackson, Kirke (2), McCarthy
DP: McKechnie-Wagner
2B: Kirk, Mckechnie, Simon
SB: Jackson, Donlin, Campbell
SH: Carey
LOB: BOS, 3; PIT, 9

K: Young, 3; Adams, 6
BB: Young, 0; Adams, 0
BF: Young, 36; Adams, 31
Umpires: Mal Eason and Jim Johnstone
Time: 1:35
Attendance: 1,208

April 14, 1915: Herb Pennock came within one out of pitching a no-hitter on Opening Day for the Mackmen in Philadelphia. The Red Sox' Harry Hooper's squibbler had eyes and found its way through the infield with two out in the ninth. The A's won, 2–0, on a winter-like day in Philadelphia.

April 15, 1915: A day after Pennock's near miss, Rube Marquard not-hit the Brooklyn Robins in a 1–0 win for the New York Giants.

April 24, 1915 Frank Allen, pitching for Pittsburgh's Rebels in the Federal League, silenced the St. Louis Terriers with a no-hitter, winning 2–0 over Bob Groom, who would throw a no-hitter of his own in 1917 for the St. Louis Browns.

October 2, 1916: Grover "Pete" Alexander threw his 16th shutout of the season, defeating Boston in the first game of a twinbill, 2–0. He downed the Braves with a three-hitter. Pat Ragan was the loser. Alexander tied George Bradley, who set the record in the NL's first year, 1876, 40 years earlier. The two will undoubtedly remain co-record holders for eons to come.

May 17, 1917: Babe Ruth, who seemed to have Walter Johnson's number in pitching matchups, bested the Senators immortal, 1–0, at Griffith Stadium. He pitched a two-hitter and drove home the contest's only run on an eighth-inning sacrifice fly. It marked the third time within a year that Ruth had beaten Johnson, 1–0.

September, 1919: The last shutouts of the Deadball Era in the National and American Leagues were logged on September 25 (AL) and 28 (NL). In the AL New York won at the expense of Philadelphia behind George Mogridge, who gave up four hits while walking three and fanning six. The loser was rookie Jimmy Zinn, who had relieved A's starter Jing Johnson.

Three days later on September 28, Pete Alexander, pitching for the Cubs at Cincinnati, baffled the Reds with a six-hit shutout on the last day of the regular season. It was his 16th win of the year. He defeated Hod Eller, 19–9 on the season for the NL champion Reds.

For the sake of technical accuracy, it should be pointed out that it was also Hod Eller who crafted a 5–0 shutout World Series victory in Game 5 on October 6, a complete-game 5–0 conquest of the Black Sox. The loser that day was Claude "Lefty" Williams in the *very* last Deadball Era shutout.

Second only to Walter Johnson with 90 career shutouts, Pete Alexander won 30 games in a season three straight times (Brace photograph).

From the first Deadball Era shutout, which occurred on April 19, 1901, at Boston, a 7–0 Braves victory over the New York Giants (future Hall of Famer Kid Nichols defeated Luther "Dummy" Taylor, 7–0), to the last shutout hurrah by Pete Alexander on September 28, 1919, a total of 4,483 regular season shutouts went into the record books. Within that span National Leaguers were responsible for a single-season high of 164 in 1908, and the AL hit a high-water mark of 146 in 1909. It was an era unto itself. One of the factors responsible, however, for its demise was the Rules Committee's decision, on February 9, 1920, to call for the banishment of "freak deliveries." Henceforth there would be clean baseballs in play, officially prepared by umpires prior to game time. Balls that were "loaded," scuffed, or lost to the field of play because they had been hit into the grandstands were replaced. In more than one respect baseball was cleaning up its act, and the result of its new code of conduct on and off the field of play would be apparent almost immediately. A new era of swinging for the fences was about to begin as home run figures would soar and the number of shutouts would dwindle.

5

From the 1920s to the 1940s

With the Roaring Twenties came the roar of The Big Shillelagh. Bunts were out and four-baggers were in. It all descended on the great pastime with a suddenness that stunned the game's followers across the country. In the space of one season the reverberations were felt in both leagues, and within a decade the numbers had reversed and all but put an end to some of the most respected and honored strategies of the hit-'em-where-they-ain't people of former times. And the fans loved it. That made going back to the one- and two-run, low-hit games passé. So the owners catered to the market and paid big bucks to keep dangerous swatsmiths like Ruth, Hornsby and Heilmann in their lineups.

A bright, shiny, livelier ball, in ready supply, made pitchers think in terms of the far edges of home plate and the strike zone. Damage control, and perhaps a hidden trick or two with a scuffed or moistened ball, also were prominent in the minds of wary pitchers who soon noticed that even hitters at the bottom of the batting order were getting to be pesky trouble makers. Survival amid the shelling pitchers were now regularly exposed to, brought on relief pitchers and diminishing numbers in almost every category of the pitching record book. The pitcher's mound was no place for the weak-hearted.

Selected from the team stats of three sample years are numbers that help sort out the old (1919) from the new (1920 and 1929). In the table following, AL statistics are listed before the slash mark and NL after.

	SHO	ERA	R	HR	SLG.%
1919	91/101	3.22/2.91	4596/4072	240/207	.359/.337
1920	80/108	3.79/3.13	5868/4893	369/261	.387/.357
1929	66/56	4.24/4.71	6140/6609	595/754	.407/.426

Those telltale numbers are eye-opening. Offense up. Pitching down. For the hitters the candy shop was open to all comers. Meanwhile, out there in the middle of the diamond, it was pitch-and-duck while fielders chased those tightened-up balls all over the lot. New gloves were marketed as the latest cure for snagging line drives and towering fly balls up against the fences. In the record book, differences like runs scored in 1919 and a decade later, or between ERAs logged ten years apart, stand out like glaring neon. Further, with respect to our primary concern in this book, check the free-fall in shutout numbers from 1919's total of 192 in both leagues, to 122 in 1929.

Aside from a few holdovers from earlier Deadball years like Pete Alexander and Walter Johnson, there just weren't many pitchers' names that stirred imaginations. In the era between the great wars there were few if any, like Lefty Grove or Carl Hubbell, who wore a mantle of instant Hall of Fame greatness and whose numbers and exceptional individual feats suggested, even before they were at mid-career, that Cooperstown was a lock once their extraordinary careers were over. That wasn't because there weren't any greats around. It is more likely that pitching greats such as Red Ruffing, Ted Lyons or Waite Hoyt didn't get the hitters out with the aplomb or flair of a Johnson or a Mathewson.

It was their lot to do their work in the 1920s and 1930s against a backdrop of superior and more flamboyant forces like Ruth, Hornsby, Foxx, Frisch, Gehrig, *et al.* David Nemec, in his 2010 edition of *Great Baseball Feats, Facts and Figures* (Nemec, 2010, 170), lists five of them, noting that they were the five pitchers with the highest ERA who were enshrined at Cooperstown. Each was essentially a post–Deadball Era hurler. Their career shutouts have been added in the table below, and Grove and Hubbell are appended:

	Yrs Active	*Wins*	*ERA*	*Career*	*SHO*
Red Ruffing	1924–42, 1945–47	273	3.80	45
Ted Lyons	1923–42, 1946	260	3.67	27
Jesse Haines	1918, 1920–37	210	3.64	24
Herb Pennock	1912–17, 1919–34	241	3.60	35
Waite Hoyt	1918–38	237	3.59	26
Lefty Grove	1925–41	300	3.06	35
Carl Hubbell	1928–43	253	2.98	36

Spread across two decades of big scores, homers and smaller shutout numbers, major league pitchers did manage to muster an outing here and there that brought the sluggers up short. A few of them follow.

> July 28, 1921: Waite Hoyt doled out four singles while his Yankees teammates pushed across four runs early in the game and went on to win against the Browns, 6–0, at the Polo Grounds. Babe Ruth, who would

go on to a monster year with 59 circuit smashes, 171 runs batted in and an .846 slugging percentage, on this day had to be satisfied with a two-run single. In his only shutout in a 19-victory season, Hoyt enjoyed his first big year in Yankees livery, posting a 3.09 ERA. His shutout was one of only eight logged by New York pitchers in 1921.

August 21, 1921: In 616 American League contests there were only 60 shutout games. Allen Sothoron hurled two of them. The second of them was a 4–0 six-hitter that beat the Red Sox' Allen Russell. Sothoron's 1921 season was notable in that he didn't allow a home run in a 13–8, 178.1-inning season split among three AL teams. That was something no other starting pitcher could boast in a year that saw the four-bagger pace stepped up to 477, an increase of 108 from the year before, and from 240 HR in 1919.

September 3, 1927: In the Year of the Yankees, 1927, the Philadelphia A's finished 19 games behind Miller Huggins' men, but that didn't mean that Lefty Grove, with his 95 mph heater, was standing idly by. In 1927 he won three out of five from the Yanks, including this 1–0 four-hitter in September (two by Ruth). It was the only time all year the New Yorkers were shut out.

September 7 and 11, 1933: Johnny Marcum started out his major league career impressively by hurling two shutouts for the Philadelphia Athletics. He was the second in the AL, and only the fourth in ML history, to do that. On September 7 he allowed Cleveland five scattered hits as Doc Cramer's two-run homer paved the way to a 6–0 win. Four days after his debut Marcum threw another five-hitter, an 8–0 victory, this time at the White Sox, with whom he wound up a seven-year career during which he was able to add but six more to his shutout total.

Three National League shutout games during the era marking the years 1920 to 1941 are worth noting:

September 21, 1934: The Cardinals ruled the baseball world in 1934. Well, not completely. One of their number, Jay Hanna Dean, if not baseball's mightiest potentate that year, came close to it. The Great Diz and his brother Paul, aka Daffy, flashed their credentials on a spectacular, late September day at Ebbets Field in a Brooklyn doubleheader. In the first of two Dizzy shut down the Dodgers on three hits, winning 13–0 to make off with his 27th win of the season. Not to be outdone, Daffy proceeded to silence the Flatbush Faithful with a no-hit, 3–0 embarrassment, coming within a base on balls of a perfect game, issuing a free pass to Dodgers outfielder Len Koenecke. The win was his 18th, and his fifth shutout. Dizzy would go on to pitch two more shutout victories at the end of the season, raising his league-leading total to seven in his 30-win year.

September 22, 1938: The mighty Cubs juggernaut of 1938 featured "Big Bill" Lee, who would certainly have been honored with the Cy Young Award had it existed in 1938. In his banner year he led the NL in wins, shutouts (9), and ERA (a sterling 2.66). A September 22 twinbill in Philadelphia saw the Cubs launch their spine-tingling, pennant-bound ten-game winning streak. In the first game of that DH, Gabby Hartnett's men were paced by the big fellow, as he notched his fourth straight shutout while whipping the Phils, 4–0. Though he gave up ten hits, he was strong in the clutch while winning his 20th of the season.

May 30, 1940: His best years were behind him, but there were flashes of brilliance to let the baseball world know that Carl Hubbell, in 1940, still had enough left to make a visit to the record book on occasion. Using but 87 pitches, Hubbell beat the Dodgers at Ebbets Field in a year that looked, that spring, as though it might be another Giants year. In his 7–0 win in the first of two, Hubbell faced only 27 hitters. The great lefty, with his famed screwball in tow, gave up a single to second baseman Johnny Hudson, then started a double play that erased the Dodgers' only baserunner. The Hudson hit prevented a perfect game. The shutout Hubbell threw was the first of two in an 11–11 season.

On the following page is a final look at the era's best pitchers, with their numbers lined up 1 to 15 according to their career winning percentages. SHO-% designates the percentage of career victories that were shutouts.

Carl Hubbell, great New York Giants left-hander (Brace photograph).

	W-L	Win.%	SHO-%	OOB%*	ERA
Grove (1925–1941)	300–141	.680	35–11.7	.311	3.06
Gomez (1930–1943)	189–102	.649	28–14.8	.321	3.34
Dean (1930–1947)	150–83	.644	26–17.3	.298	3.02
Hubbell (1928–1943)	253–154	.622	36–14.2	.291	2.98
Shocker (1916–1928)	187–117	.615	28–22.1	.311	3.17
Warneke (1930–1945)	192–121	.613	30–15.6	.304	3.18
Ferrell (1927–1941)	193–128	.601	17–8.8	.343	4.04
Pennock (1912–1934)	241–162	.598	35–14.5	.328	3.60
Vance (1915–1935)	197–140	.585	29–14.7	.308	3.24
Grimes (1916–1934)	270–212	.560	35–13.0	.331	3.53
Ruffing (1924–1947)	273–225	.548	45–16.5	.323	3.80
Harder (1928–1947)	223–186	.545	25–11.2	.334	3.80
Faber (1914–1933)	254–213	.544	29–11.4	.323	3.15
Lyons (1923–1946)	260–230	.531	27–10.4	.324	3.67
Rixey (1912–1933)	266–251	.515	37–13.9	.318	3.15

*OOB designates the percentage of base runners permitted per nine innings.

6

There's a War Going On ... and After

Pearl Harbor brought on America's second global conflict within a span of a quarter century. It was the beginning of an era in baseball that brought on a number of significant changes. Franchises were moved from sea to shining sea during this time, and new ethnic groups, principally African Americans and Latinos, moved out of the ranks of second-class baseball citizenship and into The Big Show. Beyond their belated and initially begrudging acceptance, Americans went back to work after the war's conclusion and spent a good many of their leisure hours not only in the grandstands of Organized Baseball's major and minor league ball parks, but playing the game themselves on hardball and softball diamonds across the nation. As confined and anxious-laden as the war years were, the era of transition seemed, on the other hand, just that open and ready for the winds of change. During the first months of 1942 the ballplayers left, but in 1945 and 1946 they came back, ready, as the veterans were, to get in some decent last licks before calling it a career. And the younger ones headed for training camps, bent on "making it" to spend their next 10–20 years chasing the record books while playing the game they just couldn't stay away from.

The time frame for this era includes the 1942–1945 "mini-era" of World War II, and beyond that, from the war's close in 1945, beginning with the 1946 season, to the close of the 1960 season. In sum, 19 years are included in this era. (Jim Charlton's Baseball Chronology, available on the webite Baseball Library [www.baseballlibrary.com], divides baseball history into eras, as follows: to 1900, The Early Years; 1901–1919, The Deadball Era; 1920–1941, Baseball Between the Wars; 1942–1945, The War Years; 1946–1960, Baseball In Transition; 1961–1975, Owner-Managed Growth; 1976–2005, The Free Agent Era. Eras in this book are a bit differently arranged.)

Pitchers who were active during this era fall into three groupings: (1) those whose years begin in the 1930s and end in the late 1940s or 1950s; (2) those who were primarily wartime pitchers with careers in the 1940s; and (3) those whose careers extended into the late 1950s and 1960s. Examples of each would be Bob Feller (1936–1956) and Hal Newhouser (1939–1955) from the 1930s to the 1950s; Mort Cooper (1938–1949) and Spud Chandler (1938–1949), primarily 1940s hurlers; and Allie Reynolds (1942–1954) and Johnny Sain (1942–1955), 1940s to the 1960s.

Some of the more interesting shutout games in the 1942–1945 Mini-Era include:

September 3, 1942

Louis "Bobo" Newsom, whose nomadic baseball career extended over 20 seasons, nine teams (he visited some of them more than once), and two tenures with Brooklyn, came back to the National League in 1942 after having gone from the Cubs to the St. Louis Browns in 1933. He had yet to win an NL game. That changed when he met Double No-Hit star Johnny Vander Meer, in an early September tilt in 1942, wearing, once again, a Dodgers uniform. A big, 6'3" fellow with a massive upper body, he was a pitcher given to a number of idiosyncrasies. One of those was his penchant for keeping the mound spotless while he was pitching. Opposing infielders, with tiny scraps of paper in their hip pockets, would unload them on the mound as they headed for the dugout between innings and watch in glee as old Bobo would fuss and fume over the disarray. But on this day, Mr. Newsom had it all together, shutting out the Reds with his sharp breaking pitches and a fast ball that regularly broke the 90 mph range. There were only about 4,500 spectators in the stands at Crosley Field, but those who were there saw the Dodgers score a singleton in the third frame, about all Newsom needed on a day when he gave up four scattered hits, struck out eight and benefited from two double plays to erase the few baserunners the Reds could muster. The 2–0 shutout factored into Newsom's 3.38 ERA in six games for the Dodgers in 1942. In 1942 major league rosters were already missing star players, but the Dodgers and the Cardinals, in a fierce struggle for pennant laurels, sported peace-time strength with veterans like Mort Cooper, Whit Wyatt, Lon Warneke, Johnny Allen, and Newsom on hand to help along the bright young stars and wartime replacements who came along to fill in for the Fellers and Spahns who had left.

April 21–25, 1943

The St. Louis Cardinals, defending NL champions and 1942 World Series victors over New York's vaunted Yankees, helped Cincinnati open the 1943 campaign at Crosley Field. The season opened with a new ball manufactured with a balata core (one of the materials not needed in the war effort) and it caused a furor among major league teams. Players scoffed that it felt like cement. Whether that was the direct cause of the remarkable opening series between St. Louis and the Reds is open for debate, but there was certainly a four-game scoring famine in Cincinnati as the two teams struggled mightily to put runs on the board. In the first of the four-game set Johnny Vander Meer two-hit the Cardinals, 1–0, going 11 innings to get the job done. The winning run was scored with one out on a Max Marshall single that scored Lonnie Frey. Marshall, who played for the Reds only during the war, was starting three-year career. The second game, played before 1,879 spectators (the opener drew 27,709), was another 1–0 nail-biter. This time it was 36-year-old Ray Starr who stifled St. Louis bats. Finally, in the third game of the series, the Cardinals found out how to score as they beat the Reds behind 33-year-old Harry Gumbert, 2–1. The defending champs were aided by four Cincy errors and both of the Cardinals runs were unearned.

In the series *finale* the two teams reverted to their opening 1–0 mode, as the Cards scored on a Walker Cooper triple and a Buster Adams out that drove Cooper home in the fifth stanza. Howie Pollet made that run stand up, beating Vander Meer, whose Reds had but five safe blows. During the course of the four games the two teams had scored only six runs. By the end of April the balata ball was gone and MLB had replaced it with the last of the 1941 supply of balls while they awaited a new supply of better quality baseballs. At least that much was normal in those otherwise far-less-than-normal wartime years.

September 16, 1944

There was something new in St. Louis on this day: the Browns edged their way into first place as they demolished the White Sox, 9–0, behind the one-hit craftsmanship of burly Jack Kramer. On their way to the only pennant in franchise history, the Brownies that season racked up 16 shutouts whereas their season average since the Deadball Era was around seven (in 1937 there were only two). The star bin in both leagues was, by the third full year into World War II, practically empty, with meager attendance figures. Team fielding averages were around the .970 mark and league ERAs were in the 3.50 range. But on this day all was well in the Mound City as Kramer and his teammates crushed the Pale Hose. With a 4-for-5 day, Iron Mike Kreevich led a 14-hit attack that made Kramer's 14th win that season easy pickings. It was part of a stretch of 14 wins in 17 games at the end of the season that brought the Browns into the World Series.

September 19, 1945

The year 1945 was all about winning the war and bringing the boys home. Among the many heroes who found his way back was Bob Feller, who, after nearly four years of service duty, resumed his illustrious career with the Cleveland Indians. It didn't take him long to recover his famous high, hard one, and in late August he won his first game, 4–2, over the Tigers and Hal Newhouser. In a brief, 5–3 season he found the shutout touch on September 19, blanking the Tigers and Les Mueller, a strictly wartime player. En route to his victory Feller gave up but one hit, a Jimmy Outlaw single, facing 31 batters in his no-hit bid. It was one of his 12 one-hitters in an 18-season, Hall of Fame career. Jeff Heath's 15th home run of the season was all Feller needed. The Indians had 14 shutouts in 1945, and contributed to the 110 total run up by the AL, 23 better than the 1944 total. The next season Bullet Bob would garner ten shutouts, his highest career mark. He totaled 44 in an awesome career of 266 victories, a winning percentage of .621, and 2,581 career strikeouts.

The Mini Era of wartime years ended with a World Series in 1945 that sports scribe Irving Vaughn of the *Chicago Tribune*, with tongue in cheek, said couldn't be won by either of the contestants, the Cubs or Tigers. There was, nonetheless, a shutout footnote: Hank Borowy led the Cubs in a 9–0 humiliation of the Tigers in the Series opener. Claude Passeau went him one better. In Game 3 he one-hit the Detroiters in another shutout exhibition, this time by a 3–0 count. Alas for Cubbies fans, the Tigers prevailed in the game that counted, number seven, 9–3 behind Hal Newhouser, who had been shelled in the first-game shutout.

America expected, and with great anticipation, that there would be big changes in the first of the post-war years, but not the kind Branch Rickey had in mind. America, like Organized Baseball, was forced to come to grips with its racial situation, like it or not, when "The Mahatma" inked one of the nation's finest athletes, Jackie Robinson, to a Brooklyn franchise contract. Even though he quartered Robinson in Canada with the Montreal Royals, out of sight and in the minors leagues, it was a signing that changed baseball, rocking the staid establishment to its very foundations. The effects of that liberating event were to be felt long afterward and are chronicled voluminously elsewhere. The issue is raised here as a reminder of the many changes baseball experienced in the first score of years after the second great war.

While Robinson would not appear in his first major league game until the Dodgers opened their 1947 season, both leagues were abuzz already in the 1946 spring training camps, and as the season progressed there was no lack of attention paid to north of the border where the ex–Negro Leaguer was leading the charge in Montreal's domination of the International League. Other African Americans in the Dodgers chain soon followed, notably Roy Campanella and Don Newcombe, whose first major league conquest in May of 1949, was a five-hit, 3–0 shutout of the Cincinnati Reds.

Turning to the 1946–1960 years, we find that there were also changes on the field of play, as indicated in the following pitching table. AL statistics appear first, NL behind the slash mark.

	CG	SHO	SHO%	ERA
1946	561/492	106/103	8.53/8.29	3.50/3.42
1947	503/458	100/84	8.03/6.77	3.71/4.07
1948	444/453	75/73	6.07/5.89	4.28/3.95
1949	507/472	88/89	7.12/7.15	4.20/4.04
1950	500/498	62/81	5.00/6.53	4.58/4.14
1951	479/459	78/96	6.32/7.66	4.12/3.96
1952	505/444	99/94	7.97/7.61	3.67/3.73
1953	434/430	96/73	*7.77/5.87	3.99/4.29
1954	463/377	93/83	7.49/6.75	3.72/4.07
1955	363/385	108/70	8.74/5.68	3.96/4.04
1956	398/360	70/67	5.66/5.39	4.16/3.77
1957	354/356	78/75	6.32/6.06	3.79/3.88
1958	387/356	81/64	6.54/5.19	3.77/3.95
1959	366/376	86/85	6.96/6.85	3.86/3.95
1960	312/354	75/84	6.08/6.78	3.87/3.76

Comparison years:
1880 NL	608	52	7.65	2.37
1903 both	954/955	99/69	8.93/6.16	2.96/3.26
1913 both	676/643	113/91	9.20/7.36	2.93/3.20
1935 both	559/534	70/81	5.73/6.56	4.46/4.02

By the time this era ended it was possible to make out the characteristics, as well as the evolution of the national pastime over the course of some 75 years, which made it possible to note the stark differences in the game from its playing fields to the players and the numbers they left behind. The one most critical element of the game, pitching, left the most indelible marks along the columns of records that detailed its progress (and in some cases deterioration). Note, if you will, the differences in the 1880 National League and 1903, and then on to the 1960 statistics particularly in the number of shutouts, and in the Earned Run Averages of selected years in those three eras.

From this era the salient marks of 20 hurlers are presented. Only five of them have been enshrined, and if the others are not worthy of Hall of Fame honors, at least a few of them are surely a very close, nearby echelon away. In the first column (YS) each player's years and number of shutouts are recorded. The * designates a Hall of Fame player.

	YS	W-L-Pct.	IP	ERA
Antonelli, John	1948–61 (25)	126–110, .534	1992.1	3.34
Brecheen, Harry	1940–53 (25)	133–92, .591	1907.2	2.92
Cooper, Mort	1938–49 (33)	128–75, .631	1840.2	2.97
Dickson, Murry	1939–59 (27)	172–181, .487	3052.1	3.66
Ford, E. (Whitey)*	1950–67 (45)	236–106, .690	3170.1	2.75
Friend, Bob	1951–66 (36)	197–230, .461	3611	3.58
Garcia, Mike	1948–61 (27)	142–97, .594	2174.2	3.27
Haddix, Harvey	1952–65 (20)	136–113, .546	2235	3.63
Jansen, Larry	1947–56 (17)	122–89, .578	1765.2	3.58
Lemon, Bob*	1946–58 (31)	207–128, .618	2850	3.23
Lopat, Eddie	1944–55 (27)	166–112, .597	2439.1	3.21
Maglie, Sal	1945–58 (25)	191–62, .657	1723	3.15
Newcombe, Don	1949–60 (24)	149–90, .623	2154.2	3.56
Newhouser, Hal*	1939–55 (33)	207–150, .580	2993	3.06
Pierce, Billy	1945–64 (38)	211–169, .555	3306.2	3.27
Reynolds, Allie	1942–54 (36)	182–107, .630	2492.1	3.30
Roberts, Robin*	1948–66 (45)	286–245, .539	4688.2	3.41
Spahn, Warren*	1942–65 (63)	363–245, .597	5243.2	3.09
Trout, Paul (Dizzy)	1939–57 (28)	170–161, .514	2725.2	3.23
Trucks, Virgil	1941–58 (33)	177–135, .567	2682.1	3.39

A few of the more interesting shutout games of the post-war era follow.

September 11, 1946

The host Brooklyn Dodgers and the Cincinnati Reds battled 19 innings in a game lasting 4 hours and 40 minutes that turned out to be the longest scoreless game on record. Johnny Vander Meer (15 IP) and Hal Gregg (10 IP) started for their teams. Harry Gumbert picked up the last four innings for the Reds, and three hurlers finished out the marathon for the Dodgers. The game was replayed nine days later, and Vander Meer again started for the Reds, but this time took a 5–3 loss in a game that saw the scoreless tie continue another four innings before a three-run Dixie Walker home run put the Dodgers ahead. The box score of the September 11 game:

Cincinnati	AB	R	H	PO	A	Brooklyn	AB	R	H	PO	A
Clay, cf	5	0	1	8	0	Stanky, 2b	7	0	0	4	2
Zientra, 3b	7	0	1	0	2	Reese, ss	8	0	2	4	11
Frey, 2b	6	0	1	1	8	Reiser, lf, cf	7	0	1	1	2
Haas, 1b	8	0	2	22	2	Walker, rf	8	0	1	3	1
West, lf	8	0	0	2	0	Furillo, cf	6	0	0	6	0
Mueller, c	6	0	0	17	2	Galan, lf	1	0	0	0	0
Lukon, rf	7	0	1	2	0	Lavagetto, 3b	7	0	3	1	2

Cincinnati	AB	R	H	PO	A	Brooklyn	AB	R	H	PO	A
Corbitt, ss	7	0	3	2	7	Edwards, c	6	0	0	16	1
V'r Meer, p	6	0	1	3	3	Schultz, 1b	6	0	1	19	6
Gumbert, p	1	0	0	0	0	Stevens, 1b	1	0	0	0	0
						Gregg, p	3	0	0	0	0
						Casey, p	1	0	0	3	1
						Medwick, ph	1	0	0	0	0
						Herring, p	0	0	0	0	1
						Whitman, ph	1	0	0	0	0
						Behrman, p	0	0	0	0	1
Totals	61	0	10	57	24	Totals	63	0	8	57	28

Cincinnati 000 000 000 000 000 000 0-0-10-2
Brooklyn   000 000 000 000 000 000 0-0-8-1

April 27, 1947

Sid Hudson pitched his only shutout of the 1947 season at Yankee Stadium on a day set aside to honor George Herman Ruth. It was "Babe Ruth Day" and over 58,000 fans turned out to give homage to the cancer-stricken Bambino, who graciously thanked them all in his hoarse voice. In the pregame ceremonies he finished up his brief remarks by saying, "I'm glad I had the opportunity to thank everybody." In the game that followed, a seventh-inning single by Buddy Lewis scored the tall Senators hurler for the only run of the game. Hudson stranded eight Yankees and beat Spud Chandler to remain undefeated at 2–0.

August 13, 1948

It wasn't his first appearance on major league turf, but is *was* Leroy "Satchel" Paige's first major league complete game. More than 10,000 were turned away from Comiskey park on an evening's draw of 51,013, as the Indians, en route to their first pennant in 28 years, visited Chicago's White Sox. Paige had been on hand for many a game as well as All-Star games at Comiskey Park (he was the Negro Leagues' MVP in 1935), where he led the Kansas City Monarchs and other teams with his peerless hurling.

There were no free passes from either the ageless one, or the Sox' Randy Gumbert in this matchup, as Paige won his fourth game with a masterful five-hitter. The 5–0 victory pushed his budding major league record to 4–1. The AL's first African American, Larry Doby, supported Paige with two hits, one of them a triple, two RBI and a pair of runs. Paige had attracted 72,434 fans to his first start — and there would be more. Just a week later he turned in his second straight win over the White Sox, this time at cavernous Municipal Stadium, where 78,382 Clevelanders turned out to see the sly old moundsman blank the Pale Hose 1–0. Once again Larry Doby provided offensive punch with a hit that scored manager Lou Boudreau with the only run of the game. Paige fashioned two of the AL's six 1–0 games in 1948 to go along with a sparkling 2.48 ERA.

July 25, 1950

The Philadelphia Phillies had won their only previous pennant handily in 1915 behind Pete Alexander, whose 1.22 ERA led the National League (he added 31 wins and 12 shutouts to his gold-plated record that year) and seemed to be on the brink of a dynasty. That didn't come to pass. In fact, the next 35 years brought nothing but frustration to Philly fans.

Satchel Paige might have moved slowly but his fast-ball didn't (Brace photograph).

But the Whiz Kids of 1950 put an end to all that. The new pitching leader was husky right-hander Robin Roberts, who that summer became a 20-game winner for the first time. In late July he presided over a tense, 1–0 victory that was finally won in the bottom of the ninth on a run scored by pinch runner Ralph "Putsy" Caballero. Richie Ashburn's hit sent him home with two out in the ninth, edging the Phils into first place by a half-game. It was the nightcap feature, a pivotal game in the hotly contested pennant race that summer. In the twin bill opener Emory "Bubba" Church defeated Cubs hurler Johnny Klippstein. Roberts crafted his second of three 1–0 victories that season. In 1950 the Phillies held their opponents to one run 15 times in addition to logging 13 shutouts. Their pitching staff posted a 3.50 ERA, fully 64 percentage points below the National League average of 4.14.

April 13, 1953

By the time the Milwaukee entry in the newly formed American league won its first game at home in 1901, they were already saddled with a 2–8 record. But they won their first game on home turf (they lost their first two games in Milwaukee to the White Sox by 11–3 scores) over Chicago 21–7 on May 5, 1901.

Fifty-two years later Milwaukee was back in the majors, this time opening their National League 1953 home season against the St. Louis Cardinals. It was the first franchise shift since 1903, when the Baltimore franchise of the American League was moved to New York. On March 13, 1953, the Boston Braves became the Braves of Milwaukee, and in their opening two games they were winners. A month after their franchise move's acceptance, in their home opener as Warren Spahn prevailed, 3–2, in 10 innings before 34,357 enthusiastic Wisconsin rooters. The day before, in Cincinnati, the Braves were hosted by the Reds at Crosley Field. They also won that one, the season opener, in a neat, one hour and 56 minute victory by a 2–0 score, with Max Surkont registering the first of their 14 shutouts that season. The first County Stadium whitewashing was administered by Johnny Antonelli, who beat the Cubs on May 8, 2–0.

September 20, 1958

Knuckleballer Hoyt Wilhelm astonished the baseball world when he no-hit the New York Yankees by the thinnest of margins, 1–0. The game was as tight as any seen in years, with Don Larsen of the Yankees and the angular Wilhelm, dueling through six innings of scoreless ball. Two wily managers, Casey Stengel of the Yankees and Paul Richards of the Orioles, watched their charges battle fruitlessly throughout those first six stanzas. Then Stengel called on his small but mighty reliever Bobby Shantz to hold the O's at bay. Richards had already made defensive replacements as play began in the top of the seventh inning. In the home half of the inning the first batter up was Wilhelm's battery mate, Gus Triandos. The big fellow promptly blasted a Shantz offering some 415 feet into the seats to tie Yogi Berra for the IIID-16 most home runs (30) by an American League catcher in a season, putting the O's ahead 1–0.

For the Yankees eighth, Richards brought on Brooks Robinson to play third base, replacing Dick Williams. He moved Williams to left field and replaced shortstop Foster Castleman with Willie Miranda. Hoyt Wilhelm then retired the side, including Yogi Berra, who pinchhit for Marv Throneberry. Bobby Richardson, pinch-hitter Enos Slaughter and Hank Bauer went down in order to finish off one of the most improbable no-hitters ever. Of all the things that might have happened with a knuckleball pitcher on the mound, none did. Triandos, with his specially designed, oversized glove, had but one passed ball, a near-miracle in itself.

Hoyt Wilhelm, who had come to Baltimore from Cleveland just a month before his stunning no-no, had done his first starting that year after six seasons as a reliever and went on to become the first relief pitcher in baseball history to be enshrined in the Hall of Fame. The no-hit, 1958 victory was his only shutout of that season and the first in a 21-year career that included only five shutouts.

September 28, 1960

Kansas City's Ned Garver was the last shutout artist of the 1942–1960 War and Transition Era, defeating Gaylord Perry's older brother Jim, 4–0. Leo Posada helped Garver along with his only four-bagger of the season on the same day Ted Williams finished up his career with a home run in his last trip to the plate at Boston's Fenway Park. Garver went the route, striking out one and allowing the visiting Cleveland Indians but three hits, all singles. It was the American League's 75th shutout in 1960 as compared with the Senior Circuit's 84.

Of the many changes that occurred during this very active era, marked by franchise moves from coast to coast, none affected shutouts more than the altered strike zone, which reduced it to its present armpit to top-of-the-knee distance, and advances both in glove technology and groundskeeping. Those latter changes would undergo still more refinement in the years to come which would increasingly enable pitchers to whittle away at the record book, but not necessarily at major league shutout records.

Some of that whittling was already evident, as underscored in the table above. Note the gradual increase, between 1942 and 1960 in Saves, and the decrease in Complete Games. With more and more hitters swinging for the fences, pitchers were more than ever trying to deliver the ball to home plate's outer edges and to the lower parts of the strike zone. Meanwhile, it appeared to be more and more evident that there would be fewer shutouts. The days of the Johnsons and Alexanders had surely become part of a distant and more than likely irretrievable past.

7

The Shutout During an Era of Transition: 1961–1984

Between 1961 and 1984, there was unprecedented growth in attendance; venues, equipment and facilities; the business end of the game; and the actual number of franchises in competition for the honors and accolades baseball would bestow on its leaders and champions. These and still other facets of the national pastime would obviously have an effect in one way or another on the possibilities or plausibilities of throwing low-hit and shutout games.

Each era, no matter the years or events, has its greats, and the 1961–1984 era has more than its share. Among its standouts are Juan Marichal, who won 20 games six times between 1963 and 1969, Sandy Koufax and Bob Gibson, all National Leaguers, and American Leaguers Jim Palmer (1965–1984) and Jim "Catfish" Hunter (1965–1979). Add to this list, which might easily draw another 20 greats, those who worked their pitching wizardry in both leagues like Jim Bunning, Don Sutton and reliever Rich "Goose" Gossage all Hall of Fame pitchers.

The men of the hill listed above, and many others of great accomplishment, did their hurling during a time when baseball expanded from eight teams in each league to ten, and on to 12 when the leagues split their teams into divisions. Ultimately they moved on to a total of 30 teams spread across the nation, accomplished in 1998.

Two other factors entered into the development of modern baseball. The first, the designated hitter, initiated in 1973, affected the American League only, but the second, the organization of the Major League Baseball Players Association, which in 1975 shed the shackles of the Reserve Clause, affected not only the American League, but the entire sphere of professional athletics, including major league baseball, forever. The effect on shutout records was equally profound. Consider this: an outstanding pitcher on a poor ball club could now negotiate with a pennant winner, thus increasing his chances of hurling low-run games.

As the 1961–1984 era wore on, the effects of free agency, strikes and player mobility became more pronounced. A classic example of the "new order of things" was Goose Gossage, who moved from the Pittsburgh Pirates in 1977 to the World Series with the New York Yankees in 1978. That would formerly have been impossible, except by trade. Within a month after he had been declared a free agent in October of 1977, he signed with the Yanks and subsequently became *The Sporting News*' Fireman of the Year in 1978. Being with an American League powerhouse certainly didn't hurt his chances for superior achievement any!

One other change during this era that caused differences in defensive play should be mentioned because it had an affect on the possibility of pitching shutouts. The reference here is to the installation of artificial turf, most noticeably in the National League during the 1960s and 1970s. The trend began in Houston with the construction of the Astrodome in 1965 and was soon picked up in Pittsburgh, Philadelphia and Cincinnati in 1970. The turf was laid on a cement base and caused the ball* to streak through the infield and bounce higher than it would have on dirt-based grass. This caused infielders to play deeper and baserunners to become more aggressive in running the bases. It was but one of many factors at work when making judgments about the number and quality of pitching results. When a team can't get 'em out it certainly has something to do with the pitcher's choice and the placement of his pitches, as well as how many he will have to throw.

With the rise of relief pitchers, by now a standard part of every ball club's pitching staff, there was an accompanying reduction in the number of shutouts credited to pitchers who more and more left the closing innings to others on the staff. But while there were fewer shutouts credited to starting pitchers, there was no drastic decline in the number of shutout *games*.

In *Baseball Between the Numbers* (Keri, 2006, 75) is a chapter written by Keith Woolner titled *Five Starters or Four? On Pitching and Stamina* which discusses the reasons for the demise of the complete game and other factors involved in the changes in pitchers, pitching strategies and coaching that have led to the present *status quo*. This perceptive analysis includes a table Woolner calls "Starts Resulting in Complete Games over the Past One Hundred Years." The table presents three columns, as follows: Games Started (GmsS), Complete Games (CG), and Complete Games as Percent of Starts (%S). The table:

Year	*GmsS*	*CG*	*%S*
1904	2496	2186	87.6
1924	2462	1199	48.7
1944	2484	1123	45.2
1964	3252	797	24.5

*Still another factor is the ball, discussed in the next and final era under consideration, the contemporary era.

7. The Shutout During an Era of Transition: 1961–1984 · 63

Year	GmsS	CG	%S
1984	4210	632	15.0
2004	4856	150	3.1

Note, please, that Woolner's lineup included every ten years, whereas the table above uses every 20th year. That aside, the numbers underscore in the most emphatic terms the diminution of both complete games totals and in complete games as a percentage of the number of games started. The table underscores the contentions and numbers cited previously in this book. Although relief pitching had become a part of the game many years earlier, it was during the 1961 to 1984 era that it began to be honed to a point of tactical and strategic advantage. With it came changes in the approach and responsibilities of starting pitchers. By the turn of the new millennium the starting and relieving aspects of the game became fixed in stone and every team in Organized Baseball had patterned its staff accordingly.

A representative list of the era's stars follows. GS/GC, Games started and completed; HR, home runs allowed; OBA, Opponents' batting average; and S%CG indicates the percentage of complete games that were shutouts. These are the career numbers (the * indicates a Hall of Fame member):

Southpaw Tommy John won 288 games in a 26-year career with 46 shutouts.

	Yrs	GS/CG	SHO	S%CG	HR	OBA	ERA
Jim Bunning*	1955–71	519/151	40	26	372	.242	3.27
Sandy Koufax*	1955–66	314/137	40	29	204	.205	2.76
Don Drysdale*	1956–69	465/167	49	29	280	.239	2.95
Bob Gibson*	1959–75	482/255	56	22	257	.228	2.91
Jim Kaat	1959–83	625/180	31	17	395	.264	3.45
Juan Marichal*	1960–75	457/244	52	21	320	.237	2.89
Tommy John	1963–89	700/162	46	28	302	.265	3.34
Mickey Lolich	1963–79	496/195	41	21	347	.246	3.44
Steve Carlton*	1965–88	709/254	55	22	414	.240	3.22

	Yrs	GS/CG	SHO	S%CG	HR	OBA	ERA
Jim Palmer*	1965–84	521/211	53	25	303	.230	2.86
Nolan Ryan*	1966–93	773/222	61	27	321	.204	3.19
Tom Seaver*	1967–86	647/231	61	26	380	.226	2.86

Because so many things can happen in literally countless varieties during the course of a season, a game, or even in an inning's play, there is no lack of "first-ever" events to make an era of baseball history memorable. The years 1961 to 1984 had a fair share of those kinds of games. One of them turned out to be the longest shutout game ever.

April 15, 1968

The longest shutout game ever played went into the wee hours of April 16 and threatened to become a season in and of itself, setting another of those baseball records that will most likely never be broken. Lasting until after 1:30 A.M., this game was made up of 79 at-bats by each team, 22 hits (11 by each team, which was a surprisingly small number for 24 innings of play), and nine players who made ten or more plate appearances.

Vito Stellino of *The Sporting News* (issue of April 27, 1968) opened his coverage of that Houston–New York marathon as follows:

> (Houston, Texas) Baseball's longest night was filled with moments of humor, drama, dullness and frustration — but, most of all, it was a nightmare for Al Weis.
>
> Weis, utility infielder for the Mets who was filling in at shortstop because Bud Harrelson had a sore arm, let a bases-loaded grounder go through his legs to end the longest night game — and longest scoreless contest — in baseball history April 15.
>
> The Astros and Mets matched zeroes for what seemed forever before Bob Aspromonte's grounder skipped through Weis' legs to score Norm Miller in the 24th inning. The run gave the Astros an incredible 1–0 victory in a six-hour and six minute marathon that ended at 1:37 A.M. (Houston time).
>
> No game had ever gone longer than 20 innings without scoring. No night games had ever gone longer than 22 innings before and that feat was accomplished last June 12 when the Senators edged the White Sox, 6–5. Gil Hodges was managing the Senators and had a victory to show for the long night's work. This time, as manager of the Mets, he tasted defeat.

The play-by-play account is available from Retrosheet and other baseball websites. Each account you find will have a different take on this unbelievable chain of events that led to the record books, but the most singular thing about this interminable Houston shutout victory was the 24-inning scoring drought experienced by the Mets. At the end of the day — and long night — it wound up as "just another" *W* for one team and an *L* for the other, but what an *L* it was!

July 27, 1968

In the "Year of the Pitcher" baseball eyes were riveted on Don Drysdale and Bob Gibson. Between an April 13 four-hitter and June 4, when he beat Jim Bunning and the Pirates, 5–0, Big D fired seven shutouts, including a 58.2-inning shutout streak that ended, finally, in the fifth inning of a 5–3 Dodger's victory on June 8. Bob Gibson, meanwhile, was in the midst of his record-setting season, posting an almost non-existent ERA of 1.12. It took Gibson a little longer to get started, but by the end of June he had run up five scoreless outings in a season of 13.

In the American League, it was on the date above, July 27, that Denny McLain shut out the Orioles on three hits, winning his 20th (there would be 11 more in '68) for the Tigers. In that game there were dingers by Willie Horton, twice, and one each by Don Wert, Al Kaline and Dick McAuliffe in a 9–0 romp that moved the Bengals 7½ games ahead of the Baltimore Orioles.

A week before, on July 20 at New York, Luis Tiant, aka El Tiante, blanked the Yankees, 3–0, on a three-hit shutout, one of his league-leading nine that year.

A review of some selected statistics illustrates why 1968, with Tiant, Gibson, Marichal, Sam McDowell and Drysdale, among quite a few others, is often referred to as "The Year of the Pitcher." Consider these:

1. There were 339 shutouts in 1968, 185 (NL) and 154 (AL). That is right at 10.43 percent or one out of every ten games started.
2. There were three NL and two AL no-hitters thrown in 1968.
3. Gibson with 13 shutouts; Tiant, 9; Drysdale, 8; Steve Blass and Jerry Koosman 7; and Bill Singer, Jim Nash, Ray Sandecki, Ray Culp, McLain, Dean Chance and Mel Stottlemyre, each with 6, formed the top 12 among ML pitchers.
4. The All-Star Game, played on July 9, ended in an NL, 1–0 victory, Drysdale the winner and Tiant the loser.
5. Among the top ten ERA leaders at 2.08 or less were: Gibson at 1.12; Tiant, 1.60; McDowell, 1.81; Dave McNally, 1.95; McLain, 1.96; Tommy John, 1.98; Bob Bolin, 1.99; Stan Bahnsen and Bob Veale, 2.05; and Jerry Koosman, 2.08.
6. The losing team in four of the seven 1968 World Series games was held to one run, and the Series opened with a shutout.

7. MVP Award winners in both leagues were pitchers: McLain (AL) and Gibson (NL).
8. The AL batting champion, Carl Yastrzemski, hit 71 points above the AL league BA, yet hit "only" .301. Pete Rose was 92 points over the NL BA average, hitting .335 to win the NL crown.
9. 13 of the 20 teams had team pitching ERAs under 3.00.

The listing reads like a review straight out of the early 1900s.

July–August, 1968

Jim McAndrew's start in the major leagues is one of the more poignant stories of the 1968 season. McAndrew, who came to New York's Mets in July of the "Year of the Pitcher," had the misfortune of being paired with Bob Gibson for his first major league start. He lost that one, 2–0. And he lost the next three started without his teammates scoring a run for him. The scores were: 2–0 (Mike Kekich of the Dodgers won his only career shutout in that one); Bob Bolin, Giants right hander, beat McAndrew, 1–0; and the Astros' Don Wilson also beat him, 1–0. In his next outing Juan Marichal beat McAndrew for his 23rd victory, but then he finally broke into the win column with a 1–0 win over Steve Carlton. The next time out, he once again met Carlton, but lost that one, 2–0. So, in his first seven starts in The Bigs, Jim McAndrew met future Hall of Fame pitchers four times and set a record for losing his first four big league starts via the shutout route. By the way, on September 11 of that year he beat Ferguson Jenkins, 1–0, no doubt to reassure himself that the goose egg connection hadn't entirely forsaken him! McAndrew was hailed by his teammates as "The Pride of Lost Nation, Iowa!"

There is a shutout epilogue to the McAndrew story: On October 2, 1972, Bill Stoneman of the Montreal Expos no-hit the Mets, 7–0. That's right, Jim McAndrew was the losing pitcher.

April 19 and September 3, 1972

These two dates were marked by shutouts, the first and last of Steve Carlton's incredible 1972 season. Detailed in many other publications, the taciturn southpaw's contribution to the 1972 Phillies' story was made in the midst of a dismal, last-place finish for one of the worst teams in Philadelphia history — and there were more than a few of them. Yet, Carlton threw shutout games at Bob Gibson, Juan Marichal (a one-hitter), and Tommy John, among others, totaling eight of the 13 shutouts the Phils mustered in 1972. Five of those whitewashing gems were a part of his 15-game winning streak, the last of which, during that streak, came on August 9, when Carlton's home run helped him beat Pittsburgh on a three-hitter.

Before 5,119 Atlantans, Carlton spaced five hits while coasting to an 8–0 win over the Braves on September 3. It was the 22nd of his 27 victories that year, which, when combined with a 1.97, career-low ERA and 346.1 innings pitched, gave Cy Young Award voters no choice but to present the award to Carlton. In the victory over the Braves, Carlton led off the third inning with a single and scored one of the eight tallies the Phils pieced together for the only scoring inning that day. It was one of those rare Phils days that summer when Carlton was able to waltz his way through a cakewalk.

Steve Carlton, who won nearly half his team's victories in 1972 (Brace photograph).

Among his 254 career complete games Steve Carlton threw 55 shutouts, tying him with Mordecai Brown for 12th place on the all-time list below:

Career Shutouts, the Top 20

Walter Johnson, 110
Pete Alexander, 90
Christy Mathewson, 79
Cy Young, 76
Eddie Plank, 69
Warren Spahn, 63
Nolan Ryan, 61
Tom Seaver, 61
Bert Blyleven, 60
Don Sutton, 58

Ed Walsh, 57
Pud Galvin, 57
Bob Gibson, 56
Mordecai Brown, 55
Steve Carlton, 55
Jim Palmer, 53
Gaylord Perry, 53
Juan Marichal, 52
Rube Waddell, 50
Vic Willis, 50

Jim Palmer and Gaylord Perry, tied at the 16th spot in career shutouts (Brace photographs).

April 17, 1976

On this date the Thurman Munson and Ed Figueroa battery got off to a great start in the American League race. Munson, a gifted defensive player, was a fine signal caller. His value to the Yankees was recognized when, on this day, he was named the first Yankees captain since Lou Gehrig. The handsome Puerto Rican Figueroa, acquired from California, made his second start as a Yankee a memorable one, teaming with Munson to squash the visiting Twins, 10–0, chiefly on the strength of a seven-run outburst in the second inning.

The stocky Yank captain homered and added another two hits as the Bronx Bombers won their fifth straight in the early going of the nation's Bicentennial Year. It was the first of 19 conquests for Figueroa in 1976, as well as the first of his four shutouts. He enjoyed three good years with the Yankees, culminating in successive championship years in 1977 and 1978, before he gave way to an elbow injury, thus bringing his career to a premature halt in 1981. His April 17 victory was a six-hitter, and later he fired a trio of three-hitters in his other shutouts of the season.

July 16, 1976

There were fewer than 15,000 spectators on hand when Mark "The Bird" Fidrych arrived on Planet Baseball, providing the Tigers with a 2–1 victory over the Cleveland Indians on May 15, 1976, at Tiger Stadium for his first major league victory. By July the lovable eccentric was packing them in like sardines at the corner of Michigan and Trumbull, picking up one win after another.

On the morning of July 16 his record stood at 9–2, and that day there would be in excess of 45,000 fans in attendance to see their new phenom. When The Bird was pitching seats were hard to find. Unfortunately for the visiting Athletics and Rollie Fingers, Fidrych had the whole thing going, dueling Fingers through ten innings, *mano a uccello*. In the top of the 11th frame Billy North singled for the A's' seventh hit, but Fidrych stranded the potential go-ahead run and the score remained 0–0. In the bottom of that frame Willie Horton came to the rescue with a line shot that scored Tigers swiftie Ron LeFlore, and The Bird went to 10–2, the winner of a 1–0 shutout. That season, what could have been better for Detroiters than to watch their beloved Bird beat, well, anyone? It really didn't matter as long as it was Mark Fidrych out there tending to his mound-keeping chores! The Tigers were in sad shape during the Bicentennial Year's baseball season. They came up with only 74 wins, trailing their division's leaders, the Yankees, by 24 games at season's end. Only 12 of those 74 had the distinction of being shutouts. The Bird flew off with four of those.

"The Bird," Mark Fidrych (Brace photograph).

June 11 and August 10, 1981

A pair of days, one in June, and the other in August, at the heart of the baseball season, marked the game's first in-season strike. The last games played before the strike began on June 12, featured a June 11 shutout at Montreal authored by the veteran Steve Rogers, who managed to add three during the abbreviated season out of his career total of 37. When play resumed on August 10, the man with the bionic arm, Tommy John, beat Danny Darwin of the Rangers, 2–0 in New York.

At the outset the strike-bitten season, Texas pitchers had put together a skein of four straight shutouts, April 27 to 30, spearheaded by a Darwin one-hitter on April 29 against Boston, 5–0. Thirty-nine consecutive shutout innings included that stretch of games.

April 15, 1983

Early in the season there are a significantly large number of low-hit and shutout games, put together before warmer weather heats up the hitters with their whip-handled bats. Milt Wilcox fired one of his two shutouts in 1983 on this day, a near-perfect game masterpiece. With two out in the ninth inning at Chicago, the big Tigers hurler had only pinch-hitter Jerry Hairston to retire for his 27th consecutive out. Regretfully, it didn't happen, as is the case more often than one would suspect. Hairston singled sharply to center, though the hit didn't ruin Wilcox' one-hit shutout. The weather that day? The mercury struggled to get into the 40s on a typically raw April day in Chicago.

April 26, 1983

Arm problems, which plague so many pitchers, put a crimp in the career of Larry McWilliams. However, into his sixth season, and first full season with the Pirates, Johnny Sain, one of the more astute pitching coaches in baseball history, worked with the tall lefty, changing his delivery and pitching tempo. As for 1983, the rest was, as they say, *history*. He won more games that season, 15, than in any other in his 13-year career. Among his eight complete games were four sparkling shutouts: April 9 against Houston, a 1–0 two-hitter; April 26, at Pittsburgh versus San Francisco, a one-hitter (catcher Bob Brenly in the fifth inning); a 3–0 two-hitter on July 9 at Los Angeles; and a two-hitter in New York on September 20, 4–0. In those four shutouts he was touched for only seven hits.

Of the 115 National League shutouts that season, only 47 were complete games, 41 percent. Before long the percentage would drop further and faster. The downward trend was well under way.

September, 1984

This era's final year, 1984, wound up with two remarkable performances, one in each league. On the 12th of September, Dwight Gooden blanked the Pirates, 2–0, fanning 16. The Mets wunderkind set the rookie strikeout mark at 276, as well as leading the league in OBA (opponents' batting average) at .202. His 1985 season would be even better.

What better way to close shop for another year than with a perfect game?! Mike Witt took care of those closing ceremonies on September 30 with a "Perfecto" against Charlie Hough and the Texas Rangers, 1–0. Reggie Jackson's fielder's choice scored Doug DeCinces in the seventh inning for the game's only run. It was Witt's second shutout of the season, this one a stunner witnessed by only 8,375 Texans. In 1984 the 6'7" Witt won in double figures for the first time in his 16 year career, posting 15 wins.

In the following table era figures present relevant shutout specifics. AL team statistics are listed first; NL behind the slash mark.

	SHO	SHO%	CG	ERA
1961	100/73	6.16/5.89	417/328	4.02/4.03
1962	104/95	6.43/5.85	386/458	3.97/3.94
1963	121/154	7.48/9.49	406/459	3.63/3.29
1964	134/135	8.23/8.31	349/448	3.63/3.54
1965	117/126	7.22/7.75	323/416	3.46/3.54
1966	118/128	7.32/7.91	334/402	3.44/3.61
1967	153/121	9.44/7.47	365/417	3.23/3.38
1968	154/185	9.48/11.38	426/471	2.98/2.99
1969	134/166	6.88/8.53	451/531	3.62/3.60
1970	110/124	5.71/6.38	382/470	3.71/4.05
1971	164/151	8.49/7.76	537/546	3.46/3.47
1972	193/164	10.39/8.82	502/507	3.06/3.45
1973	150/143	7.72/7.35	614/447	3.82/3.66
1974	144/142	7.40/7.30	650/439	3.62/3.62
1975	137/129	7.11/6.64	625/427	3.78/3.62
1976	161/164	8.32/8.44	590/449	3.52/3.50
1977	117/121	5.17/6.22	586/321	4.06/3.91
1978	161/144	7.12/7.41	645/389	3.76/3.57
1979	116/121	5.14/6.23	551/362	4.22/3.73
1980	132/132	5.83/6.88	549/307	4.03/3.60
1981	117/103	7.80/8.00	334/176	3.66/3.49
1982	121/117	5.33/6.02	445/289	4.07/3.60
1983	133/115	5.86/5.90	469/276	4.06/3.63
1984	124/130	5.47/6.69	398/234	3.99/3.59

The marks logged between 1966 and 1970 show a momentary crest in 1968 produced by the last corps of NL pitchers who enjoyed the use of a 15" mound elevation. The National League's shutout percentage of 11.38 that season was its highest since the shocking 1908, 13.18 percentage rating, which was the best mark of the Deadball Era. Finally, the 1968 league ERA dipped below 3.00 in both leagues, the only time that happened between 1961 and 1984.

In 1972 the Senior Circuit came along with a percentage surge in the midst of a sharp rise from 1970's 6.38 to 1972's 8.82, a mark higher by five percentage points than 1968's 11.38. And this, after all was said and done, from a 10" pitcher's mound. During that same season the American League recorded 193 shutouts (the AL shutout percentage also hit an era high at 10.39 percent). The very next season, with the Designated Hitter ruling in play, that 193 figure dropped to 150, finally to settle in the 130 range the remainder of the era.

So many numbers here might be confusing, but it would seem fair to say that lowering the height of the pitcher's mound and inserting a designated hitter into American League lineups did have the effect baseball's owners were looking for: more homers and more runs, and clubs that would produce more high-scoring games. In the AL, homer totals rose from .63 per game in 1972 to .79 in 1973, and the rate would fall below .70 only once more (1976) in the decade. After the 1968 and 1973 benchmark seasons the pitching and defensive control of the game in both leagues was diminished. Offense was, more and more, the name of the game, and by the new century the big boppers were in full bloom, blasting their way to new marks. That was something baseball's ownership approved of, citing as evidence the dramatic rise in attendance during the years McGwire-Sosa-Bonds *et al.* were pounding expensively manufactured baseballs to smithereens. The upsurge in the number of dramatic, game-ending four-baggers that began in the 1970s continued apace on into the new millennium.

8

The Modern Era: 1985–2010

There had been unrest among the ranks of the players long before baseball's first major strike of the modern era. The players, striving to extricate themselves from chattel-like contractual arrangements, formed associations of one kind or another to modify or indeed do away with the Reserve Clause, which bound players to the teams with which they had first contracted. The restrictions of the Reserve Clause went into effect in 1879. By 1889 John Montgomery Ward had had enough. In the last months of 1889 and early in 1890 he was the chief catalyst in the formation of the Players' League, in which some improvements were made in contractual arrangements. However, the Players' League folded after a single season and the "Baseball Establishment" saw to it that from 1891 forward they would maintain a vise-like grip on the business end of the national pastime. And so the festering went on and on.

Over the years there were repeated and unsuccessful attempts to organize a solid and dependable structure the players could count on to mitigate their financial status with the owners. Finally, in 1976, with a reinterpretation of the Reserve Clause, the players, thanks the Major League Baseball Players Association first formed in 1953, had the powerful antidote they had sought for nearly a century. In an era of expansion and increased revenue between 1961 and 1984, they used their organized power to forge contractual agreements both as a unit, through the MLBPA and individually with owners of the various teams in both leagues. The strike, a common but very effective union strategy, was the principal and "ultimate recourse" when negotiations bogged down in the mire of technicalities and legal considerations implicit in ownership's concern for financial profitability and the players' concern for what they considered to be a fair share of the game's—and teams financial success.

In the previous era there were strikes in 1972 and 1981, the latter much more acrimonious and damaging than the 1972 "work stoppage" as the unionized players preferred to call it. By 1985, a new era emerged in which player salaries rose, nay, leapt in such numbers that Joe Fan wondered what the players would do with all that money. In February of that year, for example, outfielder Tim Raines set a new record, since broken many times over, with a $1.2 million arbitration contract to play for the Montreal Expos. We mark that record-making agreement as the beginning of the last era under consideration in baseball's oft turbulent history, an era of Free Agency, multi-billion dollar business, and well nigh unfettered forward movement, at least as far as the money end of baseball is concerned.

This last, contemporary era can hardly be called a pitchers' era even though there have been outstanding Cy Young Award winners and no lack of pitching gems to balance the all-out attack on the offensive part of the record book. It was, to say the very least, an explosive era.

A look at baseball's most electrifying and, as some would have it, its single, most spectacular event, the home run, will bring the era's bombastic histrionics into focus with a few "most" numbers, to wit: (1) the most home runs hit by a team in a single season (in the AL, Seattle, 1997, with 264; and Houston in the NL, 2000, with 249) were hit within the last 14 seasons of play; (2) The most home runs hit at home in either league (New York Yankees, 136 in 2009, and Colorado, 149 in 1996) were walloped within the past 15 seasons; (3) 25 players have hit 500 or more home runs, 11 of them since 1985; (4) 12 of the 18 times players have hit more than 55 home runs in a single season have occurred since the 1994–95 strike; and (5) In the first month of the 2000 season, major league baseball players broke the April home run record with 931. Those few citations do not begin to tap a monster lode of recent home run statistics that stagger the minds of baseball fans. And all of them have been recorded in the recent past.

There are a number of reasons for this extraordinary power surge, one of which might well be a lack of depth in major league pitching staffs. Two pieces of equipment come to mind, however, as front-runners. One is the bat and the other is the ball. The thin-barreled handles of the bat in use today produce a whip-like thrust as the bat moves through the strike zone. In the hands of players whose supple bodies have been nurtured with special designed diets and hardened with weight training, the combination makes for blinding bat speed and thundering impact. Consequences? The 400- to 500-foot home run is not a rare event any more. These blasts get far more attention than a game-ending strikeout with the winning run at third base. Years ago it was Ralph Kiner who said that home run hitters drive Cadillacs. He was on to something.

The other half of baseball's most fundamental and essential equipment, the ball, is under investigation regularly, and especially when there is a rash of high-scoring games and home runs are being clubbed in inordinate numbers, whether in individual games or in a season. "There's a rabbit in the ball" is the claim frequently made by, as to be expected, pitchers, when their offerings are dispatched to the far corners of the planet.

Zack Hample has written an extensive treatise on the ball, entitled, quite properly, *The Baseball* (Hample, New York, 2011). Its pages detail everything about the major league baseball from its history to snagging foul balls or home runs. He acknowledges that the little sphere has been altered and doctored since time immemorial. In more modern times, going back to 1931, to stanch the flow of hits and runs that were inundating both leagues, Hample avers that the ball was deadened by raising the seams on the Spalding balls then in use. He cites the Castilian Hall of Famer Al Lopez in 1964, some 30 seasons later, as one among many who claimed the ball was too lively. Lopez was quoted as saying (ibid., 135), "The other day a pop foul struck concrete in the stands. No one was near and the ball bounced clear up to the roof."

How tightly the ball is woven, the quality of the cork and yarn used, the height (or lack) of the stitching, the pellet, or centerpiece of the ball, and many other components all affect the ball's capability of flight, trajectory and distance. And then the final variable, the human element, comes into play, all the way down to the strength of the pitcher's hands and fingers and the skill of the hitter in hitting the ball. Whether one will see a no-hitter or a home run often rides on the quality of the ball, one of the major factors at play in the pitcher's and hitter's battle for supremacy every given at-bat, indeed, every pitch of that 5–5¼-ounce sphere. Ted Williams once said that hitting a baseball was the most difficult of all things athletes to do. If he was right, making a baseball that suits everybody must be very close behind.

The years of the previous era have been stretched in this book from the usual 1976 concluding point, a time when Free Agency was enforced because of arbitration involving Andy Messersmith and Dave McNally (both were pitchers, by the way), to 1984. Thus, the present era under consideration extends from 1985 to the conclusion of the 2010 season. It is the most offense-minded era in baseball history. Yet, even in an era of big scores, with seasonal records being set almost annually, and balls jettisoned out of ball parks with regularity, there have been and continue to be masterful pitchers and masterful exhibitions of pitching. Though they have contributed to the major league shutout log in fewer numbers than during the years of the Alexanders and Mathewsons and Spahns, their accomplishments have been shining stars in the baseball firmament. Before checking into some the era's memorable shutout events, here is a look at the pertinent team stats.

The legend follows: GR represents the total number of relief appearances in a given season. You will notice the significant increase in GR numbers from 1985 to 2010. Note also the comparison years from the previous eras. AL numbers appear first, followed by the NL, behind the slash mark.

	SHO	SHO%	GR	ERA
1985	108/149	4.77/7.67	3737/3561	4.14/3.59
1986	123/113	5.42/5.83	3769/3785	4.17/3.72
1987	114/98	5.03/5.05	3917/4031	4.46/4.08
1988	139/153	6.14/7.89	3743/3588	3.97/3.45
1989	145/147	6.40/7.55	4096/3803	3.88/3.50
1990	144/116	6.35/5.97	4455/4029	3.91/3.79
1991	150/122	6.61/6.29	4780/4183	4.09/3.68
1992	141/157	6.22/8.08	4665/4374	3.94/3.50
1993	110/110	4.85/4.85	4969/5332	4.32/4.04
1994*	65/78	4.08/4.85	3600/3843	4.80/4.21
1995*	90/114	4.46/5.66	4672/5209	4.71/4.18
1996	79/117	3.49/5.16	5344/5716	4.99/4.21
1997	98/113	4.33/4.98	5559/5766	4.57/4.20
1998	101/143	4.45/5.50	5649/6314	4.65/4.23
1999	100/93	4.41/3.59	5714/6706	4.86/4.56
2000	92/112	4.06/4.32	5710/6653	4.91/4.63
2001	91/138	3.93/5.32	5711/7260	4.47/4.36
2002	122/153	5.38/5.91	5557/7205	4.46/4.11
2003	109/150	4.80/5.79	5689/7269	4.52/4.28
2004	115/136	5.08/5.25	5950/7466	4.63/4.30
2005	113/148	4.98/5.71	5930/7245	4.35/4.22
2006	124/136	5.47/5.25	6142/7694	4.56/4.49
2007	115/128	5.07/4.93	6318/8114	4.50/4.43
2008	128/143	5.64/5.52	6278/7879	4.35/4.29
2009	123/150	5.49/5.79	6338/7901	4.45/4.19
2010	127/202	5.60/7.79	6144/7780	4.14/4.02

Comparison years from previous eras:

	SHO	SHO%	GR	ERA
1901	54/70	4.91/6.23	171/156	3.66/3.32
1919	91/101	8.13/9.05	677/621	3.22/2.91
1945	110/83	8.98/6.71	910/1285	3.36/3.80
1960	75/84	6.18/6.78	1859/1734	3.87/3.76
1978	161/144	7.12/7.41	2751/3140	3.76/3.57

*Strike year

Some observations about the numbers in this table...

- The most dramatic rise in numbers has to do with the number of relief appearances made by pitchers in a season, notably from the 1985 NL low of 3561, to the major league high, to date, of 8114 by the NL in 2007.
- The number of Saves has risen in the same period of time from the low 500s to the mid–600 range per season.
- The number of team shutouts in a season has been fairly stable, hovering around the 100–110 mark. (It is no great surprise, however, the number of individual pitcher shutouts has fallen with the onset of an era that

refined the art of relief hurling to such an extent that long relievers, specialty relievers and closers became a part of every team's pitching staff.)
- Comparing the contemporary era with sample years from each era since 1900, the differences are striking. In 1901, for example, there were 18 American League Saves. That statistic rose exponentially through the following eras until the new AL record of 637 was set in 1990 (the present NL record is 697, set in 2004).

The final of the eras that make up baseball history (the nineteenth century, 1901–1919, 1920–1941, 1942–1960, 1961–1984 and 1985–2010) is an era of great pitching, studded with mound titans unlike any era save pitchers active in the Deadball Era. It is an era heavy laden with low-hit games, individual pitching heroics and record-setting feats. Some of the colorful, as well as Olympian events during that quarter century are represented by the several cameos, ordered chronologically, following.

October 6, 1985, and May 7, 2010

The 1985 season closed out with another record for the history book. On October 6 ancient Phil Niekro, by that date 46 years old, became the oldest pitcher in the AL to throw a shutout. Though he would soldier on for another two seasons, this particular shutout, the 45th and last of his career, was logged at the expense of the Toronto Blue Jays. The win, in a Yankees uniform, was his 300th to make the day quite a serendipitous affair.

Niekro's 300th victory opened up the 1985–2010 era, that was closed out in 2010 with another record-setting shutout, this one by the Phils' 47-year-old Jamie Moyer who beat the Atlanta Braves, 2–0, on May 7 in a down-to-business two-hitter in which one of his innings, the second, was a three-pitch stanza. The feat justifiably caused an outpouring of articles about the elder moundsmen of the game, fellows like Jack Quinn and Hoyt Wilhelm of years past, and more recently, Nolan Ryan and Tommy John. The shutout came in the last year of the 1985–2010 era, making for very special era bookend conquests.

September, 1988

Orel Hershiser was born in the middle of September, and on his 30th birthday in 1988 he was at the midpoint of a streak quite like none other in his life. He had completed his third straight September shutout on the 14th against the Atlanta Braves, a four-hit, 3–0 win. He went on to beat Houston,

1–0, on the 19th, and followed with a 3–0 blanking of the San Francisco Giants to make it five straight. Though the regular season was over for him, he was not yet done with shutouts. In the National League Championship Series he won a 6–0 game over the Mets and repeated that 6–0 score in the World Series against the Oakland A's in the second World Series game on October 16. In the space of six weeks he had garnered seven shutouts—and—a new major league record with 59 consecutive innings of scoreless baseball. He reaped baseball's awards, seven of them, most notably the Cy Young Award for his sparkling 1988 efforts in one of the finest individual seasons engraved into the MLB record book.

April 26 and June 11, 1990

Apparently the one-hit shutout Nolan Ryan threw in the early going of the 1990 season wasn't good enough to suit him. On June 11, only a couple months later, he reached back for the extra it always takes to fire a no-hitter, found it, and beat the Oakland Athletics, fanning 14 as he registered number six of his seven career no-nos. His early season, 1–0 win over the White Sox was a one-hitter with 16 strikeouts. What more could be asked of a 43-year-old, 24-year veteran who had already made nearly 700 career starts? Well, sir, it turns out that more yet could be asked. There was another Ryan no-hitter to be pitched, and he had another bunch of victories to put alongside his name, one of which, later in that same 1990 season, would be his 300th. More needs to be said about this extraordinary pitcher, and will be, in the discussion about No-Nos and Perfectos.

April 6, 1997

This is one of those interesting, multi-dimensional shutout stories. The story unfolded at Oakland-Alameda County Coliseum, early in 1997, and the Bronx Bombers were in town. But on this day the Yankees goliaths were being tamed, shut down without a run through seven frames of futility. Dave Telgheder, a right-hander, was largely responsible for this Yankees frustration, going almost eight innings before being lifted by the A's' skipper, Art Howe. During that time he gave up six hits, walked two and fanned one. His effectiveness was matched by David Cone, who seemed to be on his way to his first '97 win. Alas, he, too, was lifted after the seventh inning, manager Joe Torre having felt that a fresh arm in this zero-laden contest was in order to start the eighth. That meant that neither starters would be the pitcher of record.

In the eighth inning Buddy Groom replaced Telgheder after the Yanks succeeded in putting two runners on base. Groom was immediately touched for an infield single by Tino Martinez, filling up the bases.

With two out, another replacement was in order, and Howe signaled the bullpen to bring on the 6'8" Californian, Mark Acre, a right-hander, who would face dangerous Cecil Fielder. Acre wound up, threw, and the crackling sound of a sure-fire extra-base blow filled the air. Unfortunately for the hefty Yankees first-sacker, the ball screamed into the outfield directly at center fielder Damon Mashore, who gathered it in for the third out. Mark Acre, on one pitch, retired the side, and eventually became the winner on the heels of a three-run rally by the A's in the bottom of the eighth.

Winning a game on one pitch is rare enough to make headlines, but that is not the whole story regarding the 1997 Oakland Athletics. With almost an entire season yet to be played, this club managed to go through the remainder of its schedule without recording another shutout. It wasn't until May 18, 1998, that they managed another, this time against Chicago, whipping the White Sox, 14–0. The Athletics' one-shutout season became an American League record for fewest shutouts in a year.

Enough already? The A's record is *not* the major league record. The Colorado Rockies hold that one, having gone through the entire 1993 season, their first as a major league team, without a shutout victory. It wasn't until the strike-shortened season of 1994 that David Nied, on June 21, threw the only shutout of his career to put the Rockies into the shutout column with an 8–0 victory of the Houston Astros.

August 30, 2000

A 19-game winner in 2000, Randy Johnson won his 17th at the Stade Olympique in Montreal, striking out ten, walking none and otherwise deporting himself on the mound *de rigueur* as he defeated Felipe Lira and the Montreal Expos, 7–0. It was the third complete game whitewashing of the season for the lanky hurler, one of 37 he pitched in his 22-year career. That 2000 season was the third of five consecutive 300-plus-strikeout years. Between Nolan Ryan and Randy Johnson there was enough fanning to air-condition most major league stadiums. The two hold nearly all of the significant major league strikeout records, and even though their shutout totals were put together during eras short on route-going shutouts, they still managed to place high on the career shutout list, Ryan tied for seventh at 61, and Johnson tied for 57th at 37. The message: They would have been outstanding in any era.

September 16, 2005

The Dominican Pedro Martinez, with flashing dark eyes and bulldog tenacity, came upon the major league scene in late September of 1992, posting a 2.25 ERA in the eight innings he worked. It was a matter of getting his feet wet in major league waters. In his first complete season with the Dodgers he won ten games as a reliever, adding 11 in 1994 for Montreal, a year in which he nailed down his first shutout, a three-hitter over the Mets. In 1995 he added two more shutouts, plus a near-perfect game against the San Diego Padres, working his way through nine perfect innings before a tenth-inning leadoff double by Leon "Bip" Roberts caused manager Bruce Bochy to remove him with a 1–0 lead which reliever Mel Rojas preserved. The performance was the thing, however. On that day Pedro Martinez made certain everyone concerned would understand that he was going to be a pitcher who would make a difference. A big difference.

During the nine seasons from 1996 to 2004, at the top of his game, he won 147 while losing but 55. Among his 147 wins were 13 shutouts, five league-leading ERAs and minuscule opponents batting averages. His work at Boston, the most heralded part of his career, wound down with the 2004 season, having thrown his last American League shutout on August 12 in a 6–0 win over Tampa Bay during which he walked no one and struck out ten. But the word was out that perhaps Martinez' better days were behind him. Nonetheless the Mets signed him up for a four-year hitch and in 2005 he went to work in the Big Apple.

A winner, Pedro Martinez came at the hitters with all sorts of pitches and throwing angles, all of them under tight control. Another of those "sure-bet" Hall of Famers (Brace photograph).

It was during the 2005 season that he threw his last shutout, a 4–0 gem that beat John Smoltz and the Braves on September 16. It was his 17th and final whitewash job. That day he struck out ten, allowing two doubles and four well-spaced singles, as he was in command all the way. In the third, fifth, seventh and eighth innings he retired the side in order, striking out the side in the eighth reminiscent of his best days in years past.

Pedro Martinez was one of the elite, master moundsmen of his era. He matched every past pitching master in intensity and discipline. There have been some great Latino pitchers with the Martinez surname. Pedro, however, was the premier Martinez.

The 2008 Season

In discussing Brad Ziegler the topic is *not* shutouts. Rather, we're talking about a record breaker of a different kind. This fellow is in the record books because he threw scoreless innings, but not as a starting pitcher. Brad Ziegler set a major league record in 2008 by throwing 39 straight scoreless, or shutout innings at the start of his major league career. That is his rare claim to distinction. It took him until the dog days of the season in August to give up a run, but that was because he was a relief pitcher. Those 39 innings represent four-plus, nine-inning games, a decent piece of work in any man's league.

The rangy, 6′ 4″ Kansan was first called up to the Oakland A's on May 30 and got his first call to duty the very next day, when he was summoned to face Texas second baseman, Ian Kinsler, who singled in a run. But Ziegler made up for that in a hurry. He picked off Kinsler. As the season wore on and his innings mounted, so did the scoreless innings he pitched. On July 22 he set an AL record with two zeroes against Tampa Bay. Five days later he broke George McQuillan's major league mark set over a century earlier, in 1907. And when he was finally scored on in a game against — once again — Tampa Bay, on August 14, he had run up a record 39 innings in a row without giving up a run.

Quite a way to begin a career! In 2008 Brad Ziegler wound up pitching in 47 games, finishing 21 and saving 11 (though only two during his streak). The side-armer had been a record-breaking success in The Bigs. And then some!

October 2 and October 3, 2010

You will probably guess before the story is told. On these two dates, October 2 in the AL, and October 3 in the NL, the last of the era's shutouts found their way into the record books.

It was the penultimate game on Tampa Bay's 2010 schedule. The division-leading Rays were scheduled for a night game at Kansas City's Kauffman

Stadium. Some 32,484 Loyal Royals turned out hoping for some last-minute ray of light in an otherwise disappointing season. Not to be. Andy Sonnanstine headed a parade of eight Tampa pitchers who combined to blank the Royals, 4–0. Sonnanstine didn't get the win. Chad Qualls, who succeeded the Rays' starter, got a couple of outs in the third inning, as well as the victory. For Tampa Bay it was the 12th shutout of the season, and by far its most labor-intensive victory. It is rare that it takes eight pitchers to make a shutout. But those are the kind of things that happen at the tail end of the season.

In the National League on October 3, the very last game of the season was played at AT&T Park in San Francisco. There was a bit more on the line in this game than at Kansas City. The Giants needed to win this one to wrap up the NL West, and they did, four-hitting the San Diego Padres to win by a 3–0 count. In this game, as in the Tampa–Kansas City tilt, there was a procession of pitching talent on dis-

Three latter-day aces, each a solid Hall of Fame candidate. Left to right: Tom Glavine, C.C. Sabathia and Mike Mussina (Mussina: Brace photograph).

play, the Giants with Puerto Rican Jonathan Sanchez starting, followed by five relievers. The last of them, Brian Wilson, got his 48th, league-leading save in that game. For the Pads, Mat Latos started, went six innings, and was charged with the loss. He was followed by four relievers.

For the Giants, who ultimately finished their season with a World Series victory, it was their 17th shutout. Their number was a part of the NL's spike in shutout production, as the Senior Circuit posted 202 for the 2010 season, a new major league record.

As this era draws to a close we present, in conclusion, career statistics through 2010 for 19 of its top starters and three relievers. S%GC represents the percentage of shutouts pitched per the number of complete games. The SHO/SV abbreviation indicates either shutouts or saves (note: the RP designation [Relief Pitcher]).

Years	GS/CG	SHO/SV	S%/CG	ERA
Nolan Ryan	1966–1993	773/222 61	27.5	3.19
Dave Stieb	1979–1998	412/103 30	29.1	3.44
Mike Scott	1979–1991	319/45 22	48.9	3.54
Orel Hershiser	1983–2000	466/68 25	36.8	3.48
Dwight Gooden	1984–2000	410/68 24	35.3	3.51
Roger Clemens	1984–2007	707/118 46	39.0	3.12
David Cone	1986–2003	419/56 22	39.3	3.46
Kevin Brown	1986–2005	476/72 17	23.6	3.28
Greg Maddux	1986–2008	740/109 35	32.1	3.16
Tom Glavine	1987–2008	682/56 25	44.6	3.54
John Smoltz*	1988–2009	481/53 16	30.2	3.33
Curt Schilling	1988–2007	436/83 20	24.1	3.46
Randy Johnson	1988–2009	603/100 37	37.0	3.29
Mike Mussina	1991–2008	536/57 23	40.4	3.68
Pedro Martinez	1992–2009	409/46 17	36.9	2.93
Roy Halladay	1995–2010	320/58 19	32.7	3.32
Johan Santana	2000–2010	263/13 8	61.5	3.10
Roy Oswalt	2001–2010	303/20 8	40.0	3.18
C.C. Sabathia	2001–2010	322/30 11	36.7	3.57

*John Smoltz had 154 saves in four seasons as a relief pitcher.

9

Shutouts in Other Leagues and Venues

The world of professional baseball finally settled down, having sorted itself out over the winter of 1915–16, with two major leagues, the National and American, as the last leagues standing. Prior to that time there were three leagues and associations on occasion. Each was a nineteenth century competitor with the National League, except for the Federal League, which operated in two twentieth century seasons, 1914 and 1915. Back then, between 1871 and 1915, common term for shutout was "whitewashing," and there were a good-sized number of them.

Further, in each of those leagues great athletes could be found who were trying just as valiantly as the National Leaguers to come to grips with changing rules, franchises that opened up and closed down with alarming regularity, and very wobbly finances while playing, at least from time to time at major league levels.

Those leagues, named here chronologically, included the National Association, already considered in the opening chapter; the American Association, in operation from 1882 to 1891; the Union Association in 1884; the Players' League in 1890; and the aforementioned Federal League (1914–1915). Beyond those leagues, we will also take a look at several others, each a professional unit that operated with varying degrees of success both here and abroad. These include the Negro Leagues and the Japanese major leagues.

With the integration of African American and Hispanic players, which involved Caribbean, Central American, and South American ballplayers, it is not necessary to include their leagues, since so many of their players wore American uniforms. Though there some day may indeed be leagues of major league caliber, that day has not yet come, though the guess from this corner is that such may soon be the case, one way or another.

But the case for Japan as a major league venue is a wholly different one. Japanese baseball has for some time now been observed and discussed with serious interest, both here and in Nippon Land. Since the 1920s Nippon Professional Baseball (NPB) had been wildly popular in Japan, and during the past score of years has raised its caliber of play to approach modern major league standards. Consequently, its play, seasonal and championship competition, and operational viability lend us opportunities to see great home run hitters and no-hit pitchers at work in huge, major league-like stadiums that have produced, quite often, major league-level play.

As for the remainder of Asia, the baseball craze no longer produces merely marginal leagues and players. Taiwan and Korea are two such examples, playing ever more skillfully while raising the standard of play in some cases to capabilities tantamount to performance levels of the high minor leagues in America.

All of this is very interesting and, at very least, points to some significant future changes in seasonal and championship play at an international level. But our interest here is primarily in the low-hit and shutout game. So on to the bottom line: Among international venues, our interest, then, will be confined to the Negro Leagues and the NPB.

The American Association

The "Beer and Whiskey League," as the American Association was otherwise known, came into existence over the winter of 1881–1882, and by May of 1882 it was ready to open its inaugural season with games at Philadelphia, Cincinnati and St. Louis. David Nemec introduced this league to baseball buffs as follows:

> The most vibrant and freewheeling time in baseball history came during the ten years between 1882 and 1891, when the upstart American Association fought the National League tooth and nail for the right to co-exist as a major league. Although the Association ultimately lost the war, it won many battles along the road and in the process played a large hand in revolutionizing the game [*The Beer and Whiskey League* (Guilford, CT: Lyons Press, 2004), p. 1].

Nemec documents those years, as well as the games, players and franchise struggles that swirled around the new league. He would have his readers know that there was talent that matched the National League on even keel, and many of those gifted players were pitchers such as Bob Caruthers, Tony Mullane, Cannonball Crane, Silver King, Jack Stivetts, Will White, Guy Hecker and Tim Keefe, the only pitcher enshrined in the Hall of Fame after having pitched in the AA (New York, 1883 and 1884). This is the annual AA league shutout record:

	GP	SHO	SHO%
1882	233	25	10.73
1883	390	37	9.49
1884	658	81	12.31
1885	445	41	9.21
1886	557	58	10.41
1887	548	39	7.12
1888	548	63	11.50
1889	557	50	8.98
1890	538	49	9.11
1891	556	48	8.63
Total	5049	491	9.74
Comparison Years:			
1885 NL	445	72	16.18
1890 PL	529	32	6.05

Two of the pitchers named above, Charles "Silver" King and Guy Hecker, stand out as having had individual seasons among the top five all-time according to the *ESPN Baseball Encyclopedia* (Palmer and Gillette 2008, 1792). The Hecker and King seasons follow. (R designates all-time ranking.)

	W-L	GS	SHO	IP	ERA	R
Guy Hecker (Lou) '84	52–20	73	6	670.2	1.80	1
Silver King, (StL) '88	45–20	64	6	584.2	1.63	5

May 6, 1882

This was the date of the first shutout in American Association history. The game was played at Louisville and the winning pitcher was Louisville's Tony Mullane, who defeated George "Jumbo" McGinnis, St Louis Brown Stockings hurler, 4–0. Mullane, an interesting but combative character, won 30 games for Louisville's Eclipse ball club in 1882 and went on to a seven-year career in the AA before signing on in the National League. In the AA he won 30 or more games five times, logging 26 shutouts to lead all AA hurlers in career shutout games. This is the list:

AA Career Shutouts

Tony Mullane 26   Jumbo McGinnis 18
Will White 23   Dave Foutz 16
Ed Morris 22   Guy Hecker 15
Bob Caruthers 21   Ed Seward 13
Matt Kilroy 18   Adonis Terry 12

October 6, 1882, at Cincinnati

Played at Cincinnati's Bank Street Grounds, this game marked the first time that two major leagues met in a postseason series. The AA Red Stockings' rival was the Cap Anson–led Chicago White Stockings of the NL. Cincinnati forged ahead 4–0 going into the ninth inning. Ned Williamson and Abner Dalrymple then succeeded in putting together the makings of a rally with one out. That brought up the always dangerous Anson, who leaned into the first decent pitch he saw and blistered it. The blow wound up, alas for Chicago's fans, in the hands of outfielder Jimmy Macullar, who doubled Dalrymple trying to score after the catch, ending the game with the Red Stockings winning, 4–0. That wasn't exactly what the script had called for, but Will White and his red-stockinged teammates apparently didn't read the script and imposed not only a victory, but a "Chicago" on the Chicagos.

July 23, 1884, at Toledo

A relatively small number of 1–0 games found their way into the record books of the AA during its decade-long existence. There were 49, and by comparison with later ten-year stretches that is a small percentage of the total number of shutouts. One of those was fashioned by the very capable Guy Hecker, as he defeated Tony Mullane, 1–0, at Toledo's League Park.

It was mid-season in the AA and five teams were contending for first place. Louisville was one of them, and Guy Hecker, who would win 52 games in 1884, recording one of the finest individual seasons for a pitcher in major league history, was ready to go. Hecker's win was the first in an 11-game span during which the Eclipse won eight. Calling Hecker's 1884 season better than Hoss Radbourn's 59-win performance the same year may cause an eyebrow or two to be raised. The *ESPN Baseball Encyclopedia* (1472), however, rates Radbourn at number three, behind Walter Johnson in 1913 and Hecker.

In any case, this Hecker shutout was one of 15 during his career and his third among six in 1884. At the end of that day his Eclipse were riding high and only one game out of first place.

April 26, 28, 29, 1885, at Cincinnati

On these three days in 1885 the first game was played against the Pittsburgh Alleghenys at Sportsman Park in St. Louis, and the final two at the Cincinnati Base Ball Grounds (note the separated Base Ball, then in use). It turned out to be a shutout trifecta, the only time in the history of the league that a team had been successful in holding its opponents scoreless three consecutive times. In 1885 the Charlie Comiskey–led Browns, sometimes called the Brown Stockings, roared through their schedule to wind up 16 games in front of the second-place Cincinnati nine. The charge was led by Bob Caruthers, fastballing control artist, and Dave Foutz, who corralled 73 of the 79 St. Louis victories between them. Caruthers captured the second of his six blankings that summer in the first of the three shutouts against the Alleghenys, 2–0, in a fine matchup with Pittsburgh's Ed Morris (39–24 that summer). Foutz followed with a 5–0 win (he won 33 in 1885); and Caruthers (40–13 that year) beat Cincinnati 6–0 in the last of the threesome. It would take St. Louis until mid-July to win another shutout game, their total for the season coming in at 11.

August 10, 1889

Jesse Duryea was the beneficiary of a 20-run Cincinnati deluge that swamped the Baltimore Orioles in one of the worst shutout whippings ever administered in the decade-long history of the AA. Duryea, a rookie who turned 30 in September, was runner-up to Jack Stivetts, the AA's ERA leader that season, at 2.56 and won 32 games, his best major league mark. In the league's history these are the five most lopsided shutout margins:

July 6, 1883	Cincinnati 23 (Will White)
	Baltimore 0 (Hardie Henderson)
August 15, 1886	St. Louis 19 (Dave Foutz)
	Brooklyn 0 (Adonis Terry)
August 3, 1886	Pittsburgh 18 (Eddie Morris)
	Brooklyn 0 (Adonis Terry)
May 7, 1889	St. Louis 21 (Silver King)
	Columbus 0 (Al Mays)
August 10, 1889	Cincinnati 20 (Jesse Duryea)
	Baltimore 0 (Frank Foreman)

October 4 and 5, 1891, at Philadelphia and St. Louis

These are the two dates that wind up the American Association's shutout story, coming a day before the last AA outs were made on October 6 in a twin bill that Baltimore won at Washington.

On October 4 left-hander Ted Breitenstein, a St. Louisan, made his first major league start in a game against Louisville's Jouett Meekin, who had also made his first big league start that season. In that game the small left-hander staggered the baseball world by throwing an 8–0 no-hitter, defeating the

Colonels in the first game of a doubleheader. Interestingly, his feat was matched on May 6, 1953, when Alva "Bobo" Holloman of the American League St. Louis Browns made his first start in the majors and held the Philadelphia A's hitless in his *only* major league complete game.

Among the 13 shutouts thrown by St. Louis pitchers in 1891 the rookie Breitenstein's was hailed as the grandest of them all. He issued but one free pass, to first baseman Harry Taylor.

On October 5, at Philadelphia, Elton "Icebox" Chamberlain (22–23 in 1891) lost to Boston's pennant-winning Reds and 34-game winner George Haddock by the score of 6–0. In 1890 Haddock was a Players' League hurler, and lost more league games (26) than any other PL pitcher, but he turned things around with a fine 1891 season while leading the league in shutouts with five.

It was the end of the American Association's era and the last Beer and Whiskey League shutout among the 485 in its brief but colorful history.

The Union Association

In 1884 there appeared three leagues on the major league scene for the first time. Downplayed as an entry unworthy of major league status to this very day, the St. Louis–led Union Association found the going a little beyond its means and folded after one season's play in 1884. Only five of the 13 cities in the league (one of the 12 franchises played first in Chicago and then finished the season in Pittsburgh) played more than 100 games in a limited schedule that included, for example, 114 contests for the Washington and St. Louis entries, 105 for Cincinnati, and just nine for St. Paul.

Despite the uneven nature of its play and a glaring lack of competitive balance, the league worked its way through 423 contests, of which 43 were shutouts, including five 1–0 games. Probably the most fascinating person in the entire UA enterprise was not a ballplayer, but rather St. Louis franchise owner Henry V. Lucas, who constructed, on his own property, a baseball venue of unaccustomed beauty and convenience for fans of the 1880s, outdoing (if that were at all possible) another of St. Louis' baseball barons, Chris "Der Poss" von der Ahe. Lucas, who during the UA's only season became its president, brought the best players available to St. Louis, and their franchise made a mockery of the UA's pennant race. Winning 24 of its first 25 games, it nonetheless took the Maroons until May 31, when they played the Philadelphia Keystones, to win their first shutout, 5–0, behind Charley Hodnett, a 12–2 winner for the UA champions that summer.

Because of its one-season existence, the UA's shutout story is rather short as well. Its entire shutout log, with a few added notations follows. The listing is presented team by team, according to winning percentage, in each team's chronological order.

Played At	Date	Tm/Score/WP	Losing TM/SP
StL	5/31	StL 5, Hodnett	Phl, Bakely
StL	6/20	StL 5, Taylor	Chi-Pit, Daily
Phl	6/30	StL 6, Taylor	Phl, Bakley
Balt	7/12	StL 4, Boyle	Balt, Robinson
Bos	7/19	StL 1, Boyle	Bos, Shaw
StL	8/2	StL 10, Werden	KC, McLaughlin
StL	8/5	StL 8, C. Sweeney	Cinc, Bradley
StL	10/1	StL 5, C. Sweeney	Balt, Bill Sweeney
Mil	9/27	Mil 3, Porter	Wash, Geggus
Mil	9/28	Mil, 5, Cushman	Wash, Powell

Ed Cushman no-hit the Nationals, Abner Powell (LP), 5–0.

Mil	10/4	Mil 2, Cushman	Bos, McCarthy
Cinc	4/29	Cinc 5, Bradley	Chi-Pit, Daily

George Bradley threw the first Union Association shutout.

Bos	6/27	Cinc 4, Burns	Bos, Burke
Chi	7/31	Cinc 3, Bradley	Chi-Pit, Daily
KC	8/17	Cinc 7, McCormick	KC, Voss
KC	8/25	Cinc 9, McCormick	KC, Voss
KC	8/27	Cinc 6, McCormick	KC, Veach
Wash	9/22	Cinc 9, McCormick	Wash, Daily
Wash	9/23	Cinc 1, McCormick	Wash, Wise
Cinc	10/1	Cinc 7, Bradley	StP, Galvin
Cinc	10/2	Cinc 6, McCormick	Wash, Powell
Cinc	10/14	Cinc 8, McCormick	Balt, Sweeney
Chi	5/20	Balt 2, Sweeney	Chi-Pit, Horan
Chi	5/25	Balt 4, Sweeney	Chi-Pit, Daily
Altoona	5/29	Balt 13, Sweeney	Alt, Brown
Altoona	5/30	Balt 9, Sweeney	Alt, Murphy
Bos	8/18	Bos 2, Shaw	Balt, Sweeney
Bos	8/25, Gm 2	Bos 6, Shaw	Wilmington, Nolan
Bos	8/30	Bos 3, Shaw	Wilmington, Murphy
Bos	9/8	Bos 3, Shaw	KC, Black
StL	10/19	Bos 5, Shaw	StL, Sweeney

Dupee Shaw (21–15 with Boston) defeated Charlie Sweeney (24–7, St. Louis), in the last shutout of the Union Association's history. In this game Boston's Ed Crane homered. His 12th of the season was the latest date ever for a major league regular season home run.

Chi	5/18	Chi-Pit 2, Daily	Wash, Voss
Bos	7/7	Chi-Pit 5, Daily	Bos, Burke

Hugh "One Arm" Daily, who had one-hit Washington earlier, this time one-hit Boston, striking out a record 19 batters. Three days later he pitched another one-hitter against Boston's Reds.

Chi	7/24	Chi-Pit 6, Daily	KC, Hickman
Chi	7/25	Chi-Pit 4, Atkinson	KC, Overbeck
Balt	9/18	Chi-Pit 3, Daily	Balt, Beck
Wash	7/19	Wash 3, Wise	Chi-Pit, Daily
Wash	7/30	Wash 3, Wise	Phl, Fisher
Wash	8/22	Wash 14, Powell	Wilmington, Casey

This was the highest-scoring shutout in UA history.

Wash	9/6	Wash 1, Wise	KC, Veach
Wash	9/10	Wash 1, Wise	Chi-Pit, Atkinson
Phl	7/5	Phl 3, Bakley	Chi-Pit, Horan
Saint Paul	10/5	StP 1, Brown	StL, Sweeney

St. Louis pitchers Sweeney and Boyle threw a combined and rain-shortened five-inning no-hitter, but the Maroons lost when two errors enabled the White Caps' Jim Brown to win, 1–0. The no-hitter was the 12th during the 1884 season, the most ever recorded in one year of major league play.

The Players' League

Formed in the late months of 1889 under the astute leadership of attorney Monte Ward, a nineteenth century all-around player so gifted that he was awarded Hall of Fame membership in 1964, this league, though it lasted but a single season, is much respected by baseball's cognoscenti. Eight teams banded together, stocked (more than a hundred) with National Leaguers and 20 players from the AA, to play a 130-game schedule. That was about the only thing the new league had in common with the other two leagues because in many respects, beginning with playing personnel, it was superior to either of its competitors.

Notable among the ranks of pitchers who deserted the other two leagues were Pub Galvin, Silver King, Tim Keefe, Gus Weyhing, George Haddock, Charley Radbourn, Ad Gumbert and Charles Buffinton. Aside from the league's *raison d'être* and all the contributing factors that emerged from a cauldron of discontent among professional ball players, too complicated and lengthy to discuss here, there were still other factors that weighed heavily in the formation of the new league. Even though it lasted but a season, as did the Union Association, it did have its day in the sun. An interesting observation about its final disposition was made by the veteran baseball historian Marshall Wright in his *Nineteenth Century Baseball* (Wright, 1996, 195.)

After discussing the events leading up to the final arrangements for a settlement among the baseball brethren, Wright states that

> ... when the first peace offerings were made by the National League in October (1890), the Players League jumped at the chance. Wary of further losses, the

new league quickly capitulated. But in hindsight, it was revealed that perhaps the Players League had acted in haste. The National League had lost almost $500,000 — one more push and it might have gone under. One can only speculate.

Hmmm ... Interesting.

Among the 529 games played in the Players' League, 32 were shutouts, 11 fewer than recorded by the Union Association, 17 fewer than in the American Association in 1890 and 22 fewer than the 1890 National League. Its shutout percentage, a very pedestrian 6.05, was one of the lower seasonal league marks on record.

Here are a number of noteworthy dates and shutout events in the brief, but busy days of baseball's third league in 1890, the Players' League.

May 19, 1890, at Brooklyn

The Brooklyn Wonders defeated the Chicago Pirates, 6–0, behind 30-game winner Gus Weyhing, a stringy, breaking ball pitcher. It was the first of 32 Players' League shutouts. The loss went to Marcus "Fido" Baldwin, who led the PL in many categories, most notably in wins (33). Just a month after his 6–0 victory over the Pirates, on June 21, Weyhing threw an eight inning no-hitter against the same Pirates, beating Silver-King this time by a 1–0 score.

May 24, 1890, at New York

This was quite a year for Tim Keefe, the angular-visaged future Hall of Fame pitcher who became baseball's second 300-game winner on June 4. On May 24 he picked up win number 296 with a 6–0 shutout, defeating Cinders O'Brien and the Cleveland Infants. Keefe was an instrumental operative in the formation and early stages of the Players League, a good friend of John Montgomery Ward. His repertoire of pitches included a number of sharp breaking balls used effectively in his master plan against the hitters of his day, each of which he had studied at length. His 6–0 conquest of the Cleveland nine came during a skein of ten straight victories, helping him achieve a 17–11 season for New York's third-place finishers.

June 9, 1890, at Pittsburgh

By the time the Players League was organized, Pud Galvin's arm had seen better days, but the veteran campaigner, whose pitching days had gone all the way back to the last year of the National Association of Professional Base Ball Players, just knew that he had to get in on a league where owners and players would be treated as partners. So it was on to the Players' League for the 1890 season. He didn't even have to move. He had already been a big part of the Pittsburgh baseball scene for five years.

On June 9 Galvin met the Chicago Pirates and Silver King, a 30-game winner during the summer of 1890, at Exposition Park, beautifully situated on the banks of the Allegheny River. On that day old Pud was an earlier-day Galvin, retiring the Pirates without a run, while his Burgher teammates were busy scoring six tallies to make the stout future Hall of Famer's only shutout that season an easy romp in the summer sun. It was his 55th career shutout, and though there were only a couple left (he totaled 57 in his 15-year, 365-win career), he had proved, once again, that he was an upper echelon hurler. The next season he would be right back in Pittsburgh, once again in the National League, where on August 21, he would master Cincinnati, 2–0. Finally, on September 4, at home in Pittsburgh, he defeated Brooklyn in his last career shutout effort.

August 20, 1890, at Philadelphia

Bert Cunningham, in his fourth major league campaign, split his Players' League season between the Philadelphia Quakers and the Buffalo Bisons. His finest hour that year came on August 20, when the Bisons played the strong Chicago PL entry headed by Charlie Comiskey. In the twin bill opener that day he beat Chicago ace Mark Baldwin, 6–2. That went so well that manager Jay Faatz decided to go with the stocky right-hander again in the nightcap. That went even better as Cunningham this time threw a 7–0 shutout at the Pirates.

Beating any major league team twice in one day is a considerable feat, and the odds jump considerably when the opposing team is stocked with championship caliber ballplayers. The chances of winning decrease alarmingly when the opponent is as weak as the lastplace Bisons were, and more so yet when the pitcher is Bert Cunningham, who that year managed only a 3–9 mark before leaving Philadelphia in mid–July. None of that mattered on this fair August day in Buffalo. On this day Mr. Cunningham was in tight-fisted control, mowing down the likes of Windy City stars Ned Williamson, Jimmy Ryan, Hugh Duffy and Tip O'Neill. The final tally was 7–0, and the losing Chicago pitcher was Charley Bartson. Though he was no world-beater, Cunningham did put together a fine season in 1898 with the Louisville Colonels, winning 28 game. His 12-year career mark was a sub–.500, 142–167 with four shutouts, half of which were thrown with the lowly 1890 Bisons. Addendum: The Buffalo team was credited with two shutouts that season.

October 3 and 4, 1890, at Pittsburgh, Buffalo and Chicago

The 1890 Players' League shutout story ended in three cities, where Pittsburgh's Harry Staley, John Sowders of the Brooklyn Wonders, and the Chicago Pirates' Silver King all tossed shutouts. These three were added to 29 previous shutouts to bring the PL total for its lone season of play to 32. One of the teams involved in this final set of three was Pittsburgh, which led the league with seven. Another of the three was Chicago, whose Silver King led the league with four shutouts.

Two of the three blankings occurred on October 3, one at Pittsburgh, where the Burghers, behind Harry Staley, beat the Old Hoss, Charley Radbourn, 4–0. Staley that day had to be at his best to beat Radbourn, who, in his last great season, led his Boston team to the Players' League pennant with a 27–12 mark. The win was Staley's 21st for the seventh-place Pittsburghs.

While the Pittsburgh–Boston tilt was being played, Chicago was at home against the New York Giants. On the shores of Lake Michigan, Silver King had one of his finer days of the 1890 season, beating back the New Yorkers decisively, 10–0. This victory enabled King to cop the league's shutout title. Hank O'Day, probably better remembered as an umpire, was the loser that day, rounding out his 1890 record at a creditable 22–13. (It was Hank O'Day who called the 1908 play involving Johnny Evers and Fred Merkle. O'Day was an NL umpire for 35 seasons, third only to Bill Klem and Bruce Froemming in tenure.)

The Players' League 1890 season ended for all teams on October 4. One of those season-enders was played at Buffalo's Olympic Park, where the Bisons hosted the Brooklyn Wonders. John Sowders, looking to win his 19th game, was matched with Buffalo's Larry Twitchell, 5–6 going into this season finale. Brooklyn, which finished the season in second place, pleased the odds-makers that day with a 5–0 victory.

Thus ended the Players' League saga. Its untimely ending nonetheless had a trailing line: To Be Continued. The wars with owners, the struggles to ban the hated Reserve Clause, and, in a different but related way, the growth of major league baseball were all of a kind: a work in progress.

The Federal League

When there's a new kid on the block it's not too long before he's going to be compared with the others who have been around longer. Comparisons between the National League and the American Association might plausibly give the nod to the National League, however closely matched they might have been, all things considered.

That is not the case when comparisons are made between the two major leagues of 1914–1915 and the Federal League. Among knowledgeable baseball people, it is generally agreed that the existing major leagues held a clearcut edge over the Feds. Had the Federal League succeeded in getting past its first two seasons, rife with litigation and plagued by inferior financing, it might have caught up with its rival leagues and their many well-known stars. Consequently, the game but undermanned Federal League faded away, just as its predecessors had. With the last out in 1915 came these sobering bits of information.

- The Federal League put uniforms on a total of 286 players.
- 172 of them had previous major league experience, a number of them up for the proverbial cup of coffee.
- 25 of them were Fed rookies who later signed with major league clubs.
- 89 of them never played in the major leagues either before or after their days with the Feds. (This information was supplied from the Society for American Baseball Research's [SABR] internet archive in an article by Emil Rothe entitled "Was the Federal League a Major League?" The website address: http://research.sabr.org/journals/federal-league-a-major-league.)

That said, the Federal League had many major league–caliber players and many of them were moundsmen who, though in the last years of outstanding careers, contributed mightily to their teams. Eddie Plank, Jack Quinn, Guy Falkenberg, Chief Bender, Russ Ford and Mordecai Brown were some of them. Position players Joe Tinker, who managed the Chicago team, and Edd Roush joined Bender, Plank and Brown in Hall of Fame enshrinement, as did Bill McKechnie, Indianapolis and Newark third baseman, who was later honored for his outstanding managerial career.

For the sake of those on the block looking for comparisons, this table presents several pitching categories that should prove helpful. (WH/9 is the designation for baserunners per nine innings and SHO% refers to the percentage of shutouts in the total number of games played.)

	SHO	SHO%	WH/9	ERA	Tm.FA
NL 1914	119	19.04	11.4	2.78	.958
AL 1914	137	21.75	11.5	2.73	.959
FL 1914	**101**	**16.19**	**12.0**	**3.20**	**.959**
NL 1915	136	21.80	11.1	2.75	.964
AL 1915	101	16.26	11.8	2.93	.959
FL 1915	**122**	**19.71**	**11.6**	**3.03**	**.963**

A final word here on the Feds is left to Emil Rothe:

> If the Federal League was not a major league, there is room for conjecture that in 1914 and 1915, with the drain of quality players from the established leagues, maybe, in those days at least, there existed three high level minor league organizations instead.

Even though somewhat watered down, Rothe's final word seems to have hit on a way to keep everybody satisfied. That might just be the best way to celebrate the seasons and stars of all three leagues! On, then, to some of the great Federal League shutout events taken from the 1914 and 1915 annals.

April 14, 1914, at Pittsburgh

The Federal League openers were staggered, with the most interesting contest being played at Pittsburgh, where the Pittsburgh Rebels hosted the Brooklyn Tip-Tops. A typical Deadball Era pitchers' duel, the opener was won by Brooklyn's Tom Seaton, who beat left-hander Elmer Knetzer, 1–0. Seaton, a crafty knuckleball pitcher, was one of Brooklyn's prize acquisitions, having led the NL with 27 wins for the Phillies in 1913. His opponent, "The Baron," Elmer Knetzer, went on to a fine 20–12 season for Pittsburgh. Well he should have. He was well rested, having sat out the entire 1913 season over salary squabbles. Seaton, on that brisk April day, threw the first of his seven 1914 shutouts to get the win.

Pitchers in the 1914 Federal League season threw 36 1–0 games, a surprising 36 percent of the 101 shutouts thrown that year. Seaton, with four, tied Russ Ford of Buffalo for the league lead in that category.

June 20, 1914, at Chicago

Russ Ford was one of the top three Federal League hurlers in 1914, winning 21 games and losing but six in a resurgent season that turned out to be a last hurrah for the Buffalo ace. At Weeghman Park in Chicago on the day 1914's summer began, he stood the Chicago Whales on their ears, beating them, 1–0. At what later became known as Wrigley Field, at Addison and Sheffield, Claude Hendrix only allowed one run, pitching effectively yet losing to the Blues. The husky right-hander won 29 ball games during a banner season, but what might easily have been another conquest to make his season's total 30 got away from him. It was Ford, instead, with his emory ball, spitball and other doctored deliveries who was victorious on this occasion. Beyond Hendrix, Ford also threw a 1–0 cloak over Three Finger Brown, Guy Falkenberg and Elmer Knetzer among his five 1914 shutouts.

August 12, 1914, at Indianapolis

After Cy Falkenberg won 23 games for the Cleveland Naps in 1913, the Indianapolis Hoosiers knew their offer to him would have to be very good, so they laid out a lucrative offer to lure him away from the American League and into the new venture called the Federal League. They did, Falkenberg signed, and he went on to a 25–16 season, one of the workhorses of the league while leading the Hoosiers to a pennant. He led the new league in innings pitched (377.1), games started (43), strikeouts (236), and shutouts with nine. He was worth every penny Indianapolis paid him. This is his shutout log for 1914:

> April 29 vs. Pittsburgh 2–0
> May 30 vs. Chicago 5–0
> July 31 vs. Brooklyn 4–0
> August 12 vs. Buffalo 2–0
> August 22 vs. Brooklyn 5–0
> September 1 vs. Chicago 4–0
> September 14 vs. Brooklyn 10–0
> September 30 vs. Chicago 3–0
> October 7 vs. St. Louis 4–0

Notoriety came calling for Russ Ford when he perfected his emory ball, but it all came apart quickly. His 21–6 record with the Federal League Bisons in 1914 (including five shutouts) was a last but great hurrah (Brace photograph).

On August 12 the Hoosiers hosted the Buffalo Bisons in a tight race that had Chicago in first place over Baltimore, Brooklyn, and then the Hoosiers. The tall emory ball hurler outdueled spitballer Fred Anderson that day, winning 2–0 and enabling the Indianapolis nine to trim Chicago's lead. In a race that was tight all season long, the Indy club finally emerged as the Federal League's first champion by a mere game and a half. Falkenberg's win on the second-to-last day of the season was his last shutout of the season, a 4–0 victory over Dave Davenport of St. Louis that put Chicago out of reach for the pennant. Falkenberg had won his 25th and there was a champion in Hoosierland.

October 10, 1914, at Brooklyn

A peppery book about some mighty poor pitching was written by the Kaufman men in 1995 (*The Worst Baseball Pitchers*, by James C. Kaufman and Alan S. Kaufman, Citadel Press, New York). Their listings of losing seasons, careers, and pitchers with absolutely terrible statistics behind their names would be a hilarious tale were it not the true story of so many unfortunate major league pitchers who lost and lost and lost.

One of those luckless hurlers was a chap named Irvin Wilhelm who, during the days of the Deadball Era, toiled for Boston and Brooklyn of the National League. It wasn't long before he acquired the nickname Kaiser, as in Germany's emperor during those years. He broke in during the 1903 season with Pittsburgh, and carved out a 5–3 start in his debut year. Baseball's Kaiser had made a nice start in his major league career.

But then bad things started to happen. He moved on to Boston where, in the following two years, his road was downhill all the way, twice losing 20 or more with a lackluster record of 17 and 43. The Kaiser's worst year was a Boston disaster that had him in first place — 3–23 mark in 1905 — on the Kaufman and Kaufman list-

A World War I pitcher, they called Irwin Wilhelm "The Kaiser" (Brace photograph).

ing titled "The 25 Worst Seasons of the 20th Century" (Kaufman, 190). After an equally atrocious three-year hitch with Brooklyn's NL Superbas (the three-year totals were 22–42), major league teams passed on his services for several seasons and saw to it that he would suffer his next losses in the minor leagues.

But the Federal League came to his rescue in 1914. Apparently someone in Baltimore remembered, or was perhaps informed about, Kaiser Wilhelm's better days (what few there were) in years gone by. Kaufman and Kaufman documented those heroics this way:

> He was banished to the Southern League for two years [Ed. This came after his 3–23 season with Boston in 1905], where he led Birmingham to the 1906 pennant. He gave an exhibition of pitching during 1906 and 1907 that had fans linking his name with major league legends. Cy Young pitched the first perfect game of the 20th century in May 1904 for the Boston Red Sox, beating the Philadelphia Athletics 3–0. In July, 1906, Wilhelm pitched the second perfect game in organized baseball, shutting down Montgomery 7–0 for Birmingham. Only two balls were hit out of the infield. A Montgomery writer referred to his local team as "Babes in the hands of a giant," while a writer for the Birmingham News proclaimed Wilhelm, who also pitched 61 consecutive scoreless innings, as "the idol of the local fans." who has been "viewed with askance by jealous writers around the circuit" [Kaufman, 192].

In 1914 it came to pass that the weathered and wizened veteran of more than a decade of professional baseball in the era of scuffed and blackened baseballs, made his way to Baltimore. But even though he turned in another less than sensational campaign, he did put together a day that might well have made up for it all. That day came at the very end of the 1914 season, October 10, in game two of a doubleheader. For that encounter he was paired against legendary Three Finger Brown, the immortal future Hall of Famer. The Kaiser rose to that challenge with a magnificent late-afternoon exhibition of pitching prowess to squelch Brooklyn's Tip-Tops by the barest of margins, 1–0. The victory didn't do too much to improve his 12–17 record on the season, but certainly must have made for a great evening's celebration. It was, after all, a shutout ... his only one all year.

June 26, 1915

In a very special game between the Baltimore Terrapins and the St. Louis Terriers, two old friends toed the slab against each other on a very early summer day in Baltimore. The two former Connie Mack stalwarts, both of whom would become Hall of Fame pitchers in due time, were Eddie Plank and Albert "Chief" Bender. It was one of those rather typical early twentieth century duels, with St. Louis finally able to muster enough offense to push across a pair of runs and win it for the tall, lithe southpaw, Plank. And the confrontation between the two was the only occasion in which two future Famers would meet during the brief, two-season history of the Federal League.

While Eddie Plank retained his winning touch during the 1915 season, logging a 21–11 record, Bender, who the previous season with Mack's A's had led the American League in winning percentage (his .850 mark was based on a splendid 17–3 reading), seemed to have lost his pitching magic, as he suffered through a 4–16 season with the Feds in 1915.

For the record: a couple of months after Plank's win over Bender and the Terps, he became the first left-hander to win 300 games with a 12–5 victory over 21-game winner Ed Reulbach, who is probably best remembered as the only pitcher in major league history to have won two shutout victories in one day. On September 26, 1908, pitching for the Chicago Cubs, he beat Brooklyn, 5–0 and 3–0, among the seven he hurled that summer. As for Eddie Plank, he threw the last of his six 1915 shutouts on September 26, a 5–0 blanking of the Buffalo Bisons. There would only be four more, hurled in 1916 and 1917 for the St. Louis Browns, which raised his career total to 69, placing him at number five on the all time shutout honor roll.

The first portsider to win 300 games, Eddie Plank was one of Connie Mack's very best (Brace photograph).

September 29, 1915, at St. Louis

On this date lefty Gene Packard, pitching for the Kansas City Packers, beat St. Louis on his own home run in the sixth inning for the game's only score. It was the second time that season that he had beaten St. Louis hurler Dave Davenport, 1–0. Davenport, a 22–18 workhorse for St. Louis manager Fielder Jones, led the FL in shutouts that summer with ten. He also lost another 1–0 game to Nick Cullop (Kansas City again), as well as a 1–0 heartbreaker to Buffalo's Ed Lafitte, the only shutout in Lafitte's five-year MLB career.

October 3, 1915, at Chicago — A Federal League Shutout Finale: Chicago 3, Pittsburgh 0

Bill Bailey opened up the 1915 season in Baltimore, but finished it in Chicago, where he threw shutouts in the only three games he won for the Whales in rapid fire succession on September 24 (Falkenberg, Brooklyn), September 27 (Fin Wilson, also a Brooklyn hurler), and Pittsburgh on October 3, the final shutout date in FL history, this time defeating Elmer "The Baron" Knetzer in game two of a doubleheader played at Chicago.

Combined with the FL 1914 statistics, the final tally on shutouts amounted to 223 in 1,457 complete games for the 1914 and 1915 seasons. Thus, 15.31 percent of all complete games were shutouts. The figure for all games (1,243) is 17.94 percent. Of the 223 shutouts, four were no-hitters: Frank Allen (2–0), Pit vs. StL on April 24; Claude Hendrix (10–0), Chi vs. Pit on May 15; Alex Main (5–0), KC vs. Buf on August 16; and Dave Davenport (3–0) StL vs. Chi on September 7, all in 1915. One other no-hitter, on September 19, 1914, was a 6–2 Brooklyn victory (Ed Lafitte) over Kansas City. And now for an FL fini, the top shutout hurlers in its two-year history:

	SHO, 1914	SHO, 1915	Total
Dave Davenport	2	10	12
Claude Hendrix	6	5	11
Guy Falkenberg	9	1	10
Gene Packard	4	5	9
Earl Maseley	4	5	5
Nick Cullop	4	3	7
Tom Seaton	7	0	7
Fred Anderson	5	2	7

The Negro Leagues

Bob Peterson put between covers a ground-breaking history of the Negro Leagues, as they were popularly known, titled *Only the Ball Was White* (Peterson, 1970). He wrote a new Preface for the paperback edition that came out in 1990, published by Oxford University Press, and from that edition come these introductory words:

> Negro baseball was Josh Gibson standing loose and easy at the plate in Yankee Stadium and hitting the longest home run ever seen in the House That Ruth Built. And it was the touring Brooklyn Colored Giants arriving, broke and hungry, in a small Pennsylvania city where, because of a scheduling mixup, no game was arranged, and then playing a hastily called game with the local semi-

pros so they could take up a collection for a meal and enough gas to get to the next town [Peterson, 1990, 15].

It isn't the purpose of this book to discuss Negro Leagues history, or its trials and tribulations before the league's stars were finally recognized, or that the league was given tardy recognition, enabling a number of its wondrously gifted players to be rewarded, belatedly, with enshrinement in baseball's Hall of Fame. But it never hurts to remind one and all that there was a time when "Black Ball" was, in many instances and in many ways, something of a major league incarnation, even though played largely on hastily put-together ball diamonds reminiscent of nineteenth century baseball, when professional players first started making the rounds of cities and hamlets to play their game.

The pain of second class citizenship in that world of professional baseball is by now a distant memory. Not even Jackie Robinson's number 42, emblazoned on plaques and on occasion on modern uniforms in a celebration of his (and many others') difficult entrée into major league baseball, can fully bring present generations to an understanding of the struggles and frustration of those times, so it will be necessary for quite some time to come to keep those memories and the deeper meanings of that era in front of us.

There is just enough documentation to put together a few of the really lustrous accomplishments of those Negro Leagues days. Perhaps at some time years from now it will be able to draw on a statistical record that is far more complete than what we have today. Nonetheless there are some shutout events along the way that are not only worthy of note, but also reliably reported beyond the hearsay that so often distorts reality. From those sources, a few noteworthy glimpses forthwith.

The Negro Leagues and Satchel Paige in 1934

In the annual Negro Leagues All Star Game at Comiskey Park in Chicago, approximately 30,000 fans were on hand to see the best African American players from the East Division teams and the West vie for honors. Over the years 28 All-Star Games were played, 11 of them during Depression years (1933 to 1940), and all of them were well-attended. All were played in major league parks, save one, which was played in 1938 at Penmar Park in Philadelphia. Depression or no, African American fans found a way to see their favorites, sometimes drawing crowds as large as 50,000 and more on Chicago's South Side at the home of the American League's White Sox. The box score of the 1934 game follows:

East	AB	R	H	West	AB	R	H
Cool Papa Bell, cf	3	1	0	Willie Wells, ss	3	0	1
Jimmie Crutchfield, rf	3	0	0	Alex Radcliffe, 3b	4	0	0
W. G. Perkins, c	1	0	0	Turkey Stearns, cf	4	0	0
Oscar Charleston, 1b	4	0	0	Mule Suttles, 1b	4	0	3
Jud Wilson, 3b	3	0	1	Red Parnell, lf	3	0	0
Josh Gibson, c, lf	4	0	2	Sam Bankhead, rf	3	0	1
Vic Harris, lf	2	0	1	Larry Brown, c	3	0	1
Dick Lundy, ss	4	0	0	Sammy T. Hughes, 2b	2	0	0
Chester Williams, 2b	4	0	3	J. Patterson, 2b	1	0	0
Slim Jones, p	1	0	0	Theodore Trent, p	1	0	0
Harry Kincannon, p	1	0	1	Chet Brewer, p	1	0	0
Satchel Paige (WP)	2	0	0	Willie Foster (LP)	1	0	1
Totals	32	1	8	Totals	30	0	7

Errors: Wilson, Suttles
RBI: Wilson
2B: Gibson, Williams, Wells
3B: Suttles
SB-C: Bell
LOB: East 8; West 5
K: Jones 4; Trent 3; Brewer 1; Paige 5; Foster 2
BB: Brewer 1; Jones 1; Foster 1

East	000	000	010	1	8 1
West	000	000	000	0	7 1

Hall of Fame lefty Willie Foster was one of the elite pitchers of the Negro Leagues (Noir Tech Research).

This festive game was a nail-biter. A no-room-for-error affair, it went scoreless until the eighth frame, when Jud Wilson singled home Cool Papa Bell for the game's only run. The pitching hero of the day was none other than a 28-year-old right hander appearing in his first All-Star Game, Satchel Paige, in the midst of a Cy Young Award–type year. In an East uniform, Paige, who ranks right up there with the quickest to home plate, came on in the sixth inning with none out and a runner on second. He hitched up his pants and went to work on Alex Radcliffe, who became a strikeout victim, followed by Turkey Stearns and Mule Suttles who flied out, shutting the door on the number 2–3–4 hitters in the West lineup. The Satchel Man clamped down on the West the rest of the way and emerged from his debut All-Star match the winning pitcher. (In his book about the greatest fastballers in the game's history, *High Heat* [Philadelphia: Da Capo, 2010], p. 186, Wendel includes Paige with Walter Johnson, Nolan Ryan and others, and quotes a Dizzy Dean newspaper article, as follows: "[My] fastball looks like a change of pace alongside that little pistol bullet Satchel shoots up to the plate.")

Much, indeed very much, has been written about Leroy Paige, whose days as a professional go back to the mid–twenties. And rightly so. By 1934 he was already well on his way to baseball immortality, and it certainly was one of his greatest years. It was during 1934 that he was involved in what has often been called the greatest game in Negro Leagues history, a 1-1 standoff at Yankee Stadium that pitted Paige against the young Philadelphia Stars *wunderkind*, Slim Jones. The game was rescheduled and prior to the replay there was some banter "in the barbershop" about who was better, Paige or Jones. Paige, who had his Pittsburgh Crawfords ahead 3–1 as darkness and the ninth inning once again approached, this time made short work of the Stars, striking them out 1–2–3. After the game Paige is supposed to have stuck his head in the Philadelphia dugout and said, "Tell that to the boys in the barbershop."

That was also the year that Paige and Dizzy Dean, a 30-game winner at the height of his career, barnstormed together, battling one another several times, and winding up in a Los Angeles game before nearly 20,000 spectators. Paige took that one in a 13-inning thriller, 1–0, a shutout that Bill Veeck labeled "the greatest pitchers' battle I have ever seen."

The *Baseball-Reference.com* website identifies 28 Negro Leagues pitchers who hurled no-hitters. Only four of them did this twice, including Paige. In 1932 he no-hit the New York Black Yankees and in 1934 (that memorable year once again) his Pittsburgh Crawfords whipped the Homestead Grays 4–0 a game in which he struck out 17. Paige had zeroed 'em.

Negro Leagues World Series, 1924

It had to come sooner or later. Forty seasons after the formation of the first African American professional team, the New York Cubans, in 1885, there were not only many black teams, but two professional leagues, the Negro National League and the Eastern Colored League. Those two leagues staged a best-of-nine series in 1924 which was played at a number of cities where Negro Leagues baseball was popular. The series wound up in Chicago, an African American baseball mecca, on October 20, and because one of the series games ended in a tie, this game was the series' tenth. Its winner would reign as the first World Series champion in Negro Leagues Baseball.

The manager of the National Negro League's Kansas City Monarchs was a grizzled, veteran pitcher, hailed in his native Cuba as El Diamante Negro (the Black Diamond). At 37, he was at the end of the trail, closing out a distinguished career that would later merit election to the Baseball Hall of Fame. El Diamante Negro was Jose Mendez, and on this particular day he wrote his own name into the lineup as the Monarchs' starting pitcher. He proceeded to throttle the Eastern Colored League's champion, the Hilldale Daisies, who hailed from Darby, Pennsylvania, defeating Scrip Lee. The game was a tight one until the eighth inning, when the Monarchs put a five-run rally together and iced the game, and with it, the Mendez three-hit shutout, by a 5–0 score.

Mendez had locked horns previously with Joe Rogan, his teammate during the 1924 World Series, throwing a no-hitter, which enabled his Monarchs to beat the Milwaukee Bears in the second of two games on August 5, 1923, by a 7–0 score. Rogan started that game, allowing one baserunner in four innings before being lifted. The National Negro League Museum has named its Outstanding Pitcher of the Year selection for modern American and National League pitchers the Wilbur "Bullet Joe" Rogan Award. Elected to the Hall of Fame in 1998, he was the finest fielding pitcher in National Negro Leagues history, and noted also for his blazing fast ball.

May 9, 1919, at New York

It took until 1999 to enshrine Smokey Joe Williams in baseball's Hall of Fame. That was 28 years after Satchel Paige's election, which was itself many years late. The 6' 5" cannonballer, whose fast one was the equal of Paige's, was around Negro Leagues and major league exhibitions for roughly 25 seasons, throwing mostly side-armed bolts of lightning that were the talk of the town in the 1910s and 1920s. He threw an astonishing number of shutouts, their exact number unknown. One of them, however, was documented, entering

"Smokey Joe" Williams with a fast-ball second to none was named to the Hall of Fame in 1999 (Jeff Eastland).

the books as a no-hitter for New York's Lincoln Giants, a classy 1–0 affair in which he was paired against the talented Dick Redding in May of 1919. Williams won another 1–0 tilt in the late fall of 1915 against the Philadelphia Phillies, major league's World Series champions that year. In that one he fanned ten and otherwise deported himself in authentic major league fashion, as he had so often done before.

Thanks to many researchers and Negro Leagues enthusiasts, the researching goes on and on, enabling one and all to update records and bring a reliable completion to many aspects of the Negro Leagues story. One of those, germane to the main theme of this book, is a listing of no-hitters of nine innings or more. Following is a chronological listing:

No-Hit Pitcher/Team	Date	Opponent
Frank Wickware, Chicago American Giants	8/26/1914	Indianapolis ABCs
Dizzy Dizmukes, Indianapolis ABCs	5/9/1915	Chicago Giants
Dick Whitworth, Chi. American Giants	9/19/1915	Chicago Giants
Bill Gatewood, St. Louis Giants	5/13/1916	Cuban Stars
Bernardo Baro, Cuban Stars	7/21/1918	Indianapolis ABCs
Joe Williams, Lincoln Giants	5/9/1919	Brooklyn Royal Giants
Tom Johnson, Chi. American Giants	6/17/1919	Detroit Stars
Dick Redding, Bacharach Giants	8/22/1920	Chicago Giants
Bill Gatewood, Detroit Stars	6/6/1921	Cincinnati Cubans
Phil Cockrell, Hilldale	9/5/1921	Detroit Stars
Bill Force, Detroit Stars	6/27/1922	St. Louis Giants
Nip Winters, Bacharach Giants	7/26/1922	Indianapolis ABCs
Phil Cockrell, Hilldale	8/19/1922	Chi. Amer. Giants
Jose Mendez (WP), Kansas City Monarchs	8/5/1923	Milwaukee Bears

No-Hit Pitcher/Team	Date	Opponent
Joe Rogan (Save)		
Nip Winters, Hilldale	9/3/1924	Harrisburg Giants
Bob McClure, Royal Poinciana Hotel (played in Winter League in Florida)	3/5/1925 perfect game	Breakers Hotel
Andy Cooper, Indianapolis ABCs	6/28/1925	Chi. Amer. Giants
Rube Currie, Chicago American Giants	7/13/1926	Dayton Marcos
Claude Grier, Bacharach Giants	10/3/1926	Chi. American Giants
Laymon Yokely, Baltimore Black Sox	5/15/1927	Cuban Stars
Joe Strong, Baltimore Black Sox	8/4/1927	Hilldale
Willie Powell, Chicago American Giants	8/14/1927	Memphis Red Sox
Army Cooper (WP), Kansas City Monarchs Chet Brewer (Save)	6/29/1929	Chi. Amer. Giants
Paul Carter, Hilldale	9/7/1931	Baltimore Black Sox
Satchel Paige, Pittsburgh Crawfords	7/15/1932	New York Black Yankees
Satchel Paige, Pittsburgh Crawfords	7/4/1934	Homestead Grays
Hilton Smith, Kansas City Monarchs	5/16/1937	Chi. Amer. Giants
Johnny Taylor, Negro All Star Team	9/19/1937	Paige's Dominican All-Stars
Eugene Smith, St. Louis Stars	6/27/1941	New York Black Yankees
Leon Day, Newark Eagles	5/5/1946	Philadelphia Stars

Nippon Professional Baseball (NPB), the Japanese Major League

Baseball came to the Nipponese in 1873, a time when the National Association of Professional Base Ball Players was into America's third season of professional baseball. That's a long time ago. Horace Wilson, an American professor at what is now Tokyo University, introduced the game to his students and their friends. It was an immediate hit, growing in popularity and participation in quantum leaps. Ultimately, a professional league (in Japan the phrase for professional baseball is Puro Yakyu), was formed in 1936, a Puro Yakyu of teams that banded together and played to often wildly enthusiastic crowds. The first league re-formed after World War II, reorganized in 1949 and played its first championship season, 1950. Today known as the NPB, Nippon Professional Baseball is home to the best major league baseball outside the United States. Astute and exacting record keepers make it possible to trace the history of their games and leagues down to modern times, and since there have been so many professionals on location over the years, it is also possible to make comparisons between professional players on both sides of the Pacific, many of whom have gone both East and West to play in American or Japanese professional leagues.

As an example of NPB pitching records, the Baseball-Reference.com website has listed no-hit pitchers from the first one thrown on September 25, 1936, by Eiji Sawamura through the 1–0 game on November 1, 2007, a combined no-hitter, the first ever, incidentally, in a Japan Series (Japan's World Series) game. The total number of no-hitters recorded amounts to 87, and that number includes 15 perfect games.

Among the more gifted Japanese ball players, in particular the pitchers, many have been enshrined in the Japanese Baseball Hall of Fame. Appearing below is a mixed listing of American and Nipponese hurlers who have thrown the most shutouts. All listed are members of either the Japanese or American Baseball Halls of Fame. This shutout honor roll's cutoff number is 55.

Pitcher	Career SHO	Noteworthy
Walter Johnson	110	
Pete Alexander	90	
Victor Starffin	83	NPB's first 300-game winner
Masaichi Kaneda	82	NPB #1 in wins, 400
Christy Mathewson	79	
Cy Young	76	
Masaaki Koyama	74	1962: 13 SHO, 5 straight
Takehiko Bessho	72	NPB record 47 CG in 1947
Keishi Suzuki	71	Led NPB in K's eight times
Eddie Plank	69	
Jiro Noguchi	65	NPB #1 with 19 shutouts in one season
Tetsuya Yoneda	64	NPB #2, career wins, 350
Hideo Fujimoto	63	NPB #1 with 19 shutouts in one season
Warren Spahn	63	
Nolan Ryan	61	
Tom Seaver	61	
Bert Blyleven	60	
Don Sutton	58	
Tadashi Wakabayashi	57	
Pud Galvin	57	
Ed Walsh	57	
Bob Gibson	56	
Mordecai Brown	55	
Steve Carlton	55	
Minoru Murayama	55	1970: 0.98 ERA is an NPB record

Among the pitchers listed above several are singled out for special mention with respect to some of the more prominent shutout games in the NPB's history.

June 28, 1950, at Aomori Stadium and September 25, 1936, at Koshien Stadium

Hideo Fujimoto, listed above with 63 shutouts, pitching for the Yomiuri Giants, crafted the first perfect game in NPB history. He blanked the Nishi-Nippon Pirates, 4–0, striking out seven before 10,000-plus Giants fans as he faced the minimum number of 27 batters in one of the most masterful Nipponese pitching performances on record.

In connection with the first perfect game on NPB record, the very first no-hitter also deserves mention. That one was hurled in 1936 by teenager Eiji Sawamura, after whom the NPL's equivalent to the American Cy Young Award has been named since 1947. Sawamura, a Japanese Hall of Famer, enlisted in the Japanese Imperial Navy in 1943 and was the only NPB Hall of Fame pitcher killed during World War II. Between 1936, his rookie year, and 1943, his record was 63–22 in 105 career games, including two more no-hitters and a 33–10 mark in 1937.

Aside from playoff and championship games, these are the two most significant shutouts in Japanese professional baseball history.

October 11–21, 1958, the Japan Series

The equivalent of the American World Series is the Japan Series, and in 1958 it was a bona fide thriller going right on down to the closing innings of the seventh and final game. One dominating figure in that Series was 21-year-old Kazuhisa Inao, a sturdy 5'11" right hander. Pitching for the Nishitetsu Lions, he appeared in six of the seven games, winning four in succession. It was the pivotal sixth game, a three-hit shutout, that brought about a winner-take-all tilt. In the final game Inao's bid for a second straight shutout was ruined by Yomiuri third baseman Shigeo Nagashima's ninth-inning homer to make the final, Series-winning game score read 6–1, a fourth Series victory for Inao. It was no mystery that he was named the Series MVP, as he had been for the 1958 regular season. His career was deemed Hall-worthy, the honors having been awarded in 1993.

August 30, 1973, the Sayonara Game

Yutaka Enatsu, a Hanshin Tigers' southpaw who once fired 34 consecutive shutout innings at the Yomiuri Giants (1969), found himself entangled in a 0–0 game, one in which he had allowed no hits through nine innings. Through ten innings the game remained scoreless, and on into the top of the 11th the result was the same: 0–0–0, that is, no runs, no hits, no errors. In the bottom of the 11th Enatsu came up to bat, indicating that he would remain in the game. But that wouldn't be necessary because Enatsu promptly jacked one into the Hanshin seats and it was: "Sayonara," baby, game over, Hanshin; or should one say, Enatsu 1, Chunichi Dragons 0. It was one of the most memorable victories in Japanese baseball history. Enatsu was Instant Hero Number One. He had hit one that Americans today call a "walkoff" homer, and that game ended up on many a listing, as the game all-time #1.

October 1, 9, 10, 1964, the Japan Series

Each NPB team is permitted to sign up to four players who are not of Japanese descent. In 1960 Oklahoman Joe Stanka was one of the four allowed to sign a Nankai Hawks contract. By 1964 he was into his fifth season as part of the Hawks' starting rotation, and pitched so well that he wound up the year with six shutouts, a 26–7 record, and an MVP award. One of the key players in the Hawks' pennant-winning season, he was picked to pitch the Japan Series opener, which he won, beating the very able Minoru Murayama, 2–0. But he wasn't finished with his shutout business by any means. With his team on the ropes heading into Game 6 at a 3–2 disadvantage, he came back to shut down the Hanshin Hawks' offensive attack, edging Gene Bacque, also an American who hailed from Louisiana, 4–0, for his second shutout of the Series.

With all the blue chips on the table, Joe Stanka took on the Hawks in Game 7 and came through once again with a shutout, this time winning both the game, 3–0, and the Series championship. His three shutout victories, 1.23 ERA, four appearances and 29.1 innings pitched earned him the Series MVP.

The Joe Stanka–America–Japan connection, complete with a first-class shutout story, might be of more than passing interest to our readers and players in the States. Websites such as www.japanbaseball.com, www.npb.or.jp, and www.japanbaseballdaily.com, among others, chronicle Nipponese baseball and the shutout stories they have to offer.

Professional baseball players come from quite a number of foreign countries to play ball in the NPL. (In Japan there are also minor leagues for player development.) Many who do not play in their native land take Japanese citizenship. Korean and Chinese, as well as Taiwanese players, all of whom come from countries with professional leagues, including the Australian Baseball League, a vastly improved venue for professional baseball that may soon approach the higher levels of play in the United States, all look to the leader along the Pacific rim, Japan, as the "America of the East" with regard to professional baseball.

10

Zeroes in the Ball Bag

Great appreciation is due Pete Palmer, sabermetrician extraordinaire, whose contributions and insights informed this chapter.

During the course of baseball history there have been a number of teams that have distinguished themselves with respect to shutting out their opponents. They seem to have come to the ballpark with all the zeroes in their ball bags. Their prowess in this regard can be traced to a pair of major assets: great pitching and exceptional team defense. These component parts of the game have been examined in many ways from the more simplistic to the quite complicated measures of contemporary sabermetricians. However calculated, all aim at sorting out the wheat from the chaff, as it were, among baseball's teams and individual players, thus enabling a ranking of best to worst, most to least, or highest to lowest.

Acknowledging that the use of numbers and quantification is necessary in determining which teams or pitchers are the game's best, enabling a listing of those teams that rise above the others throughout history, *this* particular listing presents, rather, 29 great shutout teams derived from a listing of teams with the most single-season shutouts in baseball history. For example, three teams are tied for the most shutouts in a single season with 32: the 1909 Chicago Cubs, the 1906 Chicago White Sox and the 1907 Chicago Cubs.

Interesting, isn't it, that the team that gave rise in 1870 to the term "Chicagoed" should surface some three decades later as one of the greatest shutout teams ever? It would seem that the Windy City spawned "things shut out" and gave the whole phenomenon a name as well!

At any rate, these three teams appear at the top of the list, sorted by a hybrid sabermetric number (FPW) from the highest to the lowest. (The designation **FPW** is a combination number, calculated by adding a team's **Fielding Wins** to its **Pitching Wins**, with the highest number receiving the highest rating. An example: The 1909 Cubs had a **Fielding Wins** number of 2.6. The Cubs' 1909 **Pitching Wins**: 14.1. Added, the **sum** is 16.7, better than either the Chicago White Sox's 1906 **FPW** number or the 1907 Cubs'. Thus, the first three teams on this listing are: 1909 Cubs, 1907 Cubs and 1906 White Sox. **FW** [**Fielding Wins**] designates the total number of wins the team achieved through its fielding compared to the average [0.00] in the context of the offensive level of the league and the team's home diamond. **PW** [**Pitching Wins**] designates the total number of wins the team achieved compared to the average team in contexts mentioned above in **FW**.)

The statistics that help identify these teams as the best in shutout history give a solid foundation to their capabilities with regard to holding opponents scoreless.

It is worth noting, before presenting the Shutout Masters table below, that only three of the commonly acknowledged greatest teams in baseball history appear on the Shutout Masters' listing: the 1906 and '07 Cubs and the Philadelphia Athletics of 1910. Many of the all-time favorites like the 1927, 1939 and 1998 Yankees, the 1975 Cincinnati Reds, the 1905 New York Giants and the 1895 Baltimore Orioles had outstanding ball clubs, but not on a comparable level with the team defense and pitching staff excellence of the teams listed below.

In the following table ERA designates a team's pitching staff ERA; WH/9 indicates how many baserunners the pitching staff allowed per nine innings; and SHO% indicates the percentage of total wins that were shutouts. The FPW designation is explained above. Blackened numbers indicate best performances on *this* list.

The Shutout Masters

TM/LG/YR	FPW	SHO	SHO%	FW	PW	ERA	WH/9	FA
Chi N 1907	33	16.1	30.8	3.1	13.0	**1.73**	9.8	.967
Chi-N — 1909	32	16.7	30.8	2.6	14.1	1.75	**9.6**	.962
Chi-A — 1906	32	9.1	34.4	1.8	7.3	2.13	9.8	.963
Chi-N — 1906	30	**19.5**	25.9	4.5	**15.0**	1.75	9.8	.969
StL-N — 1968	30	7.9	30.9	0.0	7.9	2.49	10.3	.978
Chi-N — 1908	29	7.2	29.3	3.7	3.5	2.14	10.1	.969
NY-N — 1969	28	28.0	1.4	11.3	12.7	2.99	10.8	.980
LA-A — 1964	28	28.0	-.7	7.0	6.3	2.91	11.5	.978
Phl-A — 1909	27	28.4	**1.8**	8.4	10.2	1.93	9.9	.961
Clv-A — 1906	27	30.3	3.8	9.6	13.4	2.09	10.3	.967
Pit-N — 1906	27	29.0	2.2	7.7	9.9	2.21	10.5	.964
Phl-A — 1907	27	30.7	0.4	4.1	4.5	2.35	10.3	.958
StL-N — 1944	26	24.8	3.7	14.2	17.9	2.67	10.8	**.982**
Clv-A — 1948	26	26.8	1.4	13.4	14.8	3.22	12.1	**.982**
Bos-A — 1918	26	**34.7**	2.5	5.5	8.0	2.31	**10.8**	.971
Phl-A — 1904	26	32.1	0.8	5.4	6.2	2.35	10.4	.959
Chi-A — 1904	26	29.2	1.7	2.7	4.4	2.30	9.8	.964
Chi-N — 1910	25	24.0	2.1	6.0	8.1	2.51	11.0	.963
Wash-A — 1914	25	30.9	1.0	4.4	5.4	2.54	11.0	.961

TM/LG/YR	FPW	SHO	SHO%	FW	PW	ERA	WH/9	FA
Phl-N — 1916	25	27.5	0.4	4.9	5.3	2.36	10.3	.963
Phl-A — 1910	24	23.5	3.9	14.7	10.8	1.79	10.2	.965
Chi-A — 1967	24	27.0	-.3	12.4	12.1	2.45	10.4	.979
Bos-A — 1916	24	26.4	3.0	5.0	8.0	2.48	11.0	.972
Atl-N — 1992	24	24.5	0.4	8.6	9.0	3.14	11.3	**.982**
Bos-A — 1914	24	26.4	1.8	5.6	7.4	2.36	10.3	.963
LA-N — 1988	24	25.5	-.5	6.8	6.3	2.96	11.0	.977
Phl-A — 1914	24	24.2	3.5	-3.2	0.3	2.78	11.6	.966
NY-A — 1951	24	24.5	0.3	4.3	4.6	3.56	12.4	.975
LA-N — 1963	24	24.2	0.0	3.3	3.3	2.85	10.8	.975

Discussion: 66 percent of the teams (19 of the 29) in this table are Deadball Era teams. That figures. You will recall that era as a one-base-at-a-time offensive era during which doctored baseballs left in play as long as possible, squeeze plays, singles hitters adept at "hitting 'em where they ain't," and speedsters on the base paths were *sine qua nons*. During that time a five-run rally all but put a game away. Pitchers were regularly involved in one- and two-run games, and, quite often, in shutout games. The emphasis in pitching was on tight control and, afield, on heads-up defense.

All of that dissolved almost overnight when pitchers of the 1920s were obliged to throw "nothin' but horsehide," leaving emery boards, tobacco-stained balls, and scuffed baseballs behind while a steady stream of spotless baseballs was put into play. There were, of course, consequences, most all of them favorable for the fellows with the bats in their hands. That brought on an annual scoring parade, while those minuscule ERAs and shutout totals faded away into the dim recesses of the past.

You will no doubt note that it took more than a quarter century, from 1918 to 1944 to be exact, for another Shutout Masters team, the 1944 Cardinals, to earn a berth on the list of the elites. And in the recent past only the Atlanta Braves in 1992 and the Los Angeles Dodgers in 1988 have been able to line up with the other elites in the shutout ranks.

Five of the teams in this august grouping enjoyed unparalleled success with respect to shutouts and low-scoring games in baseball history. Each was a Deadball Era ball club, and their domination was largely dependent on tight defense and superior pitching. These five, Chicago's Cubs and White Sox, the Philadelphia Athletics, the Pittsburgh Pirates and the Boston Red Sox, accounted for 25 of the 38 available pennants between 1901 and 1919, and for 13 of the 19 World Series championships. Add to those accomplishments the wonders of the big McGraw years with the Giants, and you have a pretty good idea of the dominating play with which they intimidated and manhandled the rest of the league's "little Fellers." Those things considered, it suggests a closer look at these franchises and their shutout exploits. That follows.

The Chicago Cubs, 1906–1910

In his review of the Cubs franchise, *Wrigleyville,* Peter Golenbock quotes club owner Charles Murphy as remarking to Frank Chance at the outset of the 1906 campaign, "Frank, I think I've given you a pretty good team. McGraw says he'll win again, but you should give him a real fight" (*Wrigleyville* [New York: St. Martin's Griffin, 1999], p. 111).

That was an understatement *par excellence.* Not only did the Chance charges give the Giants a real fight, they swept to the 1906 National League pennant by a 20-game margin over McGraw's defending NL champions. They made a statement that resounded around the world of baseball. After standing in the wings for the better part of a quarter century, this ball club was back in pennant mode. Assembling most of the pieces by 1905, when they finished third behind the Pirates and the New Yorkers, their championship caliber ball club was ready for the laurels when the first ball was thrown to open the 1906 National League warfare. The rivalry between McGraw's Giants, the Pittsburgh Pirates and Chicago's North Siders was the main feature on the National League's bill between 1906 and 1910 — which — as those things developed, coincided with the Chicago dynasty of 1906–1910. During those years they fashioned 148 shutouts, averaging just under 30 each year, topping out in 1907 with 33 and in 1909 with 32. They won a record 116 games in 1906, a mark that might have been better yet had it not been for losing 1–0 four times and 2–1 twice, two 3–3 ties, a 1–1 tie, and two 3–2 losses. Out of those eight losses one might assume that three or four of them could as easily as not have been converted to wins. Even so, 116 out of 155 tries was more than enough to make a point. Emphatically and conclusively.

By any measure this was a dynasty for the ages. Though embarrassed in the 1906 World Series by no less than their crosstown rivals, the White Sox, baseball's hitting patsies, they overcame that fiasco with a world's championship romp in 1907 and 1908, and one more pennant in 1910. They dominated, not necessarily with overpowering offensive might, but with pitching, defense and heady play. These next to unbelievable numbers substantiate their dominating claim to fame:

> During the 1906 campaign the Cubs allowed a mere 381 runs scored against them, an average of 2.5 per game. That's the fewest in number and average of *any* major league team in a 154-game schedule.
> In 1906 they played in 13, 1–0 games, winning nine of them. Complete games were *de rigueur*: 125 was the number. Relief Pitchers did not need to apply —: Three Finger Brown was there.
> In an eight-game stretch between June 25 and July 4, when the pennant race was still a sticky affair, the Cubs persevered through 1–0 or 2–1 games each

10. Zeroes in the Ballbag

One of the most accomplished ball clubs ever, the 1906 Chicago Cubs. Standing, left to right: Brown, Pfiester, Hoffman, Gen. Mgr. Williams, Overall, Reulbach, Kling. Seated: Gessler, Taylor, Steinfeldt, J. McCormick, Mgr. Chance, Sheckard, Moran, Schulte. Front row: Lundgren, T. Walsh, Evers, Slagle, Tinker.

time, winning six of them, including back-to-back 1–0 gems over the Pirates in a July 4 twin bill. In 1906's World Series, burly Mr. Brown shut down White Sox bats on two singles in Game 4, duplicating the feat of the White Sox' Ed Walsh in Game 3, beating Nick Altrock, 1–0. Among Brown's six 1906 losses were 0–1, 1–2 and 2–3 losses. With just a little more punch here or there, Brown might have cleared the coveted 30-win mark.

Cubs rivals were held to *two* runs or less in 93 of their games, exactly three out of five. That is barely believable.

The staff ERA, 1.75 for the season, has been bettered by only two teams: the 1907 Cubs, who still possess the major league record of 1.73 and the 1909 Cubs at 1.74.

In scoring 704 runs the Cubs registered a 323-run differential that positions them fifth on that all-time listing. In a year so devoted to minimizing the offensive efforts of the opposition, it was impressive that this squad should come up with 704 markers of their own. It wasn't done with smoke and mirrors. Johnny Kling, the Cubs' able receiver, manager Chance, often referred to as P.L. for Peerless Leader, hard-hitting Harry Steinfeldt and "Wildfire" Schulte all chipped in to provide the necessary punch that chased home their league-leading 704 tallies. That said, it was nonetheless the defensive unit and superb pitching that sparked these dominators.

All of this made it possible for the 1906 Cubs to run off a stretch of games from August 6 and September 16 — six weeks — when they won 37 out of 39 games, including 19 in which they gave up one or no runs to their rivals. They played no favorites, beating each of the other teams during that six-week stretch in the dog days of the pennant race.

The Chicago National League franchise has had no club quite like it in its storied 140-season history. The same could be said for the league itself.

Presented following are the five mainstays of the Cubs' pitching staff, 1906–1910, in their five-year span of domination in the National League. The 1–0 and 2–0 columns list five-year totals of 1–0 and 2–0 victories. PW indicates the total number of Pitching Wins for the five-year period.

	W-L/%	SHO	1–0	2–0	PW
Brown	127–44/.743	38	7	8	23.5
Reulbach	91–33/.734	24	6	3	9.3
Overall	82–38/.683	27	4	8	12.1
Lundgren	41–23/.640	13	6	1	2.4
Pfiester	69–36/.657	17	4	3	6.3

The Pittsburgh Pirates, 1901–1909

During the first years of the twentieth century the Pittsburgh Pirates outshone the New York Giants as Shutout Masters six times out of nine. For those who might have been looking for the other dominating shutout franchise in the National League (beyond Chicago) during the Deadball years, it might seem not only incredible, but downright inaccurate, to put the Pirates ahead of the McGrawmen. But the numbers tell a different story:

	Pittsburgh	New York
Team Shutouts in 1901	15	11
1902	21	11
1903	16	8
1904	15	21
1905	12	18
1906	27	19
1907	24	22
1908	24	25
1909	21	17
Totals	175	152
Average per season	19.4	16.9

Mathewson, McGinnity and others of the famed Giants wrecking crew notwithstanding, the third of the mighty triumvirate that ruled the Senior Circuit in the early 1900s, Pittsburgh, brandished a potent crew of hurlers so

10. Zeroes in the Ballbag 117

Nattily attired for their 1902 team portrait, the Pittsburgh Pirates. Standing, left to right: Zimmer, Sebring, Phillippe, Merritt, Leever, Phelps. Seated, middle row: Chesbro, Bransfield, Mgr. F. Clarke, Pres. B. Dreyfuss, Wagner, Beaumont, Smith. Seated, front row: Burke, Conroy, Leach, Ritchey, McLaughlin.

accomplished that their likes have never, to this day, within the Corsairs' franchise, been duplicated. Standing in the forefront of a great defensive unit was the Pirates pitching staff. The numbers they registered with the Pirates between 1901 and 1909 follow.

Nm/Yrs	*W-L-Pct.*	*SHO*	*IP*	*PW*
Leever, 1901–09	151–59/.719	32	1905	10.4
Phillippe, 1901–09	134–77/.635	23	1879.1	10.3
Willis, 1906–09	89–46/.659	23	209	8.0
Leifield, 1905–09	77–53/.592	23	618	4.9
Camnitz, 1904–09	56–27/.675	14	757.2	3.4

MacLean Kennedy included 16 teams in a review of early baseball dynasties and great one-year clubs dating from 1872–1875 (Boston's Red Stockings) to the 1920–1928 (as he defined that dynasty) New York Yankees. Among them is the Pittsburgh team (his dating includes the years 1901–1905). This is what the veteran Detroit sportswriter, who had seen them play, had to say about them:

> There is always a reason why a team reaches the heights. For the greatness attained by Pittsburgh in 1901 to 1903, were two outstanding reasons. Frederick Clarke and Honus Wagner were the players who made Pittsburgh greater then the average great team. The team was great in its pitching department. It had an infield that worked together for many years and that worked together smoothly, powerfully and intelligently...
> Richard Wagner may have been one of the greatest musicians, and has been known to uplift thousands by the wizardry of his musical genius, but there was a namesake of his, known as Hans Wagner, who, by a single stroke of the hickory stick, has brought many thousands more to their feet and sent them home happier men and women [*The Great Teams of Baseball* (St. Louis: Sporting News, 1928; reprint, St. Louis: Horton, 1988), pp. 61 and 62. Page references for the 1988 edition].

Wagner, it should be noted, did *everything* skillfully, including pitching twice for the Pirates. But what he did best was play shortstop, and play it so well that he is, among those who know best, baseball's #1 all-time, Hall of Fame shortstop. To write his name into the lineup day after day was to put a player in the game who was better, more versatile, and more dominating than Ozzie Smith, Luis Aparicio and Cal Ripken wrapped into one. Assuredly, it made the task so much more manageable for the likes of Deacon Phillippe, Sam Leever or Lefty Leifield and the rest of the hurlers who made their way to the mound during his 21-year career.

During that marvelous ten-year span, 1900–1909, the three protagonists for championship laurels each of those years performed their wonders before excited gatherings that hung on every pitch.

The Philadelphia Athletics: 1902–1905 and 1910–1914

During the formative years of the American League, and the National as well, for that matter, baseball fans really didn't need a scorecard to know where their favorites were playing. Rosters were pretty much the same from year to year. There were changes, of course, but it was the rule rather than the exception for most of the game's better players to spend the majority of their major league years, if not all of them, with the same ball club — playing the same position and in the same spot in the batting order. And until he ran into the grim realities of a crumbling financial situation, more than once, that was especially true of Connie Mack's "White Elephants," as John McGraw called them.

In Mack's fold there were Eddie Plank, Rube Waddell and Chief Bender, Harry Davis and Stuffy McGinnis, among others, who were synonymous with the Athletics for years. Eddie Collins, Jack Barry, Jimmie Foxx, Al Simmons, Lefty Grove, Jimmy Dykes, Rube Oldring, Schreckengost, Frank Baker and Jack Coombs were all long-termers in Mack lineups. And their reign as dominators in the American League, first during the Deadball Era, and then from roughly 1925 to 1933, was one of the products of the longevity, to say nothing of their excellence as colleagues playing on some of baseball's very best ball clubs ever.

During the nine years comprising what actually were two mini-eras of supremacy in the Junior Circuit's early going, the Athletics came up with 149 shutouts, featuring high-water marks of 26 in 1904 and 24 in both 1910 and 1914. These pitchers helped amass the shutout totals:

	Rube Waddell	Chief Bender	Eddie Plank	Jack Coombs
1902	3	1		
1903	4	2	3	
1904	8	4	7	
1905	7	4	4	
1910		3	1	13*
1911		2	6	1
1912		1	5	1
1913		2	7	
1914		7	4	
Totals	22	25	38	15 (four pitchers, 100 shutouts)

*In 1910, his 31-victory year, Jack Coombs' 13 shutouts became an American League record unsurpassed to this day.

Among the nine great Athletics teams in these two eras of Mackball, the 1911 squad ranks among baseball's finest. The infield was manned by a unit dubbed the "$100,000 Infield," as able defensively as it was at bat. The pitching for this team was done by perennial stars Albert "Chief" Bender (17–5), stellar Eddie Plank (23–8), Jack Coombs (28–12), and two other double-figure winners, Cy Morgan and young Harry Krause. The staff compiled a record of three earned runs per game, led by Eddie Plank's 2.10 (Chief Bender, at 2.16, was right behind Plank).

The much-respected baseball historian Donald Honig penned these words about Mack's 1911 World Champions:

The 1910 Philadelphia Athletics. Standing: Davis, Baker, Coombs, Thomas, Bender, Houser, Derrick, Morgan, Donahue. Seated: Oldring, Lord, Murphy, Owner/Mgr. Connie Mack, Plank, Lapp, Strunk. Seated, front: Hartsel, McInnis, Atkins, Krause, bat boy Van Zelst, Dygert, Collins, Barry, Livingston.

> Of all the teams that Connie managed, it has been reported that the 1911 edition was his favorite. If true, then not a bad choice, since this was the first truly great ball club in American League history and one of the greatest ever [*Baseball's 10 Greatest Teams* (New York: Macmillan, 1982)].

The Chicago White Sox and the Boston Red Sox: 1901–1919

Virtually blanketing the Deadball Era, these two franchises, among the Junior Circuit's most stable during those years, were "in the money" for most of the seasons during that span of years. Their pennant years included: 1901, 1906, 1917 and 1919 (Chicago), and 1903, 1904, 1912, 1915, 1916, and 1918 (Boston), ten all told. Second place finishes included three for Boston and two for Chicago. Adding it up, they earned 15 first- or second-place positions out of the 38 possibilities in those 19 seasons. There were but six Future Hall of Fame pitchers sporting Red Sox or Pale Hose togs during that time, and two of them, the legendary Babe Ruth and wily Clark Griffith, were named Hall of Famers in categories other than "pitcher." That points to overall team strength and smart ballplayers who minimized weaknesses and defensive lapses as compared with their competitors. That is not to say there was a dearth of good pitching. Just a thin cut below White Sox Future Hall of Famers Ed Walsh and Urban "Red" Faber were Red Sox whizzes Smoky Joe Wood,

10. Zeroes in the Ballbag

Chicago White Sox, 1908. 1. Walsh; 2. Davis; 3. Altrock; 4. Parent; 5. Hahn; 6. Mgr. F. Jones; 7. Atz; 8. Sullivan; 9. Isbell; 10. White; 11. Frank Smith; 12. Owen; 13. Donahue; 14. Dougherty.

Carl Mays, and Bill Dinneen, plus the man who had the most of just about everything when it came to pitching, the immortal Cy Young. Other White Sox mainstays included Frank Owen, Frank Smith, Doc White, and Eddie Cicotte, who pitched for both Boston (1908–1912) and Chicago (1912–1920).

The best of the two staffs (their shutout figures guide the choices made with respect to these Boston and Chicago Deadball Era aces) are lined up alphabetically in the following table. In this Deadball Era table are included: CSHO: Total number of career shutouts. PW: Pitching Wins is a sabermetric figure that represents how many victories a pitcher achieves compared to an average (0.0) pitcher. Figures above 1 increase in seasonal value with each additional 1.0. Thus, a 4.0 season is an exceptionally good one, and a 7.00 an extraordinary one. The highest single-season PW figure since 1900 belongs to Walter Johnson: 10.9, set in 1913.

All statistics represent individual seasons except for CSHO.

Pitcher/Tm/YR	Record	SHO	CSHO	PW
Cicotte, Eddie, Chi, 1917	28–12	7	35	5.7
Collins, Ray, Bos, 1914	20–13	6	19	0.7
Dinneen, Bill, Bos, 1903	21–13	6	24	2.9
Faber, Red, Chi, 1916	17–9	3	29	1.2
Foster, George, Bos, 1915	19–8	5	15	2.9
Griffith, Calvin, Chi, 1901	24–7	5	22	4.2
Leonard, Hub, Bos, 1914	19–5	7	33	4.8
Mays, Carl, Bos, 1918	21–13	8	29	3.7
Owen, Frank, Chi, 1906	22–13	7	16	0.6
Ruth, Babe, Bos, 1916	23–12	9	17	5.7
Scott, Jim, Chi, 1915	24–11	7	26	2.9
Smith, Frank, Chi, 1909	25–17	7	27	4.1
Walsh, Ed, Chi, 1909	40–15	11	57	6.8
White, Doc, Chi, 1906	18–6	7	45	3.9
Wood, Joe, Bos, 1912	34–5	10	28	7.5
Young, Cy, Bos, 1904	26–16	10	76	3.8

From 1901 to 1919, Deadball Era teams in the American, National and Federal Leagues logged 4,483 shutouts during the regular season. The NL led the way with 2168, followed by the AL with 2092 and the Federal League with 223 in its two seasons of play. High individual season marks include 164, the National League single season record (1908), and the AL's record of 146 (1909). The Feds registered 101 in 1914 and 122 in 1915.

Among that huge number there were, of course, many significant shutout victories. Let's take the time to review just a few of them to get a taste of the important, or strange, or timely ones that were recorded during Deadball baseball. The chronological listing follows.

A young Babe Ruth with the starters on the 1915–1917 Boston Red Sox pitching staff. Left to right: George Foster, Carl Mays, Ernie Shore, Babe Ruth, and Hub Leonard (Brace photographs).

September 15, 1901

    The Chicago Chronicle reported that Cleveland was "badly beaten" and that pitcher Jack Bracken "was hit all over the field" in a merciless, 21–0 annihilation by Detroit. It was the worst shutout whipping of the Deadball Era in a game that was ended before the ninth inning so that the Blues could catch their train. In the Tigers' last home game Ed Siever limited Cleveland to five scattered hits while his Tigers teammates pounded out 24 hits including Lewis "Sport" McAllister's two doubles and a home run.

October 14, 1905

    The Deadball Era showcased three of the game's immortal pitchers, one of whom spent his entire career within its timeframe. That would be Christy Mathewson (1901–1916). The others were Walter Johnson (110) and Pete Alexander (90), who wound up their careers as the number one and two men in career shutouts. Notwithstanding, it was during the 1905 World Series that Matty unveiled his awesome three-game mastery of the mighty Philadelphia Athletics. First with 3–0 and 9–0 victories, and culminating his masterpieces with a 2–0 conquest, his third and World Series–winning shutout. Nor will we pass by this extraordinary World Series without a comment about its other two shutouts: (1) the 3–0, Chief Bender victory over Joe McGinnity in game two; and (2) "McGinnity's Redemption" in game five, a brilliant 1–0 gem that beat Eddie Plank and the Mackmen, 1–0.

May 18, 1906

Feeble at the plate but mighty afield and in the pitcher's box, baseball's Hitless Wonders, the 1906 World Champion Chicago White Sox, scraped by as best they could, but on this date they found unaccustomed thump, especially in the bat of skipper Fielder Jones, who homered in a 10–0 humiliation of Washington's Senators. In this match Frank Owen, 22–13 on the season, silenced Senators bats at American League Park. Owen that season tossed a career-high seven shutouts, tying him with Doc White for second spot among whitewashers. Ed Walsh led the club with ten.

July 17, and October 2, 1908

It was Wagner Day in Pittsburgh in the remarkable baseball year of 1908, and the Boston Doves were in town to help the local burghers honor their beloved Hans, at least before the baseball warfare afield started. The Doves weren't quite as sanguine about the game, shutting out the Pirates 4–0, Howie Camnitz dropping shutout to Tom McCarthy. Before the game Hans Wagner was presented with a $700 gold watch on behalf of the Pirates fans.

October 2, 1908

Regarded as one of all-time great games in major league history, Addie Joss no-hit the Chicago White Sox in a white-hot pennant race that wasn't decided until the final innings of the season, when neither of these two teams captured the flag, But Joss' perfect game kept the Naps in the thick of the pennant proceedings. The Cobb-led Tigers finally won out with both Cleveland and Chicago a game short of championship honors. Big Ed Walsh, the loser this day, set the single-game strikeout record, fanning 15 of the Cleveland nine.

April 14, 1910

A tradition began in Washington this day. And with it came the first ceremonial pitch of the season, usually celebrated throughout the major leagues by dignitaries, officials and, most often, a sell-out crowd of fans welcoming a new season. In Washington that dignitary is the President, and on this date, in 1910, the president was William Howard Taft, the bulking 300-pound baseball fan and the first President to throw out the first pitch. Watching the game from a special armchair, he witnessed one of Walter Johnson's better ballgames, a 3–0 one-hitter that might have been a no-hitter had it not been for a fan in the overflow crowd that caused right fielder Doc Gessler to stumble in pursuit of a Frank Baker pop fly. The ball fell safely for a double, the only hit the A's could muster in Johnson's victory over the great Eddie Plank. Quite a game. Quite a day!

September 22, 1911

How very appropriate that the last of Cy Young's 511 victories would also come as a shutout, as he defeated the Pirates in Pittsburgh, 1–0. It was also his

76th shutout. His fourth-place ranking in career shutouts places him behind Mathewson (79), Pete Alexender (90) and Johnson (110). Boston, for this season named the Rustlers, managed only five shutouts and two of them were authored by the 44-year-old Young, both over the Pirates. Young this day struck out Hans Wagner three times, walked none and bested Pirates ace Babe Adams. That piece of work would have been impressive for a 25-year-old at the top of his youthful strength and ability — but for an overweight 44-year-old? My, my! Thus, the wonders of the legendary Denton True Young!

September 24–25, 1914

The end of the season usually brought a rash of doubleheaders in days gone by. Those twin bills were caused by postponements earlier in the season. The Miracle Braves finished off their pennant-winning season with no less than eight such engagements, jammed in between September 23 and the end of the season. During that time they won 14, lost 4 and tied two games, finishing the 1914 season more than ten games ahead of their closest rival, New York. Two of those doubleheaders were played on consecutive days and Dick Rudolph hurled shutouts on those two days. The very able right-hander, nicknamed Baldy, chalked up his fifth and sixth shutouts on September 24 and 25 against Cincinnati, finishing his regular season assignments with a fine 26–10 record and a 2.35 ERA in 336.1 innings of work. His post-season log read 2–0 in a World Series that had baseball people shaking their heads in disbelief as the Braves, with Rudolph and Big Bill James leading the way (James threw a 1–0 masterpiece at the bewildered Athletics in Game 2) to the last Braves World Series championship until the 1948 Braves of Spahn and Sain once more put the National League franchise into the Fall Classic.

May 15, 1915

Succumbing to contractual, legal and financial pressures before the 1916 season began, the Federal League folded after two seasons of play. During those two seasons their teams fashioned 223 shutouts, keeping pace with their rivals in the NL and AL. One of the premier hurlers in the FL was Claude Hendrix, a strong-armed right-hander who led the league in 1914 with 29 victories. After the Feds disbanded he signed a Cubs contract, staying in Chicago, where he had led Joe Tinker's Whales pitching staff. On May 14, George "Slats" McConnell, winner of 25 games for Chicago in 1915, shut out the Pittsburgh Rebels, 6–0. On the very next day Hendrix, who totaled 11 shutouts during his FL days, had his most distinguished outing, a 10–0 no-hit gem against the Rebels. His no-hitter was one of five by FL pitchers in the two-year history of that league. Several years later he won 20 for the Cubs, who in that year, 1918, won Chicago's last world championship in the twentieth century.

May 2, 1917

This is the game made famous by Hippo Vaughn and Fred Toney of the Cincinnati Reds. Toney, a 6'2", 215-lb. workhorse, led the Reds pitching staff in 1917 with a sparkling 24–16 record. His 1–0 no-hitter over the Cubs was his career *Meisterwerke*, in a game that saw, amazingly, two nine-inning no-hitters. Unfortunately for the Cubs and Hippo Vaughn, there had to be a tenth inning, and in that frame the Reds got to Vaughn for the winning hits necessary to break up one of baseball's classic contests. The game is nicely reviewed in John McCollister's *Best Baseball Games Ever Played*. Christy Mathewson is quoted in the book as saying that it was "the greatest pitching performance I ever witnessed."

May 15, 1918

It takes stout pitching to get through 17 innings without allowing a run. Such a performance occurred in Washington where the Senators and White Sox met in a four-game series. The two teams split their four games, including two shutouts and three were extra inning ball games. This thrilling, early season series featured Walter Johnson against Claude "Lefty" Williams, the little White Sox lefty with one of the best change-ups in the majors. Johnson made it through 18 Sox at bats, spacing ten hits and kayoing nine (Wondrous Walter fanned Williams five times). Then, with one out in the bottom of the 18th, light-hitting catcher Eddie Ainsmith scored the tilt's lone run in a game that entered baseball's annals as the longest 1–0 game played to that time. Two pitchers, as contrasted to the parade of relievers present-day fans are accustomed to, and but two hours and 50 minutes of baseball for some 125 plate appearances—Deadball Era baseball at its best, as well as most efficient.

The Deadball Era Fini, September 28, 1919

The final classic in this Deadball Era folio is left in the capable hands of Grover "Pete" Alexander, whose 2–0 shutout win over Hod Eller, seeking his 20th win in Cincinnati's pennant and World Series championship year, wound down both the season and an entire era. Another of those appropriate affairs, pitchers considered, and the quality of their play—right?! In this one Fred Merkle came up with his 20th stolen base of the season and the hit that drove home the only run Alex needed to put away his 16th victory of the season. There were no boners in this one, run off in an hour and 15 minutes, showcasing great control on the part of both pitchers, each of whom issued but a single free pass. Baseball would turn a corner in 1920, heading into an era that featured hitters, not pitchers, but in this final 1919 engagement pitchers were boss, and Alexander elite.

On to a New Millennium: 2000–2010

The twentieth century shutout story ended in the American League on the last day of the 1999 season, October 3, winding up play at coastal cities east and west with a Boston win, 1–0 in 10 innings at Baltimore, and at Anaheim, where Tim Salmon's seventh-inning four-bagger was enough to get the Angels past Texas in another 1–0 duel. But October 4 goes on record as the last twentieth century regular season shutout date. In a one-game playoff for the wild-card spot at Cincinnati, the New York Mets, behind Al Leiter, shut out the Reds, 5–0. Scoring punch at the top of the order, provided by Edgar

Alfonzo and Rickey Henderson, propelled the Mets to their unique shutout achievement. It was New York's seventh of the 1999 season. The final shutout of the calendar year came on October 15, in Game 3 of the NLCS, when Tom Glavine and two Atlanta relievers combined to defeat the Mets, 1–0.

In just a matter of months the baseball wars were resumed and people were gazing at their new millennium calendars. The year 2000 and the decade following brought a continuing emphasis on a 12–13-man pitching staff used in varying capacities as starters, specialists and role-playing relievers. Fans *really did* need a scorecard this time around because not only was much of the pitching staff employed on a daily basis, but the recall system and trading maneuvers of major league teams kept rosters in a near-constant state of flux. For the average Joe Fan it was really bewildering.

There was one stunning, nigh inexplicable development during the first decade of the 2000s: the National League set a new league, team shutout record in 2010, amassing a total of 202, marking the first time any league had exceeded the 200 mark. And they shattered the 1908 major league record by an eye-popping 38 shutouts! It is hard to say what brought about such a huge spike in annual numbers ranging from 130 to 150 during the decade. Team scoring was down, pitching staffs had become more and more efficient, and relievers, especially, were more aggressive in the years preceding the quantum leap, but moving from 150 to 202 in a single season? And this, while the American League was "loafing" along at its usual 110 to 130 pace with 127 in 2010 compared to the Senior Circuit's incredible number. The 2010 statistics are included in the following table. Individual team leaders are listed behind league totals.

	National League	American League	ML Total
2000	112 (15, SF)	92 (12, Bos)	204
2001	138 (14, NY)	89 (14, Sea)	227
2002	153 (15, Atl, LA)	122 (19, Oak)	275
2003	150 (17, LA)	109 (15, Sea)	259
2004	136 (14, Fla)	115 (12, Bos)	251
2005	148 (15, Fla)	113 (14, NY)	261
2006	136 (12, Hou, NY)	124 (16, Det)	260
2007	128 (20, SD)	115 (13, Bos)	243
2008	143 (13, Hou)	128 (13, Clv, Tor)	271
2009	150 (18, SF)	123 (13, Ana)	273
2010	**202** (21, Phl)	127 (17, Oak)	**329**

The Shutout Masters of the 2000s wasted no time getting things going in the first season of the new decade. Opening game shutouts in each league were pitched by Atlanta's Greg Maddux, with help from closer Mike Remlinger, and by Steve Trachsel for Tampa Bay, who also needed bullpen help against Minnesota. In Atlanta, the Maddux-led Braves beat Colorado 2–0 on the strength of Andres Galarraga and Andruw Jones back-to-back homers in an otherwise scoreless game. At Minnesota, where 43,830 Twins partisans helped open up the season, Tampa Bay piled up seven tallies to put a wet blanket on the Twin City celebration. Among other season opening games Boston bested Seattle (Pedro Martinez vs. Denny Moyer) and San Francisco took the measure of Florida, both games played a day later than the Atlanta and Tampa Bay openers, and on April 5 San Diego's Padres humbled the Mets in New York. As was characteristic of the times, none of these games resulted in a shutout.

Another 2010 morsel: There were 62 major league, 1–0 games, representing 2.6 percent of all games played. That number may seem huge, but nonetheless almost minuscule compared with the record-setting 80 1–0 shutouts fired by pitching wizards in 1908 (6.4 percent). Finally, with respect to 1–0 games, note that three regular season-no-hitters were recorded in the first decade of the 2000s: April 27, 2003, by Kevin Millwood (Philadelphia vs. San Francisco); May 29, 2010, by Roy Halladay (Philadelphia vs. Florida) and Edwin Jackson in an interleague game, (Arizona vs. Tampa Bay) on June 25, 2010.

By the 2000s the route to a world championship for major league ball clubs had become a complicated and arduous affair. Divisional and Championship series had become October fixtures, straining World Series aspirants, especially pitching staffs, to the extreme. No longer was it a given that strong teams who had won Divisional titles would wind up playing for October's gold. From 1969 forward the playoff system was gradually lengthened by adding teams to the mix that would finally produce the two World Series contestants. In 2003, for example, the Florida Marlins were obliged to work their way through a four-game series with San Francisco before meeting the Chicago Cubs, this time in a best-of-seven series that went right on down to the final innings of Game 7 before winning the right to meet the New York Yankees in the World Series—which they also won in six games.

During the 2003 season the Florida Marlins had only 11 shutouts.

In one of those 11, Dontrelle Willis, the 2003 National League Rookie of the Year, was involved. A capsule of that game is followed by shutout victories occurring in 2004, 2005, and 2009 regular season play, each by a survivor of baseball's world series championship eliminations.

September 3, 2004: St. Louis 3, Los Angeles Dodgers 0

Scoring single runs in the second, fifth and seventh innings, the Cardinals brushed aside the LA Dodgers, 3–0, behind the two-hit pitching of Matt Morris. Singles by Dodgers pitcher Jose Lima and first baseman Robin Ventura were the only signs of offensive life the Left-Coasters could muster. Morris' shutout was one of the Cardinals' 12 in 2004.

May 18, 2005: Chicago White Sox 7, Texas Rangers 0

The record for most hits allowed in a shutout game is 14, shared by Larry Cheney of the 1913 Cubs in a September 14 game against the New York Giants, and Milt Gaston of the 1928 Senators, who somehow held the Cleveland Indians on July 10 scoreless despite their basket full of hits. Shutouts of the eight-hit and more variety are very infrequent, but this nine-hitter, fashioned by the White Sox during their world championship season of 2005, ranks up there with the rare ones. Mark Buehrle got the win, going into the eighth inning of a tiring day. Skipper Ozzie Guillen sent along the help he needed with Cliff Politte's ⅔ of an inning, and Neal Cotts' nine-inning shut-down.

September 26, 2009: New York Yankees 3, Boston Red Sox 0

In Deadball Era days a two-hitter nearly always signaled a complete game victory. Not necessarily so in the 21st century. Going by what is now reckoned as SOP for pitchers, C.C. Sabathia, one of contemporary pitching's top-rung hurlers, traveled a seven-inning route to win in a game staged before almost 50,000 frenzied Yankee loyalists. One of the most storied rivalries in the game's history, matches between these two teams usually amount to classics. In this one, C.C. went seven innings, giving up one hit. Mariano Rivera, Hall of Fame–bound Yankees closer, finished off the Carmine in this one, striking out the game's last hitter while logging his 43rd Save of the season. In this well-pitched contest, three hours and seven minutes in the making Dominican Robinson Cano, blasted a towering blow into the distant Yankee Stadium seats that put the Bronx Bombers ahead to stay.

11

The No-No

Often referred to as the No-No, the no-hitter is the acme of shutout masterpieces. Between the first one, thrown in the National Association by Joe Borden of the Philadelphia White Stockings against the Chicago White Stockings on July 28, 1875, and last one in 2010, on October 6 in a National League Divisional championship game, by Roy Halladay of the Phillies against the Cincinnati Reds, there have been 269 of these rare exceptions thrown. Among that number, scattered here and there over the years are 24 in which the team that has been no-hit has scored at least one run. Consequently, for shutout purposes, the number ought be adjusted to 245. But pay no mind. The numbers register at about 1–2 percent of all games played.

And if that is not enough, and perfection is your preference, perfect games, the epitome of pitching perfection, check in at a mere 20 through the 2010 season, and that includes Don Larsen's Perfecto on October 8, 1956, in a 2–0. New York Yankees victory over Brooklyn (World Series Game 5). Heralded far and wide whenever it happens, perfect games provide a journalistic feeding frenzy, to say nothing of many books written on the subject.

A look at major league no-hit games really should begin with: there are no-hitters and then there are no-hitters (sorry, perfectos, you will have to wait your turn). Consider this: on June 25, 2010, Edwin Jackson threw a no-hitter in an interleague game between his Arizona Diamondbacks and the AL's Tampa Bay Rays. During the course of that game Jackson threw 149 pitches and walked eight batters. The D-backs won that game 1–0. Or: In another interleague game played at Yankee Stadium on June 11, 2003, the Yanks were zeroed 8–0 by six Astros pitchers. Roy Oswalt started that game and pitched only the first inning. He was followed by a parade of five Houston relievers: Peter Munro, Kirk Saarloos, Brad Lidge (WP), Octavio Dotel and Billy Wagner.

At the other end of those rather unusual no-hit games is one thrown by Milt Pappas on September 2, 1972. With two out in the ninth inning against San Diego, leading 8–0, he retired the first two Padres batters to make it 26 up and down in a row. All he needed for a perfect game was to retire pinch-hitter Larry Stahl. Stahl worked Pappas to a full count, and on the 3–2 pitch Pappas fired what he thought was a strike, only to have umpire Bruce Froemming call it ball four. He then retired the next hitter, ex–Cub Garry Jestadt, to keep his no-hit gem intact.

As these no-hit and perfect games go, there are miles of difference between the Jackson and the Pappas no-hitters. In the Jackson no-hit game, eight Rays worked the right hander for free passes and six were fanned. Adam LaRoche provided the only score in the game with a homer in the second inning.

Pappas, some 30 seasons earlier, walked but one, struck out six, and had his infield busy recording the majority of the 27 putouts he needed. He was definitely on his A-game, and his performance that day far outshone the Jackson no-no.

Indeed, there are sometimes huge differences, even in no-hit and perfect games. One way to measure differences in these games is by pitch counts. Following is a list of perfect games with the number of pitches thrown in each game:

Pitcher	Pitch Count	Date
David Wells	120	May 17, 1998
Randy Johnson	117	May 18, 2004
Mark Buehrle	116	July 23, 2009
Roy Halladay	115	May 29, 2010
Sandy Koufax	113	September 9, 1965
Dallas Braden	109	May 9, 2010
Catfish Hunter	107	May 8, 1968
Len Barker	103	May 15, 1981
Tom Browning	100	September 16, 1988
Kenny Rogers	98	July 28, 1994
Don Larsen	97	October 8, 1956
Dennis Martinez	96	July 28, 1991
Mike Witt	94	September 30, 1984
Jim Bunning	90	June 21, 1964
Charlie Robertson	90	April 30, 1922
David Cone	88	July 18, 1999
Addie Joss	74	October 2, 1908
Cy Young	unknown*	May 5, 1904

*The Cy Young game took only an hour and 23 minutes to complete. One may safely assume it took fewer than 90 pitches to complete (cf. the Joss game, which took one hour and 29 minutes to complete).

The difference between the Wells (120 pitches) and the Joss (74 pitches) perfectos amounts to roughly four innings of pitching at an average of 12 pitches per inning. That's a lot more precision on the part of Joss, and a lot more opportunity for things to go wrong on the part of Wells. Yet both went through their opponents' lineups in 1–2–3 order nine times. Same perfect shutout, different game each time!

Another interesting phenomenon is the recurrence of multiple no-hitters in a given season. Five in one season, an unusually high number, occurred in four different seasons, 1962, 1968, and 1973. Six were thrown in four different years, 1908, 1915, 1917, 1969 and 2010. In both 1990 and 1991 there were seven no-hitters making 14 in just two seasons. Those 14 included a perfect game by Dennis Martinez and two no-nos by Nolan Ryan. And in an earlier era, when things like no-hitters were almost considered to be anomalies, there were eight in 1884, one of baseball's more remarkable years in many, many ways.

Like so many other unusual, as well as very interesting events in baseball, the no-hitter, as the song says about a woman, "is a sometime thing." Jim Bunning, who ought to know, having thrown two himself, was quoted in a "Baseball Digest" article (August 2002) by George Vass, stating, "A no-hitter is a freaky thing. You can't plan it. It's not something you can try to do. It just happens. Everything has to come together all on the same day: good control, outstanding plays from your teammates, a whole lot of good fortune on your side and a lot of bad things for the other guys."

Keeping that in mind, here are 15 of the most intriguing no-hit games in the game's history, arranged in chronological order. Remember, as you go through the list, that these games took place during regular season play only. The perfect game is not represented here inasmuch as the perfectos get their just due straight ahead.

Buffalo at Detroit, NL, August 4, 1884

In 1884 Jim "Pud" Galvin, workhorse hurler for the Buffalo Bisons, threw 12 shutouts. One of them occurred in a game against the Detroit Wolverines, the second of three straight whitewashings he authored. The victory came in a 20-game stretch during which the Bisons won 18. Galvin's no-hit victory at Detroit turned out to be the most lopsided no-hitter in the history of major baseball. Ranking second is the 15–0 embarrassment administered by Frank Smith of the Chicago White Sox, also at Detroit 21 years later. Hall of Famer Galvin had pitched an earlier no-hitter on August 20, 1880, the day after Chicago White Stockings pitcher Larry Corcoran downed Boston. The two no-hitters were the fifth and sixth on record.

Louisville at St. Louis, AA, October 4, 1891

The eighth-place Louisville Colonels visited the St. Louis Browns to play a doubleheader on the last day of the 1891 season. St. Louis manager Charlie Comiskey scheduled a rookie, southpaw Ted Breitenstein, to pitch the first game of that twin bill. Breitenstein had made brief appearances in five games for the Browns previous to his starting assignment on October 4. He was with the Browns during the season only because the Grand Rapids team of the Northwestern League, to which he had been assigned for more seasoning, folded. With the pennant beyond his grasp, Comiskey thought to give the handsome St. Louisan a start. The lefty promptly became the first player in major league history to fire a no-hitter in his first starting role. Not only did it become an 8–0, no-hit gem, it almost became a perfect game. In that game Louisville had but one baserunner, given a free pass by Breitenstein, who faced the minimum 27 batters. Coincidentally, the victory was St. Louis' last in the American Association since the league closed up shop during the off-season. The Browns moved to the National League. Since the Browns lost the second game of the season-ending doubleheader, Breitenstein also became the last St. Louis pitcher to win a shutout. The American Association's first shutout also involved the St. Louis Browns and the Louisville Eclipse. That was a 3–0 Tony Mullane victory for the Louisville nine on May 6, 1882. The final shutout in the American Association was thrown by "Gentleman George" Haddock, Boston's ace right-hander, who, on October 5, threw the last of his league-leading five shutouts, defeating Philadelphia, 6–0. It was the last of his 34 victories 1891.

July 4, 1908 Polo Grounds, New York George "Hooks" Wiltse's shutout on Uncle Sam's birthday in 1908 was a brilliant no-hit effort, a 1–0 victory over George McQuillan, who was in the midst of a 23-win year, during which he also hurled seven shutouts in 359.2 innings of work. (The nickname "Hooks" derived from his battery mate, Frank Bowerman, who used to say, "That's hooking them, George," when Wiltse would snare balls hit through the box with his long arm.)

On this particular Fourth of July Wiltse went through the Phillies batting order through 26 consecutive outs until a pitch that might easily have been called a strike was instead called a ball. The next Wiltse offering hit the batsman, sending him to first. Wiltse bore down to get the next hitter. He retired the side, but lost his perfect game, though preserving his no-hitter.

The game went into the tenth inning, which Hooks navigated in 1–2–3 order. The Giants scored in the bottom of that inning to win the game, 1–0, giving Wiltse a ten-inning no-hitter. As it happens from time to time, the umpire, Cy Rigler, who was a very good one, just might have missed one. He offered after the game that the pitch he called a ball might well have been called a strike. Well now, what might have been doesn't somehow work in baseball, but it puts its mark on important events in the game's history. In this instance one call made the difference between a no-hit game and a shutout perfecto.

The year 1908 was a banner year for Hooks Wiltse. The southpaw, who was an excellent fielder, won 23 and lost 14, toiling 330 innings and pitching the same number of shutouts as his competitor on that special Fourth of July, seven. On any other club his talent might have been more heralded, but teammates of Christy Mathewson had to be satisfied with whatever attention they could garner in the presence of the ultimate early–1900s hero. Nearly 20 percent, of Wiltse's 139 career victories were shutouts. Mathewson, by comparison, hurled 79 (third all-time). That represents 21 percent of his 373 victories. Mathewson, in a class by himself, made many another good one pale by comparison.

Weeghman Park, Chicago Cincinnati vs. Chicago Cubs, May 2, 1917

"Hippo" Vaughn, able Cub as left-hander, won 20 games five times in a 13-year career (Brace photograph).

Here is a set of no-hitters that is an original, yet to be duplicated. At what is now known as Wrigley Field, southpaw Jim "Hippo" Vaughn of the Cubs and Fred Toney, Cincinnati right-hander, pitched the only double-no-hitter in baseball history on May second, 1917. It is, arguably, the very best of all the no-hit games.

The story is so well told by sportswriter Chris Rewers (recorded as one of the greatest moments in Cubs history at www.agonyandivy.com, January 2011), that portions of the article are presented here:

In a game that lasted just 1 hour, 50 minutes, each pitcher went through the opposing lineup like a hot knife through butter. Through nine innings, neither team managed a hit.

In the 10th, Vaughn retired Cincinnati

leadoff hitter Gus Getz on a popout to catcher Art Wilson, but then his team's defense betrayed him.

Larry Kopf followed with a seeing-eye single that rolled between first baseman Merkle and second baseman Larry Doyle into right field. The next batter, Hal Chase, lifted a lazy fly that was muffed by Cubs right fielder Williams, allowing Chase to reach first safely and Kopf to advance to third. Chase then stole second.

The next Cincinnati batter was Jim Thorpe — the same Jim Thorpe who was the decathlon champion at the 1912 Olympic Games in Stockholm, Sweden, [and] had been a two-time All-American football player at Carlisle College...

The right-handed hitting Thorpe swung at a Vaughn curve and topped it off the handle of his bat. It bounced high in front of the plate and Vaughn fielded it on the third-base side of the mound. With the speedy Thorpe busting down the first-base line, Vaughn made a split-second decision to try to nail Kopf at the plate.

"(Kopf) stopped when he saw me make the throw to the plate," Vaughn later to a reporter from the *Chicago Daily News* years later. (Vaughn continued) "I didn't see him or I could have turned around and tagged him out.

"Now some of the writers said that Wilson didn't expect the throw. The truth is that Art just went paralyzed — just stood there with his hands at his sides staring at me. The ball hit him square in the chest protector — I'll never forget it — it seemed to roll around there for a moment — and then dropped to the ground. The instant Kopf saw it drop, he streaked for the plate. But Wilson still stood there, paralyzed. I looked over my shoulder and saw Chase round third and start in too. So I said to Art:

"'Are you going to let him score, too?'

"He woke up, grabbed the ball, and tagged Chase out easily. But is was too late, the one big deciding run was in."

Toney set the Cubs down in order in the bottom of the 10th to complete his feat and made Vaughn, with the exception of Harvey Haddix, the most tough-luck losing pitcher in major league history.

From that day to this, two no-hitters have never been thrown in the same game. There are many among the Cubs faithful, and their number is near countless, who would no doubt say, "Only at Wrigley. Only the Cubs!"

At Boston, Fenway Park, July 1, 1920

The 1920 season wasn't Walter Johnson's worst, but it didn't miss by much. Yet even in a mediocre season the future Hall of Famer found a way to make something remarkable happen. That took place at Boston's Fenway Park on a day when Johnson was hoping to even his season record at eight wins and eight losses. A win would be just what the doctor ordered. Indeed, it was about time to see the doctor for consultation and treatment for the arm miseries that had been plaguing the game's flamethrower supreme.

But on July's first day in 1920 all that was put aside as the great man responded to skipper Clark Griffith's call despite feeling out of sorts at game time. The pitcher he faced, Harry Harper, had been Johnson's teammate the previous seven seasons and could, on occasion, bring it with the best of them. Harper also possessed a biting curve ball that he often used as a KO punch.

All of those circumstances, plus playing away from home, augured for a tough afternoon for Johnson.

But the game moved right along with Johnson and Harper pretty much matching pitches as the two of them put one goose egg on the scoreboard after another. There was one difference in the performance of the two hurlers. Not a soul was successful in reaching base on Walter Johnson through six innings.

In the top of the seventh right fielder Braggo Roth got on base and eventually came home on a Bucky Harris single. Johnson, who knew from experience with Washington teams that he would have make that one-run lead stand up, went to work. But despite his best efforts, Boston still managed to put a runner on base in the seventh inning when second baseman Bucky Harris, usually sure-handed, misplayed Harry Hooper's grounder. So much for perfection. It was, however, a harmless error and Boston was retired without any damage to Johnson's no-hitter.

Peerless Walter Johnson, Shutout King (Brace photograph).

Six outs later the game was over and Walter Johnson had no-hit the Red Sox. His biographer, grandson Henry W. Thomas, summarized the Johnson masterpiece this way in his carefully written *Walter Johnson: Baseball's Big Train* (Lincoln, NE: Nebraska University Press, 1995, 355), a review of Johnson's 15 best games:

July 1, 1920 — Washington 1, Boston 0. Johnson's only nine-inning no-hitter missed being a perfect game by an error. It was a one-runner game, much rarer than a no-hitter. He struck out ten Red Sox and got six of them to foul out, four to the catcher. In the ninth inning Johnson struck out two left-handed pinch-hitters before Joe Judge's miraculous stop to save the no-hitter.

Ironically, Johnson started the game not feeling up to snuff and immediately following it came down with the only serious sore arm of his career. But in between "he never pitched a greater game, to my knowledge," said Bucky Harris.

The no-hit victory was Walter Johnson's last win of the 1920 season. He wound up with an 8–10 mark that season and he wouldn't return to the old Johnson form until several seasons later, when his 23–7 record paced the Senators to their first pennant in 1924.

If not the greatest no-hitter ever pitched, it was certainly the grittiest.

April 29, 1931, at League Park, Cleveland

After the smoke of battle had cleared on August 14, 1930, Connie Mack's A's stood atop the American League standings by eight games over the Washington Senators. But you wouldn't have known it was the mighty Athletics judging by the shellacking they took at the hands of Wes Ferrell. Cleveland's Indians, with Ferrell in charge, ripped into the Mackmen, slaughtering them in a 15–0 rampage. For the Indians right-hander it was another in a string of 13 consecutive victories he chalked up that season from July 9 to September 6, when Ted Lyons and the White Sox edged him, 2–1. During the 1930 season, the second of four straight 20-win campaigns at the start of his major league career, Ferrell was a 25-game winner. But there was more good news in 1931. In fact, there was no-hit good news.

Nearing the end of April, Ferrell stood at 3–1 with victories over Chicago, twice, and Detroit. On the 29th, at tiny League Park in Cleveland, he wiped out the St. Louis Browns, 9–0, fanning eight, *en route* to his no-hit masterpiece. Three of the 27 outs he needed were furnished by his brother Rick, the Brownies' catcher. Later, with brother Rick, the two Ferrells formed a formidable battery with both the Red Sox and Washington Senators.

There was more than one notable feature about Ferrell's no-hitter. His four RBI in that game were the most ever recorded by a no-hit pitcher, as he doubled and homered. In a game against Cincinnati four decades later Philadelphia hurler Rick Wise hit two homers in a no-hit game he pitched at Riverfront Stadium on June 23, 1971, making him the only pitcher in the game's history to homer twice while tossing a no-hitter. While Wise was a decent-hitting pitcher, he was a few miles removed from Wes Ferrell, the best-hitting pitcher ever. In 1931 he blasted nine home runs into American League grandstands, a Major League record, and his 38 career taters tops the list for pitchers.

The titans of the 1930s often vied against each other and that was true of Lefty Grove and Wes Ferrell, who met three times in the 1931 season. Grove won all three matchups by scores of 4–3, 6–3 and 4–3, about which one wag commented that the temperature must have been ten degrees hotter on those days with two of the fiercest competitors in baseball's history dueling one another. Grove and Ferrell were teammates in 1935, when Ferrell won a career-high 25 games, three of which were shutouts. Grove that year won 20 games, posting two of his 35 career shutouts. One can only imagine the miseries suffered by the Red Sox' locker room (and, indeed, their teammates) as they worked their way through the long, hot summer. These two worthies took no prisoners.

Wes Ferrell's no-hitter does not do too much to advance his right to Hall of Fame membership, but there are many astute baseball people who believe his case is a strong one. Perhaps some day...

June 11 and June 15, 1938, at Crosley Field, Cincinnati, and Ebbets Field, Brooklyn

The Cincinnati Reds were on the verge of something big in 1938 with a lineup that began to win regularly against the powers of the National League. Paul Derringer and Bucky Walters spearheaded a capable pitching staff, and punch in manager Bill McKechnie's offensive brigade was provided by Ernie Lombardi, Buck McCormick and a hard-hitting outfield corps led by Ival Goodman and Wally Berger. The 1938 ball club finished fourth, but a strong fourth that made Reds fans think 1939 would be *their* year. They were right.

First, however, came 1938, and with it a switch-hitting, fireballing lefty whose 1937 debut

The Double No-Hit man, Johnny Vander Meer (Brace photograph).

season gave enough promise to make McKechnie think the youngster would make his starting rotation. About pitchers and pitching McKechnie was usually right, and so he was with his young phenom, a chap named John Samuel Vander Meer.

The very mention of the name Vander Meer conjures the most unique no-hit story in the annals of the grand old game. The image is always the same: successive no-hitters thrown in two games in June 1938. The world of baseball was not really ready for what happened first in Cincinnati at Crosley Field, and then at Ebbets Field in Brooklyn, where the first night game in Brooklyn's history prompted 38,748 of the Flatbush Faithful to gather for the privilege of being "the first" to see a ball game "under the lights," as it was referred to in those days. It just so happened that watching the first Brooklyn major league game played under the lights wasn't the major event of the evening. The combination of the night-game inaugural, celebs Jesse Owens and Babe Ruth on hand for the followup to his no-hitter in Cincinnati just four days prior to the June 15 masterpiece, Vander Meer's parents and a delegation from his home town there to witness the game, and the man himself, made this event a real baseball happening. While Vandy's first no-no didn't cause too much ado other than that it was the first Cincinnati no-hitter since Hod Eller had thrown one in the Reds' last pennant year, 1919, it was a different story in advance of June 15. No one dreamed, nor was anyone expecting the lefty to knock on the door of history. A win? Maybe. A shutout? Could be possible. Another no-hitter? Nah. Won't happen.

But it did. Even though Vander Meer was uncomfortably wild in the ninth inning, loading the sacks with Dodgers runners via free passes, he got the out he needed, a lazy fly to Harry Craft that wrote *fini* to his second straight no-hitter. It wasn't perfect, but it didn't have to be. Two straight was more than enough.

Just one little bit of a curious addendum to a story written and rewritten so many times: In 1952, his major league pitching days behind him, Johnny Vander Meer was pitching for the Tulsa Oilers in the Texas League. With an 11–10 record that season, he pulled one more one more masterpiece out of the bag: a no-hit gem against Beaumont, 12–0. The Beaumont manager? Harry Craft, the fellow who caught the last out in Vander Meer's second no-no.

At Comiskey Park, Chicago, April 16, 1940, Opening Day

They called him Bullet Bob. He was later clocked at better than 100 mph. Among the premier fast ball pitchers in major league history, Bob Feller was a future Hall of Famer almost from his first major league pitch, at age 17. Fastball throwers are especially hard on hitters in raw, cold weather. It was that kind of day when the baseball season opened in Chicago with Commissioner Landis and Bob Feller's parents on hand to watch Feller's Indians play the Chicago White Sox in frigid 30-something-degree weather. Further, making the hitters' plight even worse, the wind off Lake Michigan that day was funneled directly toward home plate, making Feller's strikes doubly effective.

Chubby Eddie Smith, a portsider who would enjoy a 14–9 season with the Pale Hose in 1940, could have used a little help in opposing Bob Feller, but didn't get any. Not any. Though Feller was far from perfect, he had enough and then some to withstand the weather, Sox hitters and five free passes to first. It got his season off to a great start in a year that he won more games, 27, than during any other in his legendary career. That year he led the league in complete games (31), innings pitched (320.1) and ERA (2.61). Though debateable, his 1940 season was his very best, however close to that he might have come in 1939 or 1946. In '40 he also led the American League in shutouts with four of the 44 he pitched in his career. The box score of the only opening game no-hitter in baseball history follows:

Manager Al Lopez with pitching immortal Bob Feller.

Indians	AB	R	H	*White Sox*	AB	R	H
Boudreau, ss	3	0	0	Kennedy, 3b	4	0	0
Weatherly, cf	4	0	1	Kuhel, 1b	3	0	0
Chapman, rf	3	0	0	Kreevich, cf	3	0	0
Trosky, 1b	4	0	0	Solters, lf	4	0	0
Heath, lf	4	1	1	Appling, ss	3	0	0
Keltner, 3b	4	0	1	Wright, rf	4	0	0
Hemsley, c	4	0	2	McNair, 2b	3	0	0
Mack, 2b	4	0	1	Tresh, c	2	0	0

Indians	AB	R	H	White Sox	AB	R	H
Feller, (WP)	3	0	0	Smith, (LP)	1	0	0
				Rosenthal, ph	1	0	0
				Brown, p	0	0	0
Totals	33	1	6	Totals	28	0	0

Cleveland	000	001	000	1 6 0		
Chicago	000	000	000	0 0 1		

2B: Mack
3B: Hemsley
RBI: Hemsley
LOB: Cleveland, 7; Chicago 6
SB: Kuhel
DP: Kuhel, unassisted

K: Feller, 8; Smith, 5; Brown, 0
BB: Feller, 5; Smith, 2; Brown, 0
Umpires: Geisel, McGowan and Kolls
Time: 2:24
Attendance: 14,000

At Sportsman's Park, St. Louis, May 6, 1953

In the baseball record books and encyclopedias Alva Lee "Bobo" Holloman gets a one-line entry that's barely enough to identify the man and verify that he was a major league baseball player. Yet on May 23, 1953, he was the talk of the baseball world, making headlines the next day that many a ten-year man could only fantasize about, because he had done that pitching trick of tricks, that is, thrown a no-hit game. How improbable was that? Mighty improbable! That judgment, like the vast majority, is strictly hindsight. Although Browns owner Bill Veeck, the Huck Finn of baseball's owners, suspected early on that Mr. Holloman's destiny was not among baseball's greats, and had decided to let him go even before the big man's no-hit gem, most stories written about this rare feat seemed guided by a hidden assumption that the event was perpetrated by some kind of baseball clown cast in the Germany Schaefer mold. Not true. The gentleman was quite serious about his chosen trade. And his no-hitter, though filled with fortunate happenings (many have called them pure luck), such as screaming liners that were hit right at somebody, or a well-placed bunt that would have been a hit but rolled foul, was nonetheless legit. Ol' Bobo went the required nine, persevered to the very end, and got a well-deserved hero's treatment by his teammates when it was all over. (The Holloman story is available at the following website: www.bioproj.sabr.org. It is wonderfully and sensitively told by Len Pasculli.)

Even though the 1953 Browns lost 100 games, they did have an interesting pitching staff. A dozen pitchers combined for the 54 victories the team managed. Satchel Paige came on to save Holloman's victory on June 21, a fine piece of pitching artistry, a two-hit, 2–0 blanking of the Bosox at Fenway Park. That was one of the ten shutouts the Browns logged in 1953. Another member of that staff was Don Larsen; baseball aficionados never weary of telling and retelling about the perfecto he threw in the 1956 World Series. Others staff stalwarts who had noteworthy careers were Bob Turley, no-hit pitcher Virgil "Fire" Trucks and Harry "The Cat" Brecheen.

Beside the two scoreless game victories in which Holloman was involved, there was a 5–1 victory over Bob Lemon, another future Hall of Famer. Paige also saved that one, coming on in the sixth inning to quiet Cleveland bats. Consequently the three victories Holloman logged during his one-season MLB stint, amounted to 6–0, 2–0 and 5–1 outings. Not too shabby.

Bobo Holloman wasn't the only no-namer to hurl a no-hitter. The list he tops looks like this:

	No-No Date	Career W/L	SHO Career
Bobo Holloman	May 6, 1953	3–7	1
Bud Smith	September 3, 2001	7–8	1
George Davis	September 9, 1914	7–10	1
Mike Warren	September 29, 1983	9–13	1
Bill McCahan	September 3, 1947	16–14	2
Ernie Koob	May 5, 1917	23–31	3
Ed Head	April 23, 1946	27–23	6
Bo Belinsky	May 5, 1962	28–51	4

June 12, 1970, at San Diego

The Psychedelic Era was not yet over in 1970. Its flame was still burning brightly. Bob Dylan was popularizing hits like "Mr. Tambourine Man," and the Grateful Dead's calendar was crammed with dates in far-out places. Indeed, its influence and the antics of a determined counterculture were a throbbing part of Americana in the 1960s and 1970s. Baseball was also affected. More than just a few major leaguers were a part of that scenario, and some were either suspected or actual users.

One of the users was pitcher Dock Ellis, whose 12-year major league career was dotted with a number of great accomplishments. Dock was on the suspect list and many insiders claimed his was "on it" more than a few times.

June 12, 1970, seems to have been one of those times. Truth squad hunters, Snopes.com, ran down all the angles on Ellis' involvement and came up with a "True" status for the episode identified as the only no-hitter thrown under

11. The No-No

the influence of LSD. The most positive verification of the incident was Ellis' public admission, of pitching while "under the influence" in a statement made 14 years later, acknowledged by the Snopes people as one of the shreds of positive evidence. Since this is a no-hit story much more than a sleuthing for evidence and a final verdict, we leave all the conjecture to others. However, one of the statements in the article covering the Snopes investigation is very interesting:

> An unfortunate aspect of Dock Ellis' admission is that he is now remembered by many people (especially those too young to have seen him play during his heyday with the Pirates) as "the guy who pitched a no-hitter on drugs," a characterization which not only slights a baseball career that included some very fine moments, but also obscures the many acts of charity and conscience in which Ellis engaged both during and after his playing days; he worked with the Pennsylvania Department of Corrections to rehabilitate black prisoners, helped start the Black Athletes Foundation for Sickle Cell Research, and served as the coordinator of an anti-drug program in Los Angeles [www.snopes.com/sports/baseball/ellis.asp].

With a record of 4–4 going into this game, Ellis, who later claimed that he didn't remember too much about what was going on, had his best stuff, and that does *not* mean LSD, going for him. The Ellis arsenal included a sinking fastball, a slider, a curve, and, on occasion, a palmball. Everything he threw had movement on it, duly pointed out by catcher Jerry May.

Ellis' counterpart, Dave Roberts, was only slightly less effective than Ellis. His only problem was a problem most pitchers had: Willie Stargell. The big "Family Man" found Roberts' offerings to his liking, sending two of them over San Diego's fences to provide Ellis with all the runs he would need that night. As the innings rolled by Ellis kept getting his three outs without damage except for some rather weird wildness that put nine men on base, eight the beneficiaries of free passes and one on a hit by pitch. But when it counted most, Ellis was there with all the blue chips in place. In the bottom of the ninth, he got Chris Cannizzaro to lift a harmless fly ball to center fielder Matty Alou, and then retired the two more he needed, the last one being Ed Spiezio on strikes, to nail down his nohitter, eventually branded the most bizarre no-hitter on record.

Dock Ellis had a career 138–119 mark in 12 major league seasons. His four shutouts in 1970, the most he pitched in season were a part of his career total of 14. The no-hitter was the first of four authored in the majors in 1970. In case you might be wondering what was going on during the psychedelic 1960s, there were 34 no-hitters thrown, and Bob Gibson set the National League record for lowest ERA in one season at 1.12 in 1968. That same year Gaylord Perry beat the Cardinals, 1–0, in a no-hitter that no doubt featured the famed substance that got Perry by so often during his career, though it was no doubt a different substance than Dock Ellis used.

August 30, 1973, the Sayanora Home Run

The drugs phenomenon of the 1960s and 1970s wasn't restricted to the Americas. In Japan, for centuries a drug haven, it was in ubiquitous use during the psychedelic years, and for one of the Japanese major league's most electrifying Hall of Famers, Yutaka Enatsu, the drug scene's most vicious narcotic, heroin, became a part of his life after a Japanese baseball career that included acclaim, records, and star-status recognition. The multi-talented entertainer (he was an actor and a musician as well as a famous ballplayer) served time and, so the story goes, was given a choice to drop something from his tumultuous life to regain his composure and health. He chose none, but after a time did overcome his addiction. He was, as a pitcher and in every other respect, his own man.

The is the southpaw sidearmer who was the pivot point of the NBL's most riveting baseball story, the list-topper in a 2010 survey of the ten greatest moments ever, in Nipponese baseball. That event was a no-hitter thrown by Yutaka Enatsu at Hanshin Koshien Stadium in 1973. The game went 11 innings and would have gone into the 12th, had not Enatsu himself smashed one out of sight to beat the Chunichi Dragons in a no-hit gem that is as well-remembered in Japan as Don Larsen's perfecto is remembered in the U.S.A. To put some icing on that number one event, be informed that Enatsu also occupies the sixth and tenth spots on that auspicious top-ten listing.

In Dennis Eckersley–like fashion Enatsu moved from a starting role to the bullpen, where he added more records to his pitching portfolio. Among his accomplishments in NPB ball are 45 shutouts in 154 complete games, a stellar 29 percent; the first player to win MVP awards in both NPB leagues; and 198 Saves (the first, and probably best closer in NPB history to date).

A Clincher in the Astrodome, September 25, 1986

Barring an unforeseen disaster, the Houston Astros had the 1986 Division race in the National League West wrapped up. With a dozen games left to play they were out in front of the San Francisco Giants by nine games. Just to make doubly sure the title wouldn't get away from them, however, they turned in shutouts the next three games. The third was the clincher, and it was accomplished with a big exclamation point behind it. The *fait accompli* was artfully and dramatically achieved by Mike Scott at the Astrodome, a sparkling no-hitter that became the first of its kind to clinch a championship. The no-no came during a span of seven games during which the Astros pitching corps hurled five of its 19 shutouts in 1986. A pair of two-hitters preceded

Scott's gem, one by Jim Deshaies and one by Nolan Ryan and Charlie Kerfeld combined. Danny Darwin and Jim Deshaies started two more whitewashings days after Scott's clincher.

Before the 1986 season started, pitching coach Roger Craig convinced the big right-hander, who was capable of throwing 95 mph heat, to add the split-finger fastball to his repertoire. That, once mastered (not an easy thing), proved to be a boon extraordinaire. The splitter became an out-pitch, adding deceptive breaking stuff to Scott's assortment of pitches. (The rise of pitching coaches has been a huge factor in the pitching game. Roger Craig was one of the best. See The Pitching Coach Phenomenon appendix for further information.) In the no-hit special he tossed at San Francisco, it enabled him, with his always far better than average heater, to kayo 13 Giants hitters during that game. At one stretch during his masterpiece, he retired 19 straight batters, one of the factors that caused Craig, who was, ironically, the Giants manager, to remark that it was the most overpowering no-hitter he had ever seen.

Mike Scott was the National League's 1986 Cy Young award winner. His credentials, beyond the no-hitter he tossed, included five of his 22 career shutouts and league leadership in innings pitched (275.1), ERA (2.22), and strikeouts (306), and holding opposing hitters to a .186 batting average.

Of Scott's 1986 season, Nolan Ryan said, "If he's not the Cy Young winner, then I've never seen one." Those who cast the award's votes apparently agreed with the Strikeout King.

Number 7 on Arlington Appreciation Night May 1, 1991

Remarkable. Absolutely remarkable. It's just incredible, realizing that a 44-year-old athlete, into his 25th major league season (there would, in fact, be two more) would pitch a no-hitter in the Big Show. Interestingly, it is Cy Young, at 41 way back in 1908, who stands next to baseball's #1 strikeout man as the eldest statesman among no-hit craftsmen.

In *The Sporting News*' biography titled *Nolan Ryan: From Alvin to Cooperstown*, (Joanna Wright and Terrence Miltner, Eds. Champaign, IL: Sports Publishing, 1999, 137), a section of chapter eight is entitled *A Day When Crass Gave Way To Class*. The story has to do with Ricky Henderson's record-breaking 939th theft and his "Today I am the greatest of all time" response afterward, and Ryan's conduct after striking out Toronto victim number 16, Roberto Alomar, thus wrapping up his final no-hitter. The contrast between

Ryan's ("class") and Henderson's ("crass"), reaction to a momentous event is marked, and yet, in Ryan's case, typical. Methodical, determined, and above all humble, the man consistently went about his many record-breaking feats in a manner becoming the greatness of his persona, as well as his deeds.

Ryan's famous "#7" was put together with the support of a three-run outburst by the Rangers in the third frame, chiefly the work of outfielder, Ruben Sierra, who blasted a two-run homer off Jimmy Key. Key, teaming with Alomar, John Olerud, Joe Carter and Devon White, all top echelon major leaguers, presented the Rangers with a thorny challenge. But Ryan not only persevered, he hit the heights. After a pair of groundouts to start the ninth inning, he whiffed Alomar to end his epic no-hitter on the day he was honored on "Arlington Appreciation Night."

During his Hall of Fame career Nolan Ryan blanked opposing teams the same number of times his old Mets teammate, Tom Seaver, did — 61. That puts them in a tie for seventh place on the all-time list. Among a sampling of the major league records cited in his biography (Wright, 159) are 5,714 strikeouts, 12 one-hit games (tied with Bob Feller), the highest strikeout average per nine innings in a career, 9.55, and the oldest pitcher to strike out more than ten hitters in a game (age 45). (Ryan has since dropped to fifth in the list of strikeout average per nine innings behind Randy Johnson [10.61], Kerry Wood [10.32], Pedro Martinez (10.04), and Tim Lincecum [9.74].) But of them all, the most remarkable record will always be that #7, his May 1, 1991, conquest to the beat of a no-hitter at age 44 years, three months and one day. That was remarkable. Absolutely remarkable!

At Yankee Stadium, September 4, 1993, a Not-So Ordinary No-No

Sportswriter Tom Verducci, in the September 13, 1991, issue of *Sports Illustrated*, wrote about one of the most unusual no-hitters in baseball's long history, as follows:

> If you took every no-hitter thrown in the big leagues and arranged them in alphabetical order by pitcher, the one thrown last Saturday by James Anthony Abbott would be at the top. Should you then delineate the no-hitters according to their inspirational value, the same one would lead the list.
>
> By any measure it was a special achievement. For starters, Abbott threw his no-hitter in the heat of a September pennant race.... Mostly, though, it was a lasting moment because of who Abbott is.

What Jim Abbott was all about was the key to his not-so-ordinary feat in the Bronx during that September of 1993. That he could throw six shut-outs *at all* in an 11-year major league career, to say nothing of a no-hitter, is the heartbeat of this story. Others have played the game with handicaps that would have been all too daunting for most people. Pete Gray of the wartime St. Louis Browns comes to mind. So does Hugh Daily, the Cleveland Blues pitcher who no-hit the Philadelphia Quakes in 1883, a century before the Abbott gem, with one of his ten career shutouts. These fellows had the same courage and grit Jim Abbott did during his days in The Bigs.

Only six days prior to his whitewash job on Cleveland, those same Indians had gotten to Abbott for seven runs and ten hits, chasing him in the fourth inning. It was not a lineup of patsies. Kenny Lofton, Albert Belle, Manny Ramirez, Candy Maldonado and Jim Thome were all on hand to make life miserable for

Inspiring Jim Abbott (Brace photograph).

the sturdy fastball and sinkerball artist. As the game moved on from hitless inning to hitless inning, it became more and more evident that Big Jim was getting stronger and stronger. With only three outs to go, the final act of this drama began, and Abbott made quick work of it, getting Cleveland's last hope, Carlos Baerga, to ground out to end the game, and with it, launch a wild congratulatory melee in the middle of the diamond.

Congratulations were indeed in order. It was among the most heartwarming moments in the annals of no-hit history.

The Houston Gang of Six at Yankee Stadium, June 11, 2003

De bon augure ... Auspicious! It was not only auspicious, but this event was a first of its kind in more than one respect: (1) six pitchers combined to throw a no-hit bombshell into that *sanctum sanctorum* known as Yankee Stadium; (2) the deed, an 8–0 whitewash, was the first inter-league no-hitter in the game's history; and (3) never before had it taken six pitchers to combine on a no-hitter at the Yankee *sanctum sanctorum*. The no-hit hurt the Astros laid on the Yanks was something the Bronx Bombers hadn't experienced since September 20, 1958, when they fell victim to the Baltimore Orioles in the famous Hoyt Wilhelm no-no.

This bizarre no-hitter would not have taken place had Roy Oswalt, the Astros' starting pitcher, not pulled a groin muscle as he was facing Jorge Posada to start the second inning. He had disposed of the Yanks in order the first inning, but during the Posada at-bat summoned manager Jimy Williams, who promptly replaced Oswalt with Pete Munro. Munro got credit for the next 2.2 innings and was followed by Kirk Saarloos (1.1 innings), Brad Lidge, who chipped in the next two frames and was credited with the victory, Octavio Dotel (one inning, the eighth), and closing flamethrower Billy Wagner.

Covering the game for the *Houston Chronicle*, Jose de Jesus Ortiz wrote this about the epoch-making game's windup:

> Hideki Matsui, the Yankees' Japanese outfielder, grounded out to first to seal the no-hitter. Wagner covered first, took Jeff Bagwell's toss and pumped his left hand in joy.
>
> Second baseman Jeff Kent, not realizing what had transpired, looked at Wagner as though he were silly.
>
> "What's amazing," Wagner said, "is that most of our team didn't know about it."
>
> The crowd at Yankee Stadium was well aware, however, and the Astros appreciated the standing ovation they received. For one night, at least, the place and the history belonged to them.

For Jimy Williams to use a reliever or two in the Astros' games during the 2003 season was not unusual. After all, relievers appeared a league-leading 502 times that year, and there was only one complete game in their pitching log all season. Wade Miller threw the only complete game the Astros had, and their five shutouts were all combined pieces of work. It would be no stretch to conclude that the "Day of Relief" had arrived full-bloom in Houston during the 2003 season.

2010 Fini

Once every 750 games or so a no-hitter is thrown. That makes it a rarity, treated accordingly by reporters, historians and baseball buffs everywhere. This rare breed of shutout gets our attention. At the rate of two per season it will take another 15 years, roughly speaking, to hit number 300. Maybe more. At the rate relievers are being used it will probably be more common-

11. The No-No

place to witness combined no-hitters, which would make the complete-game, shutout no-hitter more and more an unusual pitching feat.

Following is a chronological list of 1–0 no-hit games. (P indicates Perfect Game) Unless indicated otherwise all games listed are National League games.

No-Hit Pitcher(s)	Date	Against
Lee Richmond, Worcester (P)	1880, June 12	Cleveland
Jim Galvin, Buffalo	1880, August 20	Worcester
Hugh Daily, Cleveland	1883, September 13	Philadelphia
Charles Ferguson, Philadelphia	1885, September 29	Providence
Adonis Terry, Brooklyn (AA)	1886, July 24	St. Louis
Christy Mathewson, New York	1905, June 13	Chicago
Hooks Wiltse, New York	1908, July 4	Philadelphia
Fred Toney, Cincinnati	1917, May 2	Chicago
Clyde Shoun, Cincinnati	1944, May 15	Boston
Lew Burdette, Milwaukee	1960, August 18	Philadelphia
Warren Spahn, Milwaukee	1960, September 16	San Francisco
Juan Marichal, San Francisco	1963, June 15	Houston
Ken Johnson, Houston	1964, April 23	Cincinnati (Cincinnati won this game)
Jim Maloney, Cincinnati	1965, August 19	Chicago (ten inning no-hitter)
Sandy Koufax, Los Angeles (P)	1965, September 9	Chicago
Gaylord Perry, San Francisco	1968, September 17	St. Louis
Ken Holtzman, Chicago	1971, June 3	Cincinnati
Tom Browning, Cincinnati (P)	1988, September 16	Los Angeles
Kent Mercker, Mark Wohlers, Alejandro Pena, Atlanta	1991, September 11	San Diego
Jose Jimenez, St. Louis	1999, June 25	Arizona
Kevin Millwood, Philadelphia	2003, April 27	San Francisco
Roy Halladay, Philadelphia (P)	2010, May 29	Florida
Edwin Jackson, Arizona	2010, June 25	Tampa Bay

The list of American League 1–0, shutout no-hitters:

No-Hit Pitcher(s)	Date	Against
Frank Smith, Chicago	1908, September 20	Philadelphia
Addie Joss, Cleveland (P)	1908, October 2	Chicago
Addie Joss, Cleveland	1910, April 20	Chicago
Ernie Koob, St. Louis	1917, May 5	Chicago
Walter Johnson, Washington	1920, July 1	Boston
Bob Feller, Cleveland	1940, April 16	Chicago
Dick Fowler, Philadelphia	1945, September 9	St. Louis
Bob Feller, Cleveland	1946, April 30	New York

Roy Halladay, first pitcher to throw a no-hitter in post-season playoff championships. His perfect game in 2010 was the 20th thrown in the history of the national pastime.

No-Hit Pitcher(s)	Date	Against
Allie Reynolds, New York	1951, July 12	Cleveland
Virgil Trucks, Detroit	1952, May 15	Washington
Virgil Trucks, Detroit	1952, August 25	New York
Hoyt Wilhelm, Baltimore	1958, September 20	New York
Bill Monbouquette, Boston	1962, August 1	Chicago
Jack Kralick, Minnesota	1962, August 26	Kansas City
Nolan Ryan, California	1975, June 1	Baltimore
Dennis Eckersley, Cleveland	1977, May 30	California
Mike Witt, California (P)	1984, September 30	Texas
Mark Langston and Mike Witt, California	1990, April 11	Seattle

12

Perfection

Between June 12, 1880, when Lee Richmond tossed the first perfect game, and the last to date, on May 5, 2010, by Roy Halladay, there have been 20 perfect games, which, like rare gems, have achieved a "priceless worth" tag. Below is a listing of the 20. The first three are assigned a gem-related name after the rarest and costliest gems extant. These perfect game masterpieces are presented as the best of the very best. The remainder follow in chronological order.

Perfect Game Identification	Date	Pitch Count
The Don Larsen Hope Gem	October 8, 1956	97
The Sandy Koufax Painite Gem	September 9, 1965	113
The Addie Joss Serendibite Gem	October 2, 1908	74
Lee Richmond	June 12, 1880	unknown
John M. Ward	June 17, 1880	unknown
Cy Young at Boston	May 5, 1904	unknown
Charlie Robertson	April 30, 1922	90
Jim Bunning	June 21, 1964	90
Catfish Hunter	May 8, 1968	107
Len Barker	May 15, 1981	103
Mike Witt	September 30, 1984	94
Tom Browning	September 16, 1988	100
Dennis Martinez	July 28, 1991	96
Kenny Rogers	July 28, 1994	98
David Wells	May 17, 1998	120
David Cone	July 18, 1999	88
Randy Johnson	May 18, 2004	117
Mark Buehrle	July 23, 2009	116
Dallas Braden	May 9, 2010	109
Roy Halladay	May 29, 2010	115

Yankee Stadium Extraordinaire, October 8, 1956

Some games, and the exceptional events or plays within them, are played and replayed, told and retold by succeeding generations. Several come readily to mind: Pete Alexander striking out Tony Lazzeri in the 1926 World Series; Babe Ruth's "called shot" in the 1932 Fall Classic; Gabby Hartnett's "Homer in the Gloamin"; Hank Aaron's record-breaking 715th homer on April 8, 1974; Cal Ripken's 2,131st consecutive game; and Willie Mays' marvelous catch to rob Vic Wertz of an extra-base hit in the 1954 World Series. All of these, and many more, are part of baseball's drama, as well as its historic — and indelible — moments.

Add to all of that the perfect game thrown by Don Larsen in the 1956 World Series. It is the gem of gems among no-hit games, one so perfect that its story is recalled nearly every October, especially when pitchers get into the sixth and seventh innings of post-season games that seem headed for no-hit land. Like the Hope Diamond, that game, above all other no-hitters ever thrown, will never be allowed to be forgotten, its every pitch right on down to the one that retired the 27th Brooklyn Dodger in succession, recorded with respected care. Imagination is stretched to the breaking point to find a more historic moment in baseball history — even for storied Yankee Stadium where this exceptional game took place.

The hero of the piece was not cut from the cloth of heroes, and that makes the story even more appealing and memorable. Called "Gooney Bird" by his teammates because of his late-night behavior, the big Swede had his moments, though it must be said that many of them did not come in a baseball uniform. But the moments that put together Don Larsen's *Meisterwerk* transpired in the sunlit afternoon of a day that might well have been labled a perfect, early Fall day, just right for a perfect World Series game.

Larsen obliged. Nights of late-late hours and a few too many in the years that meandered toward this unprecedented moment didn't faze Mr. Larsen in the very least. He seized that moment and made it his own.

Seven future Hall of Fame ballplayers were crammed into that one game, and the baseball gods would have you know that everything that happened was not by chance, including Mickey Mantle's amazing catch and the fortuitous bounce deflected Gil McDougald's way, enabling him to throw out Jackie Robinson.

This perfect game shutout, hurled under the pressure of World Series play, was the single most significant perfecto in the game's annals. If there ever is another, it will have to give evidence of even more significance within its parameters than Larsen's 97-pitch Miracle In the Bronx! The play-by-play account of this game is available in many books, including one of mine (*The Greatest World Series Games* [Jefferson, NC: McFarland, 2005], p. 273), as well as in website postings and the Retrosheet account in its play-by-play logs.

The Stat Board for Perfect Game Pitchers

	Years	W/L	CG	SHO	Pct.	ERA
Len Barker	1976–1987	74–76	35	7	20.0	4.34
Dallas Braden	2007–	26–36	5	2	40.0	4.20
Tom Browning	1984–1995	123–90	31	12	38.7	3.94
Mark Buehrle	2000–	161–119	27	8	29.6	3.85
Jim Bunning*	1955–1971	224–184	151	40	26.5	3.27
David Cone	1986–2003	194–126	56	22	39.3	3.46
Roy Halladay	1998	188–92	58	19	32.8	3.32
Catfish Hunter*	1965–1979	224–166	181	42	23.2	3.26
Randy Johnson	1988–2009	303–166	100	37	37.0	3.29
Addie Joss*	1902–1910	160–97	234	45	19.2	1.89
Sandy Koufax*	1955–1966	165–87	137	40	29.2	2.76
Don Larsen	1953–1967	81–91	44	11	25.0	3.78
Dennis Martinez	1976–1998	245–193	122	30	24.6	3.70
Lee Richmond	1879–1886	75–100	161	8	5.0	3.06
Charlie Robertson	1919–1928	49–80	60	6	10.0	4.44
Kenny Rogers	1989–2008	219–156	36	9	25.0	4.27
John M. Ward*	1878–1884	164–103	245	24	9.80	2.10
David Wells	1987–2007	239–157	54	12	22.2	4.13
Mike Witt	1981–1993	117–116	72	11	15.3	3.83
Cy Young*	1890–1911	511–316	749	76	10.1	2.63

*Pct. is the percentage of complete games that were shutouts; the * indicates a Hall of Famer.*

The table above will provide you with a reference guide to the career achievements of the 20 pitchers through the 2010 season who have entered the record books with perfect game performances. (The statistics for the three active pitchers—Braden, Buehrle, and Halladay—are current through the end of the 2011 season.) Notice that their numbers hardly seem to fit in the same listing, nor do they. Putting Cy Young on any list almost always wilts the names and numbers of the others. Therefore, it is best to keep in mind that the only thing these fellows have in common is having pitched a perfect game.

The table gives convincing evidence of the recent tendency to let pitchers finish games only under special circumstances. One factor in the decision to let the pitcher go the distance is how close he is to finishing off a low-hit game. That wasn't a factor in earlier days, as the Cy Young, Lee Richmond and Addie Joss numbers tend to indicate. Here are two more of the three best perfect games.

Los Angeles 1, Chicago 0: The Painite Perfect Game at Dodger Stadium

Only a few hundred faceted stones of the world's rarest gem, painite, exist. When cut to exacting standards, it is a near-priceless jewel of rare beauty. To veteran baseball observers, the Sandy Koufax–Bob Hendley duel on September 9, 1965, was just that, a painite thing of rare beauty.

What almost ranks the Koufax perfecto on an even plane with Don Larsen's masterpiece, is not only that he retired 27 Cubs in 1–2–3 order, nor that he struck out 14, or even that he was so overpowering on this particular outing. Beyond all that, the southpaw Hall of Famer *had to be that good* because his opposite number, Bob Hendley,* also a left-hander, gave up but one run, an unearned run at that, while battling Koufax pitch for pitch in an unbelievably fine performance of his own which eventuated, ultimately, in a heart-breaking (for Hendley) one-hitter. It was the rarest of rare baseball perfectos, broadcast, recorded, replayed via audio production and written about time and again, so distinctively elegant was this perfection of pitching artistry.

> Sandy Koufax was perfect. He had fanned the last six in a row. He had punched out 14. He had thrown his fourth no-hitter. He had out-dueled Hendley, who had thrown a one-hitter. He had faced 27 batters. He had gotten them all without a walk.
>
> The perfect game was Koufax's Hamlet, his Ninth Symphony, his Mona Lisa. It is the game for which he will be forever remembered and marveled [John Klima, *Pitched Battle* (Jefferson, NC: McFarland, 2002), 119].

Five days later, when the Cubs and Dodgers met again, Hendley out-dueled Koufax, beating the Dodgers, 2–1. This time Hendley threw a four-hitter, while Cubs future Hall of Famer Billy Williams beat the Dodgers with a two-run clout off Koufax.

The Serendibite Perfecto, October 2, 1908, at Cleveland's League Park

Another of the world's rarest gems is October 2, 1908 believed to be the cyan-hued serendibite, a jewel that when properly cut is a thing of breathtaking elegance. Similarly, this game played so many, many years ago at the corner of East 66th (formerly known as Dunham Avenue) and Lexington, was, in its own way, about as rare an exhibition of flawless professional baseball as an exquisite cut of serendibite.

More than 10,000 die-hard Forest City denizens made their way out to

12. Perfection

old League Park on a 50-degree October day to see their Naps take on the hard-charging Chicago White Sox in a pennant race that was marked by tissue-thin margins between three contending American League teams with five games still to be played:

	Won	Lost	Pct.	GB
Detroit	87	61	.588	–
Cleveland	87	62	.584	.5
Chicago	85	62	.579	1.5

Into that cauldron stepped the two teams vying to overtake Detroit's Bengals. At that point it was Detroit's pennant to lose, but a Cleveland win and a Tigers loss on October 2 would put the Cleveland nine in charge of the final furlong of this tightly contested pennant chase.

Manager Nap Lajoie named Cleveland's ace, Addie Joss, to pitch the big game coming up. Joss, winner of his previous six starts, wouldn't have wanted it any other way. Since September 1, at a time when his Naps were in fourth place, only three and a half games behind Detroit, his pitching log shaped up as follows:

September 1	1–0 over Boston (Winter)
September 5	Lost 7–0 to Ed Walsh (Chicago)
September 7	Beat Ed Walsh 6–0
September 11	Beat Harry Howell (St. Louis) 4–1
September 14	10–4 over Chicago (Frank Owen)
September 17	Beat Cy Young (Boston) 1–0
September 22	Beat "Wild Bill" Hogg (New York) 7–0
	Joss' eighth shutout of the season
September 26	5–4 over Washington ("Long Tom" Hughes)
October 2	Walsh and Joss meet for the fourth time in 1908, Joss having won two of the previous three duels.

Ed Walsh won his 39th game in a gargantuan season of 464⅔ innings pitched, a twentieth-century major league record for a single season, only three days prior to the Joss matchup. He had been absolutely indefatigable, and as effective as he was omnipresent in White Sox games. The two best pitchers in the American League would meet head-on in the most important and noteworthy game of the Deadball Era.

After the titanic battle had exacted its last casualty, one tainted run separated the two teams on this day of reckoning, the run belonging to the homestanding Naps, making the final count, 1-0. Since Detroit beat St. Louis, they remained in first place at the end of the day. But Cleveland had not lost ground, hanging on to the Tigers heels by just a half-game.

There is one rather mysterious item about this perfect game that begs for attention, and that is the Joss pitch count in this game. The pitch count did not become a regularly kept baseball statistic until the 1980s. So who counted Joss' pitches? The answer is in his biography, penned by historian Scott Longert (*Addie Joss: King of the Pitchers*. Cleveland: SABR, 1998, 101).

> A man named Peter Witt had brought a registering device to the game. For his own enjoyment, he decided to track the number of pitches thrown. At the end of the game his machine recorded seventy-four pitches thrown by Addie, an average of just 2.74 per batter.

That count is almost as remarkable as the game itself. It seems that just about everything about that game was as remarkable as it was unforgettable.

The Saturday, October 3, edition of the *Boston Post* summarized the Joss victory this way: "Adrian Joss leaped into exclusive society in the family of American pitchers when he defeated the White Sox today." Terse, but finely cut like a Serendibite jewel, that comment says it all.

Something special might be said of each of the remaining 17 perfect games on record. Several of them, in fact, could be touted as serious contenders with the three chosen. Mark Buehrle's perfecto came in the midst of a record-breaking streak of 45 consecutive shutout innings. Then there was the ceremony-laden game that fate chose to endow with epic perfection. In a game that many feared would never get going, what with parades, speeches and jokes by old-timers, and Yankees comraderie all around, David Cone somehow mustered the élan and fortitude in front of an august assemblage of former Yankees greats to see his way through nine innings of runnerless ball against a National League team, the Montreal Expos, in an interleague game.

Or the Randy Johnson slice of perfection. Older even than Cy Young, who at 37 threw a perfect game against Rube Waddell and the Philadelphia Athletics way back in 1904, Johnson paralyzed the Braves from Atlanta with a 2–0 *coup de maître* at age 40.

Other contenders for Top

Addie Joss, who crafted a perfect game in the thick of a pennant race against Ed Walsh and the Chicago White Sox.

Three honors might be Jim Bunning's Father's Day masterpiece on June 21, 1964, or the perfect game put together by "El Presidente," the Nicaraguan Dennis Martinez. Each of the 20 in its own way was an extraordinary achievement. Of those 20, five were 1–0 games, hurled by Lee Richmond, Addie Joss, Mike Witt, Tom Browning and Roy Halladay.

Upwards of 200,000 games in seven major leagues have been played during the regular season between 1871 and 2010. Roughly 4,400 of them have been 1–0 shutouts, including five of the 19 perfectos (19 of the 20 perfect games occurred during regular season play; the 20th was Larsen's.), a little better than two percent. Inaugural 1–0 games are listed for each league below:

The National Association of Professional Base Ball Players

May 11, 1875 at St. Louis: Chicago 1 (George Zettlein, WP); St. Louis Reds 0 (Joe Blong, LP)

The American Association

July 13, 1882 at Baltimore: Cincinnati 1 (Harry McCormick); Baltimore 0 (Sam "Doc" Landis)

The Union Association

July 19, 1884 at Boston: St. Louis 1 (Henry Boyle, WP); Boston 0 (Fred Dupee Shaw)

The Players League

June 21, 1890 at Chicago, eight-inning no-hit game: Brooklyn 1 (Gus Weyhing); Chicago 0 (Charles "Silver" King)
September 9, 1890 at Brooklyn: Philadelphia 1 (Ben Sanders); Brooklyn 0 (George Hemming)

The National League

May 5, 1876 at St. Louis: St. Louis 1 (George Bradley); Chicago 0 (Al Spalding)

The American League

July 27, 1901 at Detroit: Detroit 1 (Joe Yeager); Baltimore 0 (Joe McGinnity)

The Federal League

April 14, 1914 at Pittsburgh: Brooklyn 1 (Tom Seaton); Pittsburgh 0 (Elmer "Baron" Knetzer)

There remains one of the more exciting types of shutout, the 1–0 game in which a thrilling home run puts the game in the "W" column. Some of them are on review in the next chapter.

13

When Titans Clash

Here we celebrate the consummate artistry of Hall of Fame pitchers who have been immortalized by their Olympian achievements. This shutout saga begins in 1880, when, on June 17 in Buffalo, John Montgomery Ward faced off against "Gentle Jeems" Galvin. On that pleasant, late Spring day, Ward and his Providence teammates subjected their rival nine to a perfect game, permitting not a single Bisons batter to reach first base. Now, that is a rather extraordinary way to start off a history to say the least.

Ward, elected to baseball's Valhalla in 1964, threw the second perfect game in baseball history just five days after Lee Richmond had turned the trick, and it came in the form of a 5–0 win against a lineup featuring several of the day's great stars, not least of which was Galvin. Ward that season won 39 games, and among them were a league-leading eight shutouts. On the other hand, Galvin, fronting a weak Buffalo entry in 1880, managed 20 wins, including five shutouts. His great days were still ahead of him in a career netting 365 victories. Ward, despite his perfect game effort and 39 wins in 1880, went on to a more varied career, playing a number of positions, managing, and moving around the baseball world of his day in labor leadership, ownership and league development scenarios. He is the only Hall of Famer with 150+ wins and 2,000+ hits. To be able to start off the shutout story among Hall of Famers with these two pitchers and a perfect game sets the bar at a very high level. Galvin, incidentally, was selected for Hall of Fame honors a year following Ward's, in 1965.

In the following pages we've assembled a unique part of Hall of Fame pitching history. It begins, appropriately, with the peerless leader among shutout Titans, Walter Johnson. Pete Alexander and 13 other Famers follow, each of whom registered 55 or more career blankings. Their individual shutout careers against other Hall of Famers add up to 185 games, 60 of which ended in 1–0 scores (nearly one out of three).

Walter Johnson

During his incredible career, the Washington Senators master craftsman pitched a major league-leading 110 shutouts, just a bit more than 25 percent of his 417 major league victories. That number is also 20 more than Grover Cleveland Alexander's rather distant runner-up at 90, which is also the pacemaker among National League shutout artists. These numbers, each enormous in terms of pitching records, set both Johnson and Alexander apart from the pitching mainstream as well as the Shutout Titans.

SHO Gms vs. HOF Pitchers: 23 (Most among Top 15)
W/L: 13–10
1–0 games: 13, won 6, lost 7
Most Appearances with: Plank, five and Ruth four

Sixty-five of the great Johnson's 696 decisions were of the 1–0 variety, resulting in 39 victories and 26 losses. With all due respect to the many fine major leaguers who donned Senators togs during Johnson's career, it must be said that many of his victories came in troublesome circumstances, when, considering Washington and its opponents, they appeared on the field as so many Davids against an array of Goliaths. There was one "David," however, who made all the difference in the world: Mr. Johnson. Even at that, the stream was a good deal more choppy when Big Ed Walsh or Babe Ruth appeared on the mound against him. Those two fellows knocked off the Big Train six times by scores of 1–0, three times each. The 1916 season must have been particularly disheartening. During that season two players, more famous by far for their hitting than for their pitching, beat the Washington Wonder by 1–0 scores: The Babe twice and George Sisler once.

What became the last of Johnson's shutout victories against other Hall of Fame pitchers was forged against Waite Hoyt at Griffith Stadium on June 28, 1922, when he scattered seven hits in a paper-thin, 1–0 squeaker for his 94th career shutout.

Following is a list of Johnson's record against Hall of Famers:

	Opp. Pitcher	*Score*
September 4, 1908	Chesbro	3–4
September 7, 1908	Chesbro	4–0
September 18, 1908	Ed Walsh	0–1
July 25, 1909	Rube Waddell	0–6
August 4, 1909	Addie Joss	1–0
August 17, 1909	Charles "Chief" Bender	1–0
August 29, 1909	Ed Walsh	0–1
April 14, 1910	Eddie Plank	3–0

The pitching staff of the world champion 1924 Washington Senators featuring the incomparable Walter Johnson. Standing: Tom Zachary, Walter Johnson, George Mogridge, Firpo Marberry. Kneeling: Warren "Curly" Ogden, Paul Zahniser, Byron "By" Speece, "Oyster Joe" Martina (Brace photographs).

	Opp. Pitcher	Score
May 14, 1910	Joss	1–0
August 23, 1910	Ed Walsh	0–1
October 3, 1911	Eddie Plank	2–0
April 30, 1913	Eddie Plank	2–0
June 1, 1916	Babe Ruth	0–1
July 7, 1916	Eddie Plank	0–5
August 15, 1916	Babe Ruth	0–1
September 17, 1916	George Sisler	0–1
May 7, 1917	Babe Ruth	0–1
August 6, 1917	Eddie Plank	1–0
August 10, 1917	Red Faber	1–0
October 3, 1917	Babe Ruth	6–0
June 18, 1922	Red Faber	1–0
June 28, 1922	Waite Hoyt	1–0
July 5, 1924	Herb Pennock	0–2

Grover Cleveland "Pete" Alexander

SHO Gms vs. HOF Pitchers: 12
W/L: W 9, L 3
1–0 Games: 3, W 3, L 0
Most Appearances with: Grimes, 4, Won 3, Lost 1

The Alexander log is half the length of Walter Johnson's, but had old Pete gone to work a few years earlier, he would have encountered a greater number of Famers. As it is, he shut out Hall of Fame opponents much more often than they shut his team out, winning at an .800 clip. During his rookie year Alexander's September 7 clash with Cy Young, heading to less active days in retirement and the latter, the youngster bristling with superb equipment in the form of a sinking fast ball and a sharply breaking curve ball, was just starting out on his Hall of Fame career. Their much-heralded 1–0 game featured two grimly determined competitors focused intensely on winning, making for the kind of game Deadball Era aficionados would pay to see over and over again.

Alexander possessed, and used wisely, a variety of speeds and arm angles. This is what Rogers Hornsby, a fellow who knew what he was talking about when it came to pitching and hitting, had to say about Alex in a "Baseball Magazine" article in 1919 (quoted in *The Neyer/James Guide to Pitchers*, New York: Simon and Shuster, 2004, 118): "Alexander has as much speed as anybody in the National League. *He is the best pitcher I ever saw.*"

Even on those days when home plate might have been a bit blurry, he showcased near-perfect control, putting his pitches just off the edges of home plate and bedeviling the hitters with his wizardry. He was under no circumstances to be taken lightly. The Yankees found that out in the 1926

National League shutout leader Pete Alexander, who pitched 90 shutouts, appearing here as the smiling hero of the 1926 St. Louis Cardinals World Series champions (Brace photographs).

World Series, when Alex brushed aside rumors about his drunkenness the night before he was brought into the Series' climactic game seven and struck out Tony Lazzeri with the bases loaded. Alexander's shutout numbers in competition with other Hall of Famers follow:

	Opp. Pitcher	Score
September 7, 1911	Young	1–0
July 1, 1913	Marquard	0–10
September 12, 1914	Marquard	1–0
September 2, 1915, Gm 2	Mathewson	2–0
September 3, 1917, Gm 1	Marquard	5–0
May 24, 1920	Rixey	6–0
August 28, 1920	Grimes	1–0
July 26, 1921	Grimes	0–3
September 2, 1921	Rixey	7–0
September 12, 1923	Rixey	0–4
August 7, 1926, Gm 2	Grimes	3–0
April 12, 1928	Grimes	5–0

Christy Mathewson

SHO Gms vs. HOF Pitchers: 8
W/L: W 2, L 6
1–0 Games: 2, Won 1, Lost 1
Most Appearances with Mordecai Brown, 3, won 1, lost 2

Two New York Giants pitchers, both Hall of Fame hurlers, used unusual pitches, and used them to perfection. Carl Hubbell, who pitched 36 shutouts during a distinguished career, used his famous screwball with astonishing effect. The other was John McGraw's favorite, Christy Mathewson, whose fadeaway tied National League batters in knots. One of the game's all-time greats, Mathewson won better than 30 games in a season four times, and totaled 373 victories. But beyond his athletic gifts and amazing achievements was his most invaluable strength, his character. And that was a shining light during rough and tumble times in professional baseball. That he was an accomplished pitcher was so much icing on the cake.

Titanic struggles with Chicago's pitchers, particularly Mordecai Brown, brought out droves of Chicago and New York baseball fans, as was the case when confrontations between Honus Wagner, who hit *all* pitchers well, and the Bucknell Beauty took place in Pittsburgh or New York. It was against the three-fingered one, Brown, that his only 1–0 game against a future Hall of Famer took place. This one, which might well have been billed as another of those the "Games of the Century," took place in that very special campaign of 1908, heavy with awesome wonders in both leagues. In the heat of a tight pennant race the two met in a midsummer pairing during a four-game July series in Chicago. The race was a tangled 1-2-3 struggle between Pittsburgh, which led the league after the day's play was completed on July 17, New York, a half-game behind, and then Chicago, after the victory over Mathewson, within a game of the Pirates. The game was typical of the many 1–0 and one-run thrillers in 1908. Sadly for Giants fans, Brown beat him in this one.

Christy Mathewson put 79 shutouts into the record books, 11 of them in 1908, a number that led the National League. Additionally, nine times in 1908 he allowed but a single run, winning eight of them and losing only to Brown in July. He might not have been so fortunate in his shutout bouts against Hall of Fame pitchers, but rest

The fellow all ball-playing youngsters wanted to become in the early 1900s, Christy Mathewson.

assured: his overall record against those same opponents glistened with winning numbers with the exception of Three Finger Brown. The shutout record follows:

	Opp. Pitcher	Score
August 13, 1901, 10 inn.	Charles "Kid" Nichols	0–3
July 12, 1902	Jack Chesbro	0–4
June 13, 1905	Mordecai Brown	1–0
September 7, 1905, Gm2	Vic Willis	3–0
July 17, 1907	Vic Willis	0–2
August 2, 1907	Mordecai Brown	0–5
July 17, 1908	Mordecai Brown	0–1
September 2, 1915, Gm 2	Grover Alexander	0–2

Denton True "Cy" Young

SHO Gms vs. HOF Pitchers: 17
W/L: W 3, L 13 and 1 scoreless tie
1–0 Games: 5, W 1, L, 4
Most Appearances with Waddell, 5, Plank, 3

With a record of only four wins in 21 tries against Hall of Fame pitchers it would seem that explanations are in order. What do we have here? An anomaly? A set of numbers that belie the respect and lofty status accorded one of the game's royalty? No other Hall of Fame pitcher, after all, has such atrocious numbers in shutouts against his distinguished contemporaries as does Cy Young. Involved in five 1–0 games, he only won one. That lone bright spot came in his National League days against another NL pitcher who moved over to the American League, Rube Waddell, edged by Young, 1–0, on one of the last days (the exact date was September 24, 1900) before the American League's inaugural in 1901. He lost his first one to fireballer Amos Rusie in 1890, while in the National League, and his last one there, as well, in 1911, to Pete Alexander. In between he lost to some mighty fine pitchers in both leagues, luminaries like Kid Nichols, Eddie Plank, Ed Walsh and Addie Joss. And when it came to shutout games, they all seemed to have his number.

The big exception would be the first American League game on record that was letter perfect, and the first perfect game at the distance of 60'6". On May 5, 1904, during a season when he led his league in shutouts for the sixth time, this time with a career-high ten, he met his nemesis, Rube Waddell, at Boston's Huntington Grounds before a crowd numbering better than 10,000. Polishing off the Mackmen in less than an hour and a half, the last of the 27 he needed, Rube Waddell himself, was retired on a fly ball to center fielder Chick Stahl to finish off the first perfecto in American

Cy Young, "Mr. Most," Hall of Fame, 1937.

League history. That one, like the other 19 perfect games on record to date, was no mean achievement.

Though it might be pointed out that in nine of his 16 losses, and the scoreless tie, he held his opponents to three runs or less, those games went into the "L" column nonetheless. The list of those Hall of Famers who made a shambles of Cy Young's brilliant record follows. Numbers in parenthesis indicate the number of appearances for each.

Amos Rusie (2)	Rube Waddell (5)
John Clarkson (1)	Eddie Plank (3)
Kid Nichols (1)	Addie Joss (1)
	Ed Walsh (2)
Joe McGinnity (1)	Pete Alexander (1)

Eddie Plank

SHO Gms vs. HOF Pitchers: 12
W/L: W 6, L 6
1–0 Games: 3, W 2, L 1
Most Appearances with Walter Johnson, 5, Won 1, Lost 4

Taciturn and fidgety, Eddie Plank, Gettysburg's gift to the Hall of Fame, was baseball's premier southpaw during the first quarter of the 20th century. His career began with the birth of the American League and continued through 1917. During that time he garnered 69 shutouts, recording at least one in each season he pitched. His first shutout, which was also the Philadelphia Athletics' first, was a 6–0 triumph in Philadelphia on June 13, 1901, against the Milwaukee Brewers. His shutouts against Hall of Fame hurlers numbered six, including one Federal League conquest over his old Athletics teammate, Chief Bender.

One of the finest games in Plank's career came in a 13-inning affair with the Boston Red Sox at Philadelphia's Columbia Park on September 10, 1904. That day he defeated Cy Young in one of those remarkable extra-inning Deadball Era ball games. In the tenth inning of a scoreless game Young allowed a leadoff triple to Danny Murphy, but then proceeded to strike out Monte Cross, Mike Powers, and Plank, a powerfully skillful achievement. But Gettysburg Eddie caught up with Young a couple innings later, singling home the winning run to win this magnificent pitcher's duel, 1–0.

In the twilight of his career, Plank met Walter Johnson in his last appearance against a Hall of Fame pitcher in a shutout game. The two crossed swords on August 6, 1917, in Washington. In that game old Eddie, at that point in his career pitching for the St. Louis Browns, lost to Johnson, 1–0.

These are the Famers Eddie Plank met in shutout games:

        Cy Young (3)   Ed Walsh (1)
        Addie Joss (1)   Chief Bender (1)
        Jack Chesbro (1)   Walter Johnson (5)

Warren Spahn

Baseball's leading portsider in career wins, 363, has also won more shutouts, 63, than any other National League lefty, ranking sixth on the all-time list. His numbers against Hall of Fame pitchers include five wins against four losses. Spahnie is also the first modern era pitcher on this elite listing.

SHO Gms. vs. HOF Pitchers: 9
W/L: W 4, L 5
1–0 Games: 4, Won 2, Lost 2
Most Appearances with Roberts, 3 Won 2, Lost 1

Warren Spahn was an award winner long before his career ended in 1965. As a member of the 176th Combat Engineers Division he fought with distinction in the European Theater of War, winning Purple Heart and Bronze Star medals for valorous action in the Battle of the Bulge. He often said that his battlefield experience made pitching a pleasure. It was easy by comparison.

Among his nine matchups with Famers there is certainly one that stands out over all the others, and that is his "old-timer" vs. "youngster" game against Juan Marichal on July 2, 1963. On that occasion he toiled long into the night until another Hall of Famer, Willie Mays, broke up a scoreless duel in the 16th frame with a game-winning blast that sent the San Francisco fans home in the wee hours of the next morning. (The story of that game is reviewed by John McCollister in *The Best Baseball Games Ever Played*, pp. 110–117.) Both pitchers had thrown in excess of 200 pitches, something that would make pitchers of the recent past faint dead away. But for a man who had been in the Battle of the Bulge, and further, at age 42, it is best to keep in mind that Spahn, who that season won 23, was just having fun!

The great Milwaukee left hander started out his Hall of Fame appearances with three games in succession on his shutout list. A worthy opponent, Robin Roberts, dueled with him twice in 1949 and again in 1954, the year in which he finally bested Spahn, 4–0, on a one-hitter, masterfully pitched, in Milwaukee. Robin Roberts that night executed to perfection one of Spahn's foremost pitching tenets, stated this way by the great lefty: "Hitting is all about timing, and pitching is all about upsetting the hitter's timing."

Earlier in that same 1963 season, Warren Spahn took on Don Drysdale at Dodger Stadium in a night game on June 28 that saw the only scoring take place in the first inning. On a pair of singles, a walk, and a sacrifice fly by Joe Torre, the Braves scored what turned out to be the winning run. That evening Spahn took a perfect game to the seventh inning permitted but three well-spaced singles in a convincing display of pitching supremacy as he racked up his 11th win in the early season going.

Winningest lefty in major league history Warren Spahn attired in a Boston franchise uniform. Moving to Milwaukee in 1953, the Spahn-led Braves were world champions in 1957 (Brace photographs).

Warren Spahn's final encounter in a Hall of Fame shutout game was in his final season, this time with the Mets, winners of only 50 games in 1965. On May 5 he matched pitches with Jim Bunning of the Phillies. But one run separated winners and losers, and that was the product of a leadoff homer in the top of the sixth inning at Shea Stadium. It was hit by Jim Bunning, enabling the Phils to beat Spahn, 1–0.

The Spahn list against Hall of Fame pitchers in shutout encounters follows:

        Roberts (3)   Gibson (1)
        Marichal (2)   Drysdale (1)
        Koufax (1)   Bunning (1)

Nolan Ryan and Tom Seaver

They persevered. Through thick and thin these two "gamers" found their way to Cooperstown on the strength of very special gifts, as well as grit, speed, and unique deliveries that fueled superb careers. Tom Seaver and Nolan Ryan both chalked up 61 shutouts in careers that endured 20-plus seasons filled with great moments and trying times. Ryan, with seven skirmishes involving Hall of Fame pitchers, and Seaver, with nine, joined the amazing New York Mets pitching staff within a year of each other and remained there together through the Mets' improbable 1969 World's Championship, and on through the 1971 season. In 1972 Seaver was still in New York, but Ryan moved on to the golden west, where Cowboy Gene Autry's men wore the uniform of the California Angels.

Interestingly, if not curiously, the two never pitched against each other though both were around for many years after their New York days ended. Their record in shutout games involving other Hall of Fame pitchers follows:

Seaver	Ryan
SHO Gms, HOF Pitchers: 10	SHO Gms, HOF Pitchers: 6
W/L: W 8, L 2	W/L: W 2, L 4
1–0 Games 3, W 2, L 1	1–0 Games 1, W 0, L 0
Most Appearances: Niekro 5, W 4, L 1	Most Appearances: Jenkins, 2

Nolan Ryan started out his 1970 season with a sparkling one-hitter that belabored the Phils' Jim Bunning, 7–0, at New York, aided no little by a pair of Mets taters, one by Ken Boswell and the other by Tommie Agee. Ryan fanned 15, nailing the heart of Philadelphia's batting order eight times. Second sacker Denny Doyle, the Phils' leadoff hitter, started the game with a single—and that was it. There were no Philadelphia hits the rest of the game.

But bad news followed this impressive engagement. Nolan Ryan and his 100 mile an hour heater lost four of his next five encounters with Hall of Fame hurlers, beating only Fergie Jenkins in 1979, 5–0. Bert Blyleven (1973), Jenkins (1973), Steve Carlton (1980), Phil Niekro (1981).

Tom Seaver's shutout encounters started much like Nolan Ryan's with a 1–0 masterpiece. In this one against Don Sutton in Dodgerland, the winning run came on a tenth-inning single by Al Weis, after which Seaver took down the Angelinos without a hit in the Dodgers' tenth. It was one of his five shutouts in a 16–12 year.

Years later, in a July 27, 1986, match when Seaver was finishing out his career with the Boston Red Sox, Sutton, in a six-inning stint, caught up with Seaver, defeating him this time for his ninth win of the season in a 15–11 year with the California Angels.

Ryan and Seaver. They gave hitters pause as they contemplated standing in against them. Representing two very different pitching styles, and with widely differing numbers, these two master craftsmen, by dint of disciplined work, great care, endurance and fierce determination, posted some mind-boggling numbers that prompted Hall of Fame voters to usher them into baseball's pantheon of immortals *ex post haste*. It would have been a baseball sin if they hadn't.

Rik Albert "Bert" Blyleven

After the completion of the 2010 season, Bert Blyleven, who hailed from Zeist, Netherlands, became the most recent electee to the Hall of Fame in Cooperstown. The portfolio he brought with him included 60 shutout victories, good for the ninth spot on that prestigious list. Among them were 10 games involving other Hall of Fame pitchers. The record:

SHO Gms vs. HOF Pitchers: 7
W/L: W 3, L 4
1–0 Games: 2, W 0, L 2
Most Appearances with Eckersley and Ryan, 2

Bert Blyleven's first experience with a future Famer was a successful one, as he beat Nolan Ryan on June 29, 1973. Pitching for the Minnesota Twins at California on a pleasant June evening, he locked horns in a tight duel that put goose egg after goose egg on the scoreboard until the Twins managed to load up the sacks in the top of the eighth inning. Then Twins right fielder Bobby Darwin, batting cleanup, cleaned up, launching a booming shot beyond recall to make the score 4–0 in one swat. That was just what the doctor ordered for Blyleven, who disposed of the Angels to emerge victorious for the tenth time in the only season of his career that he won 20 games. It also happened to be the only season he led his league in shutouts (nine).

Blyleven's fastball, decent but not overwhelming, was often used as a setup for his curveball, one of the best, if not the very best, in the game's history. Many a slugger and future Hall of Famer looked silly fanning away at Uncle Bert's hook. It was obviously in good working order a few years later, when, pitching for Texas against Dennis Eckersley and the Indians, Blyleven shut them down on June 13, 1977, with but four hits, all singles, zeroing the Indians, 3–0.

Would that the remainder of his shutout games had ended as well as one of his encounters with Ryan and The Eck. Ryan caught up with Big Bert in a 1976 game, shutting him out by a 1–0 score as he got by on a three-hitter while walking seven, aided considerably by three twin killings. That was one of the four shutout losses he labored through against Hall of Fame pitchers.

Others who lowered the boom on the big right hander were Jim Palmer, Tom Seaver, and the final of his seven shutout games with Hall of Fame pitchers, against Don Sutton in 1986. One other in which he was involved was a game started by Claude Osteen but ended by Goose Gossage at the tail end of the 1975 season. In that game a pair of Minnesota singles caused Chicago White Sox manager Chuck Tanner to take starter Osteen out of the game and bring on the big fellow, Gossage, who got Twins shortstop Danny Thompson to ground into a double play. Pitching the remaining five innings, Gossage was credited with the win. The Chicago twin killing was the key play of the game, ultimately sending Blyleven to his defeat.

Bert Blyleven had to stand in line longer than most to make it to the final home of baseball's best. At the very end of his eligibility, the Hall's voters finally acknowledged his superior contributions to the game via 22 seasons and five different teams. So much better late than never!

Don Sutton

Don Sutton, winner of 324 games in a Hall of Fame (1998) career with 58 shutouts.

The current expression is *all in*, meaning, that whatever a person is into, he's in it all the way. Don Sutton was all in. When it came to baseball in general and pitching in particular, Sutton was totally engaged, sharply focused and thoroughly committed to the task at hand. He was around for 23 seasons in the Big Show, a testimony not only to his ability — not meager, yet not overwhelmingly outstanding — but to his tenacious determination. During his 23-year career he managed the magic number of wins it takes to get the nod in Cooperstown, but it took into his 21st season to get there. Not satisfied with 300 wins, he soldiered on to his final and 324th two seasons later despite being way past his prime and in the "hanging on" stages of his career. The numbers:

SHO Gms vs. HOF Pitchers: 12
W/L: W 6, L 8
1–0 Games: 1, W, L 1
Most Appearances with Seaver, 4, Won 1, Lost 3

Much has been made of Sutton's doctoring the ball, and most of that was no doubt true. Umpire Tom Gorman averred that the solidly built right-hander scuffed and marred baseballs regularly — but was never really caught in the act. Whether or not that was needed in his arsenal of pitches is hard to say. His sharply breaking curve ball was his primary out pitch and among the very best in his generation, and he found home plate's black edges more often than most. All of that was in demand in this test against a future Hall of Fame pitcher.

Gaylord Perry, even better known for doctoring pitches than Sutton, was paired with the Dodgers' Sutton on August 28, 1967, at Candlestick Park. The Giants that day whipped the Dodgers, 7–0, getting to the youngster for six tallies, three in the third, when the two Willies, Mays and McCovey, raised havoc, and three in the sixth inning. Meanwhile, Perry's sinking pitches, or doctored deliveries if that is what they actually were, set down Dodgers hitters on strikes nine times while submitting weakly in Perry's 11th win of the season.

During the next season Sutton ran into Tom Seaver, who bested him in a taut, 1–0 game that went ten innings before New York won out. It was the first of four encounters between the two. Don Sutton's best game with Seaver came in another 1–0, ten-inning tilt on July 17, 1970, in the City of the Angels. Seaver left that game after nine scoreless innings, but Sutton stayed on to get the win over reliever Tug McGraw, which disqualifies it from inclusion in the chart.

Others involved in shutouts with Sutton included Bert Blyleven, Phil Niekro, Bob Gibson and Juan Marichal. Against those worthies he went 2–4.

Don Sutton's tenth place ranking on this august listing also rounds out the top five modern era pitchers who follow Walter Johnson and Co., among the five very best Hall of Fame Shutout Titans. The remaining five include three early pitchers: Pud Galvin, Mordecai Brown and Ed Walsh. Hurlers Bob Gibson and Steve Carlton round out this elite 15.

James "Pud" Galvin "The Little Steam Engine" and Ed Walsh

Jim Galvin and Ed Walsh combined for 114 shutouts, splitting them evenly at 57, while accomplishing those numbers during baseball's earlier days. Galvin achieved his total before the 60'6" distance from pitcher's box to home plate was established, and Walsh after. Between them, these two patriarchs were engaged in 39 games against Hall of Fame pitchers, Galvin 18, and Walsh 21. Though a generation apart, Galvin (1875–1892) and Walsh (1904–1917) were dominant pitchers in their time, each featuring a devastating pitch: Galvin with his rising fastball and Walsh with his spit-ball. Both were relentless competitors, the one a stocky, 5'8" pitcher with many pitches and arm angles, and the other, Walsh, a handsome, well-built six-footer who, it was said, strutted while sitting down. Both are best remembered for seasons with outlandish numbers in wins, innings pitched and games started.

Pud Galvin engaged in shutout clashes with Charles "Old Hoss" Radbourn six times, Mickey Welch five times, John Ward four times and Tim Keefe three. Ed Walsh's list of Hall of Fame hurlers was more varied: Addie Joss (7), Rube Waddell, Walter Johnson, Chief Bender, Cy Young (2 each), and Jack Chesbro and Eddie Plank once each, all within a compact period of four seasons (1906–1909). Their numbers:

Galvin	*Walsh*
SHO Gms vs. HOF Pitchers: 18	SHO Gms vs. HOF Pitchers: 21
W/L: W 6, L 12	W/L: W 12, L 9
1–0 Games: 1, Won 1	1–0 Games: 5, W 4, L 1
Most Appearances with Radbourn 6	Most Appearances with Joss 8

It was Pud Galvin who was on the losing end of John Montgomery Ward's 1880 perfect game, a game Galvin never forgot, commenting that it was a wake-up call to as near perfection as he could manage each time he began a game. That was surely a part of his great success during a relatively short, 15-year career, at least for those enshrined at Cooperstown.

Galvin met one of the other great nineteenth-century pitchers, Old Hoss Radbourn, on July 13, 1888, in the second game of a doubleheader against Boston's Beaneaters, downing them, 6–0. It was his last shutout victory against a Hall of Fame pitcher. He was not too successful against his Hall of Fame competitors, but there is no denying the enormous success he enjoyed during his major league days.

The most famous single game in Ed Walsh's career was his 1–0 loss in the white-hot 1908 pennant race to Cleveland's brilliant ace, Addie Joss, who tossed a perfect game at Chicago's pennant hopes. The lone run in that game was unearned, and despite Big Ed Walsh's 15 Ks, this much celebrated game between the two future Hall of Famers came down, finally, to Joss' perfection, simply too much for Walsh and his White Sox teammates. Of this tension-laden game, sportswriter Franklin Lewis' trenchant comment perhaps summed it best: "A thousand fingernails hit the floor of the dugout during the ninth inning."

Big Ed had begun the last leg of the 1908 season with a 1–0 nail-biter against Walter Johnson on September 18, following up against Philadelphia, 2–0, New York in a 1–0 loss, a victory over Eddie Cicotte, 3–0, and a twin-killing against Boston by 5–1 and 2–0 scores, all of which amounted to 54 innings of work in 12 days in which he allowed but two runs. After he lost to Joss in Cleveland, he earned a 6–1 victory over Detroit in the Sox' next to last game of the season. That victory made him the last of the 40-game winners, at the same time setting up his White Sox for a one-game showdown with Detroit for pennant laurels in the season's last game. The flag wound up in Detroit.

Walsh and Joss met twice more in 1909, and on both occasions Joss lost 2–0 games to the great spitball pitcher. Their record in shutout games wound up at Walsh, 4 wins, and Joss, 4. It is also worth noting that in both 1908 and 1909 Walsh defeated Cy Young in 1–0 and 4–0 games, linking him with two of the three all-time outstanding shutout pitchers, Walter Johnson and Young. Though he won only 195 games, far shy of the Johnson and Young totals, Walsh won better than .600 percent of his major league decisions in a distinguished career that still ranks as the very best among all Chicago White Sox pitchers.

Bob Gibson

There weren't many ballplayers in the game's history who were more intense, combative or intimidating than Bob Gibson. And at the end of his Hall of Fame career he was no less that way than he was as a rookie. Usually players like Gibson either have extraordinary careers or they wind up doing something else for a living before too long. In the very athletic Gibson's case, there were five 20-win seasons (two more netted 19), 56 shutouts and that other-planetary season of 1968, which was one of the prime factors in his 1981 election into the Hall of Fame. Possessed of a sizzling fastball and an especially wicked slider, Gibson was the main St. Louis Cardinals attraction after Stan Musial's departure. He ranked right up there with the famous Saarinen Arch as one of the Mound City's stellar attractions. His primary shutout numbers follow:

SHO Gms vs. HOF Pitchers: 18
W/L: W 1, L 8
1–0 Games: 7, W 3, L 4
Most Appearances with Koufax and Marichal, 3 each

Among the greats in the game, many are remembered for one season that towers over all their other seasons, for example, Ruth's 1921, Radbourn's

1884, Pedro Martinez' 2000, and Bob Gibson's 1968. During that season he added three 13 wins to his total, including one each against Fergie Jenkins (1–0), Juan Marichal (3–0) and Phil Niekro (again, 1–0). During that magic season it would take a pitcher's very best to beat him. On one occasion in particular it did, when on September 17, 1968, Gaylord Perry came up with a no-hitter that beat the Cardinals 1–0. A Ron Hunt first-inning bomb left the premises at Candlestick Park for a home run that Perry used to win the no-no. Eight of Gibson's nine losses that season were by one or two runs, including two 1–0 games.

Over the course of 13 seasons between his first Famer shutout game and his last in 1973, he was paired with Sandy Koufax and Juan Marichal three times each; Don Drysdale, Perry, Phil Niekro and Fergie Jenkins twice each; and Don Sutton, Jim Bunning, Steve Carlton, and Warren Spahn one each, a formidable array of pitching talent.

Standing out among his victories were games in 1963 and 1967, the first of which was the nightcap of a July 7 doubleheader played at San Francisco during Stan Musial's last season. It was a scoreless duel until the seventh frame, when Stan the Man clouted a two-run homer to put the Cardinals out in front of the Giants. Gibby himself came along with a two-run single two innings later to ice it, defeating Juan Marichal, 5–0. The other of these two triumphs came in the 1967 opener, when, once again, Marichal and the Giants were victimized, this time by a 6–0 count before a packed St. Louis house, with 38,117 in attendance. On this occasion Gibson turned in a five-hit, 13-strike out performance.

The Cardinals' franchise pitching staff included a number of Cooperstown residents: Jesse Haines, the one and only Pete Alexander and Dizzy Dean among others. It's no stretch to make the claim that Bob Gibson was the pick of the litter.

Mordecai Brown and Steve Carlton

Pitching opposites in eras, style and career records are represented in these two Hall of Fame twirlers. Three Finger Brown, bellcow of the immortal 1906–1910 Chicago Cubs (see above in Teams) and Steve Carlton are the two Hall of Famers linked in this rather awkward pairing. However, Brown, whose career ranged from his rookie season with the St. Louis Cardinals in 1903 to 1916, and Carlton (1965–1988), both finished their careers with 55 shutouts, thus pairing them as the 14th and 15th Hall of Famers on this list.

During Mordecai Brown's career every game between the Cubs and the Giants was a first-class tussle. Better termed: all-out warfare. Three Finger and Matty were in the forefront of those friction-laden skirmishes. They met ten times within four seasons, resulting in three shutouts and it took until their last pairing in a shutout game on July 17 of 1908 for Brown to shut out Mathewson. The score was 1–0, just the way their shutout log started in 1905. There was a difference in the two 1–0 games. Mathewson's was a no-hitter, in keeping with his lofty status no matter the comparison. Brown also split two shutouts with Joe McGinnity, the other half of John McGraw's dynamic duo in the early 1900s. The only other Famer on the Brown shutout list was Vic Willis, who logged seven shutouts for Pittsburgh during the wildly sensational 1908 season. They also split the two shutout games in which they were involved. Brown won the August 12, 1908, encounter, and Willis returned the favor just a month later in the Pirates' lair with a razor-sharp, 1–0 outing that added still more fire to the pennant race. As an added note to that incredible 1908 race, that Brown's Cubs were engaged in 43 shutout games (there was also a scoreless tie) out of the 158 they played (the Cubs tied 40 games including the scoreless tie). That comes down to better than 25 percent, one out of every four games that resulted in a shutout. They won 29 of those shutout games, by the way.

Many years later Mordecai Brown, in retirement as one of Terre Haute, Indiana's, solid citizens, was asked about his best year in major league baseball. He replied that there could be only one choice for him, 1908, and that "it was just absolutely crazy from beginning to end!"

For Steve Carlton there was also one season above all others, 1972, when he won almost half of his team's games and a Cy Young Award. During that 1972 campaign he won eight of his 27 victories via the shutout route, and fired a one-hitter at Juan Marichal and the Giants on April 25. The lone hit was a leadoff single by Chris Speier. Facing only 28 batters in that game, the lefty with one of the more celebrated sliders in the game's

Mordecai Peter Centennial Brown, aka "Three-Finger Brown," the mainstay of the Cubs pitching staff during their 1906–1910 dynasty (Brace photographs).

annals, struck out every hitter he faced except Chris Arnold, including pinch-hitter Willie Mays. The strikeout total was 14. It was Juan Marichal who also served as Lefty's first Hall of Fame shutout opponent. While with the Cardinals in 1968 that first encounter resulted in a Marichal victory, 3–0. Carlton's 1972 masterpiece evened that score, with some to spare.

Fergie Jenkins (1969) and Tom Seaver (1976) also bested Carlton by 1–0 scores. Joining these luminaries during the Carlton years were Jim Bunning (a 3–0 Carlton win in 1970), Bob Gibson (a 1–0 Carlton win in 1972), Phil Niekro (a 4–0 Carlton loss in 1978) and finally Nolan Ryan (a 3–0 Carlton win in 1980).

With his nasty slider and awesome powers of concentration, Carlton brought more than enough credentials to baseball's pantheon, including winning streaks, 4,136 strikeouts, over 5,000 innings pitched, four Cy Young Awards and 55 shutouts among his 329 career victories. He wasn't on the Cooperstown ballot very long. The electors put him on the Hall of Fame wall the first chance they had.

Shutout Titans in Championship Play

The table below presents a review of baseball's most prolific Shutout Titans who pitched in post-season games. The review includes only the 15 Titans whose shutout records against Hall of Fame pitchers are detailed in this chapter (above). All games listed are World Series games except the first and last.

Pitcher/Tm/Lg/Score	Date	Opp. Pitcher/Tm/Lg
Young, Cleveland, (NL) scoreless tie	10–17–1892	Stivetts, Boston (NL), 11-inning game
Mathewson, New York (NL)	3–0 10-9-1905	Plank, Philadelphia (AL)
Mathewson, New York (NL)	9–0 10–12–1905	Coakley, Philadelphia (AL)
Mathewson, New York (NL)	2–0 10–14–1905	Bender, Philadelphia (AL)
Walsh, Chicago (AL)	3–0 10–11–1906	Pfiester, Chicago (NL)
Brown, Chicago (NL)	1–0 10–12–1906	Altrock, Chicago (AL)
Brown, Chicago (NL)	2–0 10–12–1907	Mullin, Detroit (AL)
Brown, Chicago (NL)	3–0 10–13–1908	Summers, Detroit (AL)
Mathewson, New York (NL)	3–0 10–8–1913	Plank, Philadelphia (AL), 10 inning game
Johnson, Washington (AL)	4–0 10–11–1925	Yde, Pittsburgh (NL)
Spahn, Milwaukee (NL)	3–0 10–5–1958	Ford, New York (AL)
Gibson, St. Louis (NL)	6–0 10–8–1967	Santiago, Boston (AL)
Gibson, St. Louis (NL)	4–0 10–2–1968	McLain, Detroit (AL)
Sutton, Los Angeles (NL)	3–0, NLCS 10–5–1974	Reuss, Pittsburgh (NL)

Discussion: Not since Don Sutton's triumph over the Pittsburgh Pirates in 1974 has there been a World Series shutout pitched by one of the top 15 Shutout Titans. Christy Mathewson with four, and Mordecai Brown's three shutouts are the most registered by these Hall of Fame pitchers. Mathewson's four included victories over Hall of Fame Athletics pitchers Eddie Plank and Chief Bender. Bob Gibson, with World Series wins in two successive seasons, is the only other multiple winner among the eight Titans cited above.

The only 1–0 shutout came in the famous 1906 Series pitting the Cubs of Frank Chance and the "Hitless Wonders" White Sox led by Fielder Jones. In that game, the fourth of an electric. Series, the fabled Cubs infield went to work in the seventh inning. Chance led off with a single, was sacrificed by Harry Steinfeldt to second and then moved on to third on a bunt by Joe Tinker. John Evers then ripped a single to left field, scoring Chance with the only run of the game. "Miner" Brown then squelched the Pale Hose the rest of the way to win a superbly pitched two-hitter.

Among still other games that might be noted, the Warren Spahn victory over Ed "Whitey" Ford in the 1958 World Series is presented here as another of those great World Series contests among many all the marbles on the table. In the Series' fourth game the two teams went through five scoreless innings before the Braves scored an unearned run to take a 1–0 lead. Scoring on a Spahn single in the seventh frame and then again in the eighth, the Braves added to their lead. Meanwhile, Spahnie kept on mowing down the powerful Yankees crew until finally there were none left standing, victimized by a brilliant Spahn two-hitter. His final out was a hard-hit ball off the bat of Mickey Mantle that was converted into an infield out. Though future Hall of Fame pitcher Whitey Ford pitched well, it wasn't good enough on this day. The great portsider, Spahn, had prevailed. The box score follows:

Milwaukee Braves	AB	R	H	RBI	*New York Yankees*	AB	R	H	RBI
Schoendienst, 2b	5	1	1	0	Siebern, lf	3	0	0	0
Logan, ss	5	1	1	0	McDougald, 2b	4	0	0	0
Mathews, 3b	4	0	1	1	Bauer, rf	4	0	0	0
Aaron, cf, rf	4	0	2	0	Mantle, cf	4	0	1	0
Adcock, 1b	3	0	0	0	Skowron, 1b	3	0	1	0
Torre, ph, 1b	1	0	0	0	Berra, c	3	0	0	0
Crandall, c	3	1	2	0	Richardson, 2b	2	0	0	0
Covington, lf	3	0	0	0	Howard, ph	1	0	0	0
Bruton, pr, cf	0	0	0	0	Carey, 3b	0	0	0	0
Pafko, rf, lf	4	0	1	0	Kubek, ss	2	0	0	0
Spahn (WP)	4	0	1	1	Slaughter, ph	1	0	0	0
Dickson, p	0	0	0	0	Ford (LP)	1	0	0	0

Milwaukee Braves AB R H RBI   *New York Yankees* AB R H RBI
                                 Kucks, p   0 0 0 0
                                 Lumpe, ph, ss   1 0 0 0
Totals   36 3 9 2   Totals   29 0 2 0

        Milwaukee   000   001   110   3 9 0
        New York   000   000   000   0 2 1

2B: Aaron, Pafko, Logan, Mathews   BB: Spahn 2; Ford 1; Kucks 1, and Dickson, 0
3B: Schoendienst, Mantle   ER: Spahn 0; Ford 2; Kucks and Dickson 0
DP: McDougald, Kubek, Skowron   IP: Spahn 9; Ford 7, Kucks and Dickson, 1
LOB: Milwaukee 8; New York 4   Attendance, 71,563
K: Spahn 7; Ford 6; Kucks and   Umpires: Flaherty HP, Barlick 1B, Berry 2B,
  Dickson, 0   Gorman 3B, Umont lF, Jackowski RF

14

Shutout Summitry

19th Century Championships

Nineteenth century fans who attended championship games were just as thrilled during those formative baseball years as we are today when the best teams line up against each other and play for pennant or World Series laurels. The big events of those years of yore began with the first game ever played for a professional championship on October 30, 1871. Billed as the Championship of the National Association of Professional Base Ball Players, and played at New York's Union Grounds, it featured the Philadelphia Athletics against the Chicago White Stockings. On that rather cold October day, the Athletics prevailed, 4–1, claiming a prestigious "Whip Flag" emblematic of the league's championship.

As professional play evolved and became one of America's classic sporting events toward the end of the century, stakes were provided for championship play between existing leagues, and later by the Temple family in series between the top teams in the National League. The winner received a championship cup (The Temple Cup, 1894–1897). The last of these special championship awards was staged in 1900 in a series played for the Chronicle-Telegraph Cup.

Finally, the post-season championship we know as the World Series today was initiated in 1903, when the National and American League pennant winners agreed to meet in a best of nine series. The American League's Boston team, known variously as the Pilgrims, Invaders, Somersets, or Red Stockings, and by 1908 as the Red Sox, the team name with which we are familiar today, took on the Pittsburgh Pirates and defeated them in what was almost immediately called "The World's Series." The rest, as is often said, is history. Following the 1903 lead, there would be plenty of World Series and league championship play in post-seasonal extravaganzas that have become a hugely popular part of America's sports world.

After the first professional playoff, won by Philadelphia, the next championship series was played between the Providence (NL) and New York (AA) teams in 1884. The very first game of that series resulted in a shutout, Charley

Radbourn two-hitting the New York Metropolitans of the American Association for the Providence Grays. That shutout heads our post-season listings, and others (All-Star Games and tie-breaking playoffs are included), from 1884 through the 2010 season:

Year	Series Gm	Win.Tm/Score/Pitcher	Losing Tm/Pitcher
1884	Game 1	Providence 6 (Radbourn)	New York (Keefe)
1886	Game 1	Chicago 6 (Clarkson)	St. Louis (Foutz)
1886	Game 2	St Louis 12 (Caruthers)*	Chicago (McCormick)
1887	Game 4	Detroit 8 (Baldwin)	St. Louis (King)
1887	Game 6	Detroit 9 (Getzein)	St. Louis (Foutz)
1888	Game 2	St. Louis 3 (Chamberlain)	New York (Welch)
1890	Game 1	Brooklyn 9 (Terry)	Louisville (Stratton)
1892	Game 1	Cleveland 0 (Young)†	Boston (Stivetts)
1892	Game 4	Boston 4 (Nichols)	Cleveland (Cuppy)
1895	Game 4	Baltimore 5 (Esper)	Cleveland (Cuppy)
1896	Game 4	Baltimore 5 (Corbett)	Cleveland (Cuppy)
1900	Game 3	Pittsburgh 10 (Phillippe)	Brooklyn (Howell)

*Caruthers pitched a one-hitter in this game.
†This was an 11-inning, scoreless game.

League Championship Playoffs

Beginning with the 1969 season the major leagues initiated a playoff series to determine league champions. The system was refined with the passage of time, becoming progressively more elaborate. The ultimate end, however, remained the same: determining league champions who would meet in the World Series. Those playoff shutouts follow. Blackened team/score/winning pitcher indicates a 1–0 game.

Year	Series/Gm	Win.Tm/Score/ Winning Pitcher	Los.Tm./ Losing Pitcher
1969	ALCS/Gm 2 (11 ins)	**Baltimore 1 (McNally)**	Minnesota (Boswell)
1970	NLCS/Gm 1 (10 ins)	Cincinnati 3 (Nolan)	Pittsburgh (Ellis)
1972	ALCS/Gm 2	Oakland 5 (Odom)	Detroit (Fryman)
1972	ALCS/Gm 3	Detroit 3 (Coleman)	Oakland (Holtzman)
1973	ALCS/Gm 1	Baltimore 6 (Palmer)	Oakland (Blue)
1973	ALCS/Gm 5	Oakland 3 (Hunter)	Baltimore (Alexander)
1973	NLCS/Gm 2	New York 5 (Matlack)	Cincinnati (Gullett)
1974	ALCS/Gm 2	Oakland 5 (Holtzman)	Baltimore (McNally)
1974	ALCS/Gm 3	**Oakland 1 (Blue)**	Baltimore (Palmer)
1974	NLCS/Gm 1	Los Angeles 3 (Sutton)	Pittsburgh (Reuss)
1974	NLCS/Gm 3	Pittsburgh 7 (Kison)	Los Angeles (Rau)
1978	NLCS/Gm 2	Los Angeles 4 (John)	Philadelphia (Ruthven)

14. When Titans Clash

Year	Series/Gm	Win.Tm/Score/ Winning Pitcher	Los.Tm./ Losing Pitcher
1979	ALCS/Gm 4	Baltimore 8 (McGregor)	California (Knapp)
1980	NLCS/Gm 3 (11 ins)	**Houston 1 (D. Smith)**	Philadelphia (McGraw)
1981	ALDS/Gm 1	Oakland 4 (Norris)	Kansas City (Leonard)
1981	NLDS/Gm 5	Montreal 3 (Rogers)	Philadelphia (Carlton)
1981	NLDS/Gm 2 (11 ins)	**Houston 1 (Sambito)**	Los Angeles (Stewart)
1981	NLDS/Gm 5	Los Angeles 4 (Reuss)	Houston (Ryan)
1981	ALCS/Gm 3	New York 4 (Righetti)	Oakland (Keough)
1981	NLCS/Gm 2	Montreal 3 (Burris)	Los Angeles (Valenzuela)
1981	ALDS/Gm 2	New York 3 (Righetti)	Milwaukee (Caldwell)
1982	NLCS/Gm 1	St. Louis 7 (Forsch)	Atlanta (Perez)
1983	ALCS/Gm 2	Baltimore 4 (Boddicker)	Chicago (Bannister)
1983	ALCS/Gm 4 (10 ins)	Baltimore 3 (T. Martinez)	Chicago (Burns)
1983	NLCS/Gm 1	**Philadelphia 1 (Carlton)**	Los Angeles (Reuss)
1984	ALCS/Gm 3	**Detroit 1 (Wilcox)**	Kansas City (Leibrandt)
1984	NLCS/Gm 1	Chicago 13 (Sutcliffe)	San Diego (Show)
1985	ALCS/Gm 5	Kansas City 2 (Jackson)	Toronto (Key)
1986	NLCS/Gm 1	**Houston 1 (Scott)**	New York (Gooden)
1987	NLCS/Gm 2	San Francisco 5 (Dravecky)	St. Louis (Tudor)
1987	NLCS/Gm 6	**St. Louis 1 (Tudor)**	San Francisco (Dravecky)
1987	NLCS/Gm 7	St. Louis 6 (Cox)	San Francisco (Hammaker)
1988	NLCS/Gm 7	Los Angeles 6 (Hershiser)	New York (Darling)
1991	NLCS/Gm 2	**Atlanta 1 (Avery)**	Pittsburgh (Z. Smith)
1991	NLCS/Gm 5	**Pittsburgh 1 (Z. Smith)**	Atlanta (Glavine)
1991	NLCS/Gm 7	Atlanta 4 (Smoltz)	Pittsburgh (Smiley)
1991	NLCS/Gm 6	**Atlanta 1 (Avery)**	Pittsburgh (Drabek)
1995	ALDS/Gm 2	Cleveland 4 (Hershiser)	Boston (Hanson)
1995	ALCS/Gm 4	Cleveland 7 (Hill)	Seattle (Benes)
1995	ALCS/Gm 6	Cleveland 4 (Martinez)	Seattle (Johnson)
1995	NLDS/Gm 4	Atlanta 6 (Avery)	Cincinnati (Schourek)
1996	NLCS/Gm 5	Atlanta 14 (Smoltz)	St. Louis (Stottlemyre)
1996	NLCS/Gm 7	Atlanta 15 (Glavine)	St. Louis (Osborne)
1997	ALCS/Gm 1	Baltimore 3 (Erickson)	Cleveland (Ogea)
1997	ALCS/Gm 6 (11 ins)	**Cleveland 1 (Anderson)**	Baltimore (Benitez)
1997	NLCS/Gm 4	Atlanta 4 (Neagle)	Florida (Leiter)
1998	ALDS/GM 1	New York 2 (Wells)	Texas (Stottlemyre)
1998	ALDS/Gm 3	New York 4 (Cone)	Texas (Sele)
1998	ALCS/Gm 4	New York 4 (Hernandez)	Cleveland (Gooden)
1998	NLCS/Gm 2	San Diego 3 (K. Brown)	Atlanta (Glavine)
1998	NLCS/Gm 6	San Diego 5 (Hitchcock)	Atlanta (Glavine)
1999	ALDS/Gm 1	New York 8 (Hernandez)	Texas (Sele)
1999	ALDS/Gm 3	New York 3 (Clemens)	Texas (Loaiza)
1999	NLCS/Gm 3	**Atlanta 1 (Glavine)**	New York (Leiter)
2000	ALDS/Gm 2	New York 2 (Pettitte)	Oakland (Appier)
2000	NLDS/Gm 4	New York 4 (B. J. Jones)	San Francisco (Gardner)

Year	Series/Gm	Win.Tm/Score/ Winning Pitcher	Los.Tm./ Losing Pitcher
2000	ALCS/Gm 1	Seattle 2 (F. Garcia)	New York (Neagle)
2000	ALCS/Gm 4	New York 5 (Clemens)	Seattle (Abbott)
2000	NLCS/Gm 5	New York 7 (Hampton)	St. Louis (Hentgen)
2001	ALDS/Gm 1	Cleveland 5 (Colon)	Seattle (F. Garcia)
2001	ALDS/Gm 2	Oakland 2 (Hudson)	New York (Pettitte)
2001	ALDS/Gm 3	**New York 1 (Mussina)**	Oakland (Zito)
2001	NLDS/Gm 2	**Atlanta 1 (Glavine)**	Houston (Mlicki)
2001	NLDS/Gm 1	**Arizona 1 (Schilling)**	St. Louis (Morris)
2001	NLCS/Gm 1	Arizona 2 (Johnson)	Atlanta (Maddux)
2003	NLDS/Gm 1	San Francisco 2 (Schmidt)	Florida (Beckett)
2003	NLCS/Gm 5	Florida 4 (Beckett)	Chicago (Zambrano)
2004	ALDS/Gm 1	Minnesota 2 (Santana)	New York (Mussina)
2004	NLDS/Gm 3	Los Angeles 4 (Lima)	St. Louis (Morris)
2004	NLCS/Gm 5	Houston 3 (Lidge)	St. Louis (Isringhausen)
2006	ALDS/Gm 3	Detroit 6 (Rogers)	New York (Johnson)
2006	NLDS/Gm 2	St. Louis 2 (Weaver)	San Diego (Wells)
2006	ALCS/Gm 3	Detroit 3 (Rogers)	Oakland (Harden)
2006	NLCS/Gm 1	New York 2 (Glavine)	St. Louis (Weaver)
2006	NLCS/Gm 3	St. Louis 5 (Suppan)	New York (Trachsel)
2007	ALDS/Gm 1	Boston 4 (Beckett)	Anaheim (Lackey)
2008	ALCS/Gm 1	Boston 2 (Matsuzaka)	Tampa Bay (Shields)
2009	NLCS/Gm 3	Philadelphia 11 (Lee)	Los Angeles (Kuroda)
2009	ALDS/Gm 1	Anaheim 5 (Lackey)	Boston (Lester)
2010	NLDS/Gm 1	Philadelphia 4 (Halladay)*	Cincinnati (Volquez)
2010	NLDS/Gm 3	Philadelphia 2 (Hamels)	Cincinnati (Cueto)
2010	NLDS/Gm 1	**San Francisco 1 (Lincecum)**	Atlanta (Lowe)
2010	NLCS/Gm 3	San Francisco 3 (Cain)	Philadelphia (Hamels)
2010	ALDS/Gm 2	Texas 6 (Wilson)	Tampa Bay (Shields)
2010	ALCS/Gm 3	Texas 8 (Lee)	New York (Pettitte)

*This was the first no-hit game in league divisional and league championship play.

Number of shutouts, 1969–2010: 85
Number of 1–0 games, 1969–2010: 17
Percentage of 1–0 games: 20

The Playoff Tie-Breaker Shutout Log

October 2, 1951, Brooklyn at New York
National League Pennant, Game 2 of 3

Brooklyn, 10–13–2, (Labine)
New York, 0–6–5, (S. Jones)

October 1, 1962, Los Angeles at San Francisco
National League Pennant, Game 1 of 3

San Francisco, 8–10–0, (Pierce)
Los Angeles, 0–3–1, (Koufax)

October 4, 1999, New York at Cincinnati
Wild Card NLDS spot, one game

New York, 5–9–0, (Leiter)
Cincinnati, 0–2–0, (Parris)

September 30, 2008, Minnesota at Chicago
Central Division championship, one game

Chicago, 1–5–0, (Danks)
Minnesota, 0–2–0, (Blackburn)

The All-Star Game Shutout Log

Game Number 8 at St. Louis, Sportsman's Park, July 9, 1940
National League 4–7–0 (Derringer); American League 0–3–1 (Ruffing)

Game Number 13 at Boston, Fenway Park, July 9, 1946
American League, 12–14–1 (Feller); National League, 0–3–0 (Passeau)

Game Number 29 at New York, Yankee Stadium, July 13, 1960
National League, 6–10–0 (Law); American League, 0–8–0 (Ford)

Game Number 39 at Houston, Astrodome, July 9, 1968
National League, **1–5**–0 (Drysdale); American League, 0–3–1 (Tiant)

Game Number 58 at Oakland-Alameda County Coliseum, July 14, 1987
National League, 2–8–2 (Lee Smith); American League, 0–6–1 (Jay Howell)
13-inning game

Game Number 61 at Chicago, Wrigley Field, July 10, 1990
American League, 2–7–0 (Saberhagen); National League, 0–2–1 (Brantley)

Game Number 67 at Philadelphia, Veterans Stadium, July 9, 1996
National League, 6–12–1 (Smoltz); American League, 0–7–0 (Nagy)

The World Series Shutout Log

The Mount Everest of major league baseball is the World Series. One of the most scintillating of America's gala sporting extravaganzas, its annual following lives and breathes with every pitch, every out, every victory until a champion is declared — and then the celebrations *really* begin. *En route*, or indeed, as climax to a World Series championship, those individual acts of the drama that is "*The* Series," unfold game by game. And among the more unforgettable games are those that are so masterfully pitched that one of the teams is held scoreless, unable to muster even the semblance of an attack. Those would be the shutouts, epitomized by the Don Larsen perfecto that marked the 1956 Series as the rarest of the rare gems in World Series play.

During the years of the modern World Series from 1903 to 2010, there have been 611 games played. Among those 611 one finds that 109 have been shutouts (17.84 percent), or nearly one game in five. That is a significantly higher percentage than in regular seasonal competition. One would expect that to be the case inasmuch as the Fall Classic regularly matches pitching staffs that are among the very best in both leagues. That suggests that there is a strong likelihood that fans will see a shutout in each World Series played.

Because of the large number of games *en toto* only 1–0 games (blackened) and those games won by Hall of Fame starting pitchers are listed, as well as the first shutout in World Series history, as follows:

Date/Game Number	Winner/Score/Winning Pitcher	LosingTm/Losing Pitcher
October 2, 1903, Gm 2	Boston 3 (N) (Dinneen)	Pittsburgh (Leever)
October 9, 1905, Gm 1	New York 3 (N) (Mathewson)	Philadelphia (Plank)
October 10, 1905, Gm 2	Philadelphia 3 (A) (Bender)	New York (McGinnity)
October 12, 1905, Gm 3	New York 9 (N) (Mathewson)	Philadelphia (Coakley)
October 13, 1905, Gm 4	**New York 1 (N) (McGinnity)**	Philadelphia (Plank)
October 14, 1905, Gm 5	New York 2 (N) (Mathewson)	Philadelphia (Bender)
October 11, 1906, Gm 3	Chicago 3 (A) (Walsh)	Chicago (N) (Pfiester)
October 12, 1906, Gm 4	**Chicago 1 (N) (M. Brown)**	Chicago (Altrock)
October 12, 1907, Gm 5	Chicago 2 (N) (Brown)	Detroit (Mullin)
October 13, 1908, Gm 4	Chicago 3 (N) (Brown)	Detroit (Summers)
October 8, 1913, Gm 2	New York 3 (N) (Mathewson), 10 inn.	Philadelphia (Plank)
October 10, 1914, Gm 2	**Boston 1 (N) (James)**	Philadelphia (Plank)
October 6, 1920, Gm 2	Brooklyn 3 (Grimes)	Cleveland (Bagby)
October 11, 1920, Gm 6	**Cleveland 1 (Mails)**	Brooklyn (S. Smith)
October 12, 1920, Gm 7	Cleveland 3 (Coveleski)	Brooklyn (Grimes)
October 6, 1921, Gm 2	New York 3 (A) (Hoyt)	New York (N) (Nehf)
October 13, 1921, Gm 8	**New York 1 (N) (Nehf)**	New York (Hoyt)
October 12, 1923, Gm 3	**New York 1 (N) (Nehf)**	New York (A) (S. Jones)
October 11, 1925, Gm 4	Washington 4 (Johnson)	Pittsburgh (Yde)
October 5, 1926, Gm 3	St. Louis 4 (N) (Haines)	New York (Ruether)
October 6, 1930, Gm 5	Philadelphia 2 (A) (Grove)	St. Louis (Grimes)
October 9, 1934, Gm 7	St. Louis 11 (N) (Dean)	Detroit (Auker)
October 6, 1948, Gm 1	**Boston 1 (N) (Sain)**	Cleveland (Feller)
October 5, 1949, Gm 1	**New York 1 (N) (Reynolds)**	Brooklyn (Newcombe)
October 6, 1949, Gm 2	**Brooklyn 1 (Roe)**	New York (Raschi)
October 4, 1950, Gm 1	**New York 1 (A) (Raschi)**	Philadelphia (Konstanty)
October 9, 1956, Gm 6	**Brooklyn 1 (N) (Labine)**, 10 inn.	New York (Turley)
October 7, 1957, Gm 5	**Milwaukee 1 (Burdette)**	New York (Ford)
October 5, 1958, Gm 4	Milwaukee 3 (Spahn)	New York (Ford)
October 1, 1959, Gm 1	Chicago 11 (A) (Wynn)	Los Angeles (Craig)
October 6, 1959, Gm 5	**Chicago 1 (A) Shaw**	Los Angeles (Koufax)
October 8, 1960, Gm 6	New York 10 (A) (Ford)	Pittsburgh (Mizell)
October 12, 19260, Gm 6	New York 12 (A) (Ford)	Pittsburgh (Friend)
October 4, 1961, Gm 1	New York 2 (A) (Ford)	Cincinnati (O'Toole)
October 8, 1961, Gm 4	New York 7 (A) (Ford)	Cincinnati (O'Toole)
October 16, 1962, Gm 7	**New York 1 (Terry)**	San Francisco (Sanford)
October 5, 1963, Gm 3	**Los Angeles 1 (Drysdale)**	New York (Bouton)
October 1, 1965, Gm 5	Los Angeles 7 (Koufax)	Minnesota (Kaat)
October 14, 1965, Gm 7	Los Angeles 2 (Koufax)	Minnesota (Kaat)
October 6, 1966, Gm 2	Baltimore 6 (Palmer)*	Los Angeles (Koufax)
October 8, 1966, Gm 3	**Baltimore 1 (Bunker)**	Los Angeles (Osteen)
October 9, 1966, Gm 4	**Baltimore 1 (McNally)**	Los Angeles (Drysdale)
October 8, 1967, Gm 4	St. Louis 6 (Gibson)	Boston (Santiago)

Date/Game Number	Winner/Score/Winning Pitcher	LosingTm/Losing Pitcher
October 2, 1968, Gm 1	St. Louis 4 (Gibson)	Detroit (McLain)
October 14, 1969, Gm 3†	New York 5 (Gentry)	Baltimore (Palmer)
October 18, 1972, Gm 3	**Cincinnati 1 (Billingham)**	Oakland (Odom)
October 18, 1986, Gm 1	**Boston 1 (Hurst)**	New York (N) (Darling)
October 27, 1991, Gm 7	**Minnesota 1 (Morris)**	Atlanta (Pena)
October 28, 1995, Gm 6	**Atlanta 1 (Glavine)**	Cleveland (Poole)
October 24, 1996, Gm 5	**New York 1 (Pettitte)**	Atlanta (Smoltz)
October 26, 2005, Gm 4	**Chicago 1 (F. Garcia)**	Houston (Lidge)

*In the 1966 World Series the Baltimore pitching staff combined to pitch 33 consecutive scoreless innings, a World Series record.
†Nolan Ryan pitched in relief in this game

Appendix A

The First Ones

There is usually curiosity, if not serious interest, in a first-time event. So, too, with the shutout. This listing presents the first shutout achievement in a number of settings. Examples would be a shutout in a league like the American Association, or in a major event, like the World Series.

The National Association of Professional Base Ball Players

First NA Shutout
May 4, 1871 at Fort Wayne, 2–0
Mathews (Fort Wayne), WP; Pratt (Cleveland), LP
Professional Baseball's first shutout and its first season-opening game shutout

First NA No-hitter
July 28, 1875 at Philadelphia, 4–0
Borden (Philadelphia) WP; Golden (Chicago) LP

First NA 1–0 Game
May 11, 1875 at St. Louis, 1–0
Zettlein (Chicago) WP; Blong (St. Louis), LP

The National League

First NL Shutout
April 25, 1876 at Louisville, 4–0
Spalding (Chicago) WP; Devlin (Louisville) LP
Major League Baseball's first shutout and its first season-opening game shutout

First NL No-hitter
July 15, 1876 at St. Louis, 2–0
Bradley (St. Louis) WP; Bond (Hartford) LP

First NL 1–0 Game
May 5, 1876 at St. Louis, 1–0
Bradley (St. Louis) WP; Spalding (Chicago) LP

The American Association

First AA Shutout
May 6, 1882 at Louisville, 3–0
Mullane (Louisville) WP; McGinnis (St. Louis) LP

First AA No-hitter
September 11, 1882 at Cincinnati, 2–0
Mullane (Louisville) WP; White (Cincinnati) LP

First AA 1–0 Game
July 13, 1882 at Baltimore, 1–0
McCormick (Cincinnati) WP; Landis (Baltimore) LP

The Union Association

First UA Shutout
April 29, 1884 at Cincinnati, 5–0
Bradley (Cincinnati) WP; Daily (Chicago-Pittsburgh) LP

First UA No-hitter
August 26, 1884 at Kansas City, 3–1
Burns (Cincinnati) WP; Black (Kansas City) LP

First UA 1–0 Game
July 19, 1884 at Boston, 1–0
Boyle (St. Louis Maroons) WP; Shaw (Boston) LP

The Players' League

First PL Shutout
May 19, 1890 at Brooklyn, 6–0
Weyhing (Brooklyn) WP; Baldwin (Chicago) LP

First PL 1–0 Game*
June 21, 1890 at Chicago, 1–0
Weyhing (Brooklyn) WP; King (Chicago) LP
* *There were no no-hitters in the Players' League*

The American League

First AL Shutout
May 15, 1901, at Boston, 4–0
Lee (Washington) WP; Cuppy (Boston) LP

First AL No-hitter
September 20, 1902, at Chicago, 3–0
Callahan (Chicago) WP; Egan (Detroit) LP

First AL 1–0 Game
July 27, 1901, at Detroit, 1–0
Yeager (Detroit) WP; McGinnity (Baltimore) LP

Federal League

First FL Shutout
April 14, 1914, at Pittsburgh, 1–0
Seaton (Brooklyn) WP; Knetzer (Pittsburgh) LP
This game was also the FL's first 1–0 game.

First FL 9-inning No-hitter*
April 24, 1915, at St. Louis
Allen (Pittsburgh) WP; Groom (St. Louis) LP
*On September 19, 1914, at Brooklyn, Ed Lafitte was WP in an 8-inning no-hit game vs. Kansas City (Cullop), 6–2.

First MLB All Star Game Shutout
July 9, 1940, at St. Louis, 4–0
Derringer (National League) WP; Ruffing (American League) LP

First NL Interleague Shutout
June 14, 1997, at Montreal, 1–0*
Martinez (Montreal) WP; Thompson (Detroit) LP
*This was also the first 1–0 game in Interleague play

First AL Interleague Shutout
June 16, 1997, at Milwaukee, 1–0
Wickman (Milwaukee) WP; Alan Benes (St. Louis) LP

First AL Interleague No-Hitter
July 18, 1999, at New York
Cone (New York) WP; J. Vazquez (Montreal) LP

First MLB Tie-Breaker Shutout
Game 2, October 2, 1951 at Brooklyn, 10–0
Labine (Brooklyn) WP; Jones (New York) LP

First NL Post-Season Playoffs Shutout
Game 1, NLCS, October 3, 1970 at Pittsburgh, 3–0 (10 innings)
Nolan (Cincinnati) WP; Ellis (Pittsburgh) LP

First AL Post-Season Playoffs Shutout*
Game 2 ALCS, October 4, 1969 at Baltimore, 1–0 (11 innings)
McNally (Baltimore) WP; Boswell (Minnesota) LP
*This was also the first 1–0 game in Post Season Playoffs history.

First MLB Post-Season Playoffs No-Hitter
Game 1, NLDS, October 6, 2010 at Philadelphia, 4–0
Halladay (Philadelphia) WP; Volquez (Cincinnati) LP

First NL Shutout in Canada
April 29, 1969 at Montreal, 2–0
Ryan (New York) WP; Grant (Montreal) LP

First AL Shutout in Canada
April 24, 1977 at Toronto, 9–0
Jenkins (Boston) WP; Singer (Toronto) LP

First MLB World Series Shutout*
October 2, 1903 at Boston, 3–0
Dinneen (Boston, AL) WP; Leever (Pittsburgh, NL) LP

*19th century Championships: at Providence, October 23, 1884, 6–0
Radbourn (Providence) WP; Keefe (New York) LP*

19th century Championships, Scoreless tie, 11 innings:
at Boston, October 17, 1892
Young (Cleveland) and Stivetts (Boston)

First MLB World Series 1–0 Game
Game 4, October 13, 1905 at New York
McGinnity (New York, NL) WP; Plank (Philadelphia, AL) LP

First MLB World Series No-Hitter (Perfect Game)
Game 5, October 8, 1956 at New York, 2–0
Larsen (New York AL) WP; Maglie (Brooklyn, NL) LP

Appendix B

From 50' to 60'6"

Bill Deane, baseball historian and research consultant at baseball's Hall of Fame in Cooperstown, New York, has discussed the 60'6" distance from the pitcher's box to the center of home plate, suggesting that the distance from which the pitcher actually releases the ball under the present regulations is really *not* that much farther than the 1892 distance of 50'.

This is his reasoning: Prior to 1893, the front of the pitcher's plate was set into a rectangular box 50' away from the center of home plate, but the pitcher actually began his delivery to home base 55'6" away, at the back of the pitcher's box (along its rear line). However, since home plate was set *inside* the diamond, the center of home base was really 8½ inches *closer* from the point our present-day distance is measured. That adjustment makes our present day measurement slightly more than 7 percent farther than the pre-1893 distance. Consequently, while much is made of the pitching and hitting adjustments players had to make from 1892 to 1893, those adjustments were actually less demanding than supposed.

While there was a spike in hitting statistics, it didn't last very long. Batters and pitchers soon settled into their own "comfort zones" with the new measurements.

Appendix C

Crushed and Chicagoed

Since June 21, 1871, there have been 36 games in which major league teams have scored 18 or more runs while holding their opponents scoreless. The scores follow.

League	Date/Site	Winner/Score/Loser	Pitchers (WP/LP)
NA	6/21/1871, Boston	Boston (**21**)–Fort Wayne	Spalding/Mathews
NA	5/9/1872, Brooklyn	Boston (**20**)–Brooklyn	Spalding/McDermott
NA	6/8/1872, Philadelphia	Phila (**19**)–New York	McBride/Cummings
NA	6/27/1873, Baltimore	Canaries (**20**)–Marylands	Cummings/Stratton
NA	10/1/1874, Boston	Boston (**29**)–Brooklyn*	Spalding/Bond
NA	5/1/1875, Washington	Boston (**24**)–Washington	Spalding/Stearns
NA	5/3/1875, Washington	Phila (**21**)–Washington	McBride/Stearns
NA	6/9/1875, Philadelphia	Phila (**23**)–Brooklyn	McBride/Cassidy
NA	10/4/1875, New Haven	Hartford (**18**)–New Haven	Cummings/Nichols
AA	7/6/1883, Cincinnati	Cincinnati (**23**)–Baltimore	White/Henderson
AA	8/3/1886, Pittsburgh	Pittsburgh (**18**)–Brooklyn	Morris/Terry
AA	8/15/1886, St. Louis	St. Louis (**19**)–Brooklyn	Foutz/Terry
AA	5/7/1889, St. Louis	St. Louis (**21**)–Columbus	King/Mays
AA	8/10/1889, Cincinnati	Cincinnati (**20**)–Baltimore	Duryea/Foreman
PL	7/16/1890, Boston	Boston (**19**)–Buffalo	Gumbert/Cotter
PL	8/29/1890, Boston	Boston (**18**)–Pittsburgh	Radbourn/Maul
NL	7/20/1876, Chicago	Chicago (**18**)–Louisville	Spalding/Devlin
NL	8/21/1883, Providence	Providence (**28**)–Philadelphia	Radbourn/Hagan
NL	8/4/1884, Detroit	Detroit (**18**)–Buffalo†	Galvin/Meinke
NL	5/28/1886, Washington	Chicago (**20**)–Washington	McCormick/Crane
NL	6/28/1887, Indianapolis	Philadelphia (**24**)–Indianapolis	Ferguson/Morrison
NL	7/8/1896, Pittsburgh	Pittsburgh (**19**)–Washington	Hughey/Mercer
NL	6/7/1906, New York	Chicago (**19**)–New York	Pfiester/Mathewson
NL	7/11/1910, Pittsburgh	Philadelphia (**18**)–Pittsburgh	McQuillan/Leifield
NL	8/10/1930, Cincinnati	Phila (**18**)–Cincinnati	Willoughby/Wysong
NL	7/14/1934, Philadelphia	Philadelphia (**18**)–Cincinnati	Hansen/Brennan
AL	8/13/1939, Philadelphia	New York (**21**)–Philadelphia	Ruffing/Pippen
NL	6/10/1944, Cincinnati	St. Louis (**18**)–Cincinnati	M. Cooper/Lohrman
NL	8/3/1961, St. Louis	Pittsburgh (**19**)–St. Louis	Haddix/Cicotte

Appendix C: Crushed and Chicagoed 193

League	Date/Site	Winner/Score/Loser	Pitchers (WP/LP)
NL	8/8/1965, Cincinnati	Cincinnati (**18**)–Los Angeles	Maloney/Drysdale
NL	4/22/2010, Pittsburgh	Milwaukee (**20**)–Pittsburgh	Wolf/McCutchen
AL	7/10/1936, New York	New York (**18**)–Cleveland	Ruffing/C. Brown
AL	4/30/1950, Boston	Boston (**19**)–Philadelphia	Dobson/Fowler
AL	5/18/1955, Boston	Cleveland (**19**)–Boston	Score/Nixon
AL	5/10/2002, Anaheim	Anaheim (**19**)–Chicago	Schoeneweis/Wright
AL	8/31/2004, New York	Cleveland (**22**)–New York	Westbrook/Vazquez

*29–0 is the greatest margin recorded in baseball's shutout history.
†This 18–0 shutout game was also a No-Hit Game.

Selected Bibliography

Achorn, Edward. *Fifty-Nine in '84.* New York: Smithsonian Books, 2002.

Acta Sports. *The Bill James Handbook, 2011.* Chicago: Acta, 2010.

Anderson, David. *More Than Merkle.* Lincoln: University of Nebraska Press, 2000.

Attiyeh, Mike, *Who Was Traded for Lefty Grove?* Baltimore: Johns Hopkins University Press, 2002.

Bready, James H. *Baseball in Baltimore*: Baltimore: Johns Hopkins University Press, 1998.

Browning, Reed. *Cy Young: A Baseball Life.* Boston: University of Massachusetts Press, 2000.

Buckley, James, Jr., and Phil Pepe. *Unhittable.* Chicago: Triumph Books, 2004.

Cairns, Bob. *Pen Men.* New York: St. Martin's Press, 1992.

Ceresi, Frank, and Mark Rucker with Carol McMains. *Baseball in Washington, D.C.* Charleston, SC: Arcadia, 2002.

Clark, Dick, and Larry Lester, eds. *The Negro Leagues Book.* Cleveland: SABR, 1994.

Coffey, Michael. *27 Men Out.* New York: Atria Books, 2004.

Darling, Ron, with Dan Paisner. *The Complete Game.* New York: Alfred A. Knopf, 2009.

Dorfman, H. A., and Karl Kuhel. *The Mental Game of Baseball*, 3d ed. South Bend, IN: Diamond Communications, 2002.

Enders, Eric. *Baseball's Greatest Games.* Minnetonka, MN: MLB Insiders Club, 2008.

Feller, Bob, with Bill Gilbert. *Now Pitching, Bob Feller.* New York: Birch Lane Press, 1990.

Freyer, John, and Mark Rucker. *Chicago Aces.* Chicago: Arcadia, 2005.

Gibson, Bob, and Reggie Jackson with Lonnie Wheeler. *Sixty Feet, Six Inches.* New York: Doubleday, 2009.

Gillette, Gary, and Pete Palmer, eds. *The ESPN Baseball Encyclopedia*, 5th ed. New York: Sterling, 2008.

Goldenbock, Peter, *Wrigleyville*, St. Martin's Griffin, New York, 1999.

Goldstein, Warren. *Playing for Keeps.* Ithaca: Cornell University Press, 1989.

Grayson, Harry. *They Played the Game.* New York: A. S. Barnes, 1944.

Hageman, Bill. *Baseball Between the Wars.* Chicago: Contemporary Books, 2001.

Helyar, John. *Lords of the Realm.* New York: Random House, 1995.

Holtzman, Jerome, and George Vass. *Baseball, Chicago Style.* Chicago: Bonus Books, 2001.

Holway, John. *The Complete Book of Baseball's Negro Leagues.* Fern Park, LA: Hastings House, 2001.

Honig, Donald. *The October Heroes.* Lincoln: University of Nebraska Press, 1984.

House, Tom. *The Winning Pitcher.* Chicago: Contemporary Books, 1988.

James, Bill. *The Bill James Gold Mine.* Skokie, IL: Acta, 2010.

_____. *The Bill James Historical Abstract.* New York: Villard Books, 1985.

_____, and Rob Neyer. *The Neyer/James Guide to Pitchers.* New York: Fireside, 2004.

Johnson, Randy, with Jim Rosenthal. *Randy*

Johnson's Power Pitching. New York: Three Rivers Press, 2003.
Jordan, Pat. *Pitching*. New York: Harper and Row, 1985.
Kahn, Roger. *The Head Game*. New York: Harcourt, 2000.
Kaplan, Jim. *Lefty Grove: An American Original*. Cleveland: SABR, 2000.
Kaufman, James C., and Alan S. Kaufman. *The Worst Baseball Pitchers of All Time*. Jefferson, NC: McFarland, 1993.
Kavanagh, Jack. *Grover Cleveland Alexander*. New York: Chelsea House, 1990.
Kennedy, MacLean, *The Great Teams of Baseball*. St. Louis: Sporting News, 1928; reprint edition of 1988.
Keri, Jonah, ed. *Baseball Between the Numbers*. New York: Perseus Book Group, 2007.
Klima, John. *Pitched Battle*. Jefferson, NC: McFarland, 2002.
Lanigan, Ernest. *The Baseball Cyclopedia*. New York: Baseball Magazine Company, 1922.
Larsen, Don, with Mark Shaw. *The Perfect Yankee*. Champaign, IL: Sagamore, 2001.
Leavy, Jane. *Sandy Koufax: A Lefty's Legacy*. New York: HarperCollins, 2002.
Leventhal, Josh. *The World Series*. New York: Black Dog and Leventhal, 2001.
Lieb, Fred. *The Baltimore Orioles*. New York: G.P. Putnam's Sons, 1955.
Longert, Scott. *Addie Joss*. Cleveland: SABR, 1998.
Mayer, Ronald A. *Perfect! Biographies and Lifetime Statistics of 14 Pitchers of "Perfect" Baseball Games, with Summaries and Boxscores*. Jefferson, NC: McFarland, 1991.
Mazzone, Leo. *Pitch Like a Pro*. New York: St. Martin's Griffin, 1999.
McCollister, John. *The Best Baseball Games Ever Played*. New York: Citadel Press, 2002.
Melville, Tom. *Early Baseball and the Rise of the National League*. Jefferson, NC: McFarland, 2001.
Myers, Doug, and Mark Gola. *The Complete Book of Pitching*. Chicago: Contemporary Books, 2000.
Nemec, David, with Scott Flatow. *Great Baseball Feats, Facts and Firsts*. New York: Signet, 2010.
_____. *The Great Encyclopedia of 19th Century Major League Baseball*. New York: Donald L. Fine, 1997.
Neyer, Rob, and Bill James. *The Neyer/James Book of Pitchers*. New York: Simon and Schuster, 2004.
Okkenen, Marc. *The Federal League of 1914–1915*. Cleveland: SABR, 1989.
Palacios, Oscar. *Diamond Diagrams*. Skokie, IL: STATS Pub. Co., 1997.
Peterson, Robert. *Only the Ball Was White*. New York: Oxford University Press, 1970.
Pietrusza, David, Matthew Silverman, and Michael Gershman, eds. *Baseball: The Biographical Encyclopedia*. Kingston, NY: Total/Sports Illustrated, 2000.
Poremba, David. *Baseball in Detroit, 1886–1968*. Charleston, SC: Arcadia, 1998.
Rader, Benjamin. *Baseball: A History of America's Game*. Urbana: University of Illnois Press, 1992.
Rains, Rob, ed. *Nolan Ryan: From Alvin to Cooperstown*. St. Louis: Sporting News, 1999.
Ritter, Lawrence. *The Glory of Their Times*. New York: William Morrow, 1984.
Roth, Allan, ed. *1970 Who's Who in Baseball*. New York: Harris Press, 1970.
Segar, Charles, ed. *The 75th Anniversary of the National League*. New York: Jay, 1951.
Snyder, John. *Red Sox Journal*. Cincinnati: Emmis Books, 2006.
Solomon, Burt. *The Baseball Timeline*. New York: DK, 2001.
Spink, Alfred H. *The National Game*. St. Louis: National Game Publishing Company, 1910.
Stewart, Wayne. *Pitching Secrets of the Pros*. New York: McGraw-Hill, 2004.
Sugar, Bert Randolph, ed. *The Baseball Maniac's Almanac*, 2d ed. New York: Skyhouse, 2010.
Thomas, Henry W. *Walter Johnson: Baseball's Big Train*. Lincoln: University of Nebraska Press, 2005.
Thorn, John, ed. *The National Pastime*, New York: Warner, 1981.
Thorn, John, and John Holway. *The Pitcher*. New York: Prentice-Hall, 1987.

Trucks, Rob. *The Catcher.* Cincinnati: Emmis Books, 2005.
Wendell, Tim. *High Heat.* Cambridge, MA: DaCapo Press, 2010, 2011.
Wilbert, Warren N. *A Cunning Kind of Play.* Jefferson, NC: McFarland, 2002.
_____. *What Makes an Elite Pitcher?* Jefferson, NC: McFarland, 2003.
Will, George. *Bunts.* New York: Scribner's, 1998.
Williams, Peter. *When the Giants Were the Giants.* Chapel Hill, NC: Algonquin Books, 1994.
Wright, Marshall. *Nineteenth Century Baseball.* Jefferson, NC: McFarland, 1996.

Periodical Sources

Baseball Digest
Baseball Research Journal
Boston Globe
Chicago Sun Times
Chicago Tribune
ESPN: The Magazine
New York Clipper
New York Times
St. Louis Post Dispatch
Sporting Life
The Sporting News
Sports Illustrated

Website Resources

baseballguru.com
baseballhalloffame.org
baseballhistorypodcast.com
baseballlibrary.com
baseball-reference.com
baywell.ne.jp
bb-almanac.com
chicagonow.com
hardballtimes.com
hickocksports.com
japaneseballplayers.com
japantimes.co.jp
mlb.com
mlbblogbuzz.com
nationalpastime.com
negroleaguebaseball.com
retrosheet.org
sabr.org
snopes.com

Name Index

Aaron, Hank 152, 177–178
Abbott, Jim 146–147, 182
Acre, Mark 79
Adams, Babe 43
Adams, Buster 53
Adcock, Joe 177
Agee, Tommy 2, 168
Ainsmith, Eddie 126
Alexander, Doyle 180
Alexander, Grover, "Pete" 31, 38, 43–44, 47, 58, 60, 67, 108, 123–126, 152, 158–161, 163–165, 174
Alfonzo, Edgar 126–127
Allen, Babe 43
Allen, Dave 42
Allen, John 52
Allen, Nick 189
Alomar, Roberto 145–146
Alou, Matty 143
Alston, Walter 22
Altrock, Nick 41, 115, 121, 176, 184
Amoros, Sandy 22
Anderson, Brian 181
Anderson, Dave 42
Anderson, Fred 97, 101
Andujar, Juan 24
Anson, Adrian, "Cap" 17, 87
Antonelli, Johnny 56, 59
Aparicio, Luis 118
Appier, Kevin 181
Appling, Luke 140
Arnold, Chris 176
Asgburn, Richie 58
Aspromonte, Bob 2, 64
Atkins, Tommy 120
Atkinson, William, "Bill" 90–91
Atz, Jake 121
Auker, Eldon 184
Autry, Gene 168
Avery, Steve 181, 191

Baerga, Carlos 147
Bagby, Joe, Sr. 184
Bagwell, Jeff 148
Bahnsen, Stan 65
Bailey, Bill 101
Bakeley, Edward 90–91
Baker, Frank 24, 118–120, 124
Baldwin, Marcus, "Fido" 92–93, 180, 188
Bankhead, Sam 103
Bannister, Floyd 181
Barker, Len 153
Barlick, Al 178
Barnes, Ross 17, 34
Baro, Bernardo 106
Barry, Jack 118–120
Barston, Charles 93
Bauer, Hank 59, 176
Beaumont, Clarence, "Ginger" 117
Bechtel, George 16
Beck, Rod 6
Beckett, Josh 24, 182
Behrmann, Hank 57
Belanger, Mark 24
Belinsky, Bo 142
Bell, "Cool Papa" 103–104
Belle, Albert 147
Bender, Albert, "Chief" 24, 39, 95, 99–100, 118–120, 124, 159, 172, 177
Benes, Alan 189
Benes, Andy 181
Benitez, Armando 24, 181
Bentley, Cy 14
Berger, Wally 138
Berra, L., "Yogi" 22, 25, 59, 176
Berry, Charlie 178
Besho, Takehiko 108
Billingham, Jack 24, 185
Black, Bob 188
Blackburn, Ron 182

Blass, Steve 65
Blong, Joe 16–17, 157, 182
Blue, Vida 180
Bluege, Ossie 24
Blyleven, Bert 67, 108, 168–171
Bochy, Bruce 80
Boddicker, Mike 181
Bolin, Bob 65–66
Bond, Tommy 15–16, 18, 24, 34–35, 38, 192
Bonds, Barry 72
Borbon, Pedro 24
Borden, Joe 130, 171, 187
Borowy, Hank 54
Boswell, Andy 40
Boswell, Ken 168, 180
Boudreau, Lou 58, 140
Bouton, Jim 184
Bowerman, Frank 133
Boyle, Henry 90–91, 157, 188
Bracken, Jack 123
Braden, Dallas 153
Bradley, George 16–18, 31, 34–35, 43, 91, 157, 187–188
Brainard, Asa 14–15
Bransfield, William, "Kitty" 117
Brantley, Cliff 183
Brecheen, Harry, "The Cat" 56, 142
Breitenstein, Ted 37, 87–88, 133
Brenly, Bob 70
Bresnahan, Roger 25
Brewer, Chet 103, 107
Bridwell, Al 43
Britt, Jim 14
Brock, Lou 2
Brouthers, Dan 24
Brown, Clint 141, 193
Brown, Jim 90–91

199

Name Index

Brown, Larry 103
Brown, Mordecai 39, 42, 67, 95–96, 99, 108, 111, 115–116, 171, 174–175, 177
Browning, Tom 149, 157
Bruton, Bill 176
Buehrle, Mark 156
Buffinton, Charles 36, 90, 92
Bumgarner, Madison 9
Bunning, Jim 61, 63, 65, 132, 157, 167–168, 174
Burdette, Lew 149
Burdock, Jack 24
Burke, Lefty 26, 117
Burns, Britt 161
Burns, Dick 188
Burns, Jim 90
Burris, Ray 181
Byrne, Bobby 43

Caballero, Ralph, "Putsy" 58
Cain, Matt 182
Caldwell, Ray 41, 181
Callahan, Nixey 37, 188
Camnitz, Howie 24, 40, 124
Campanella, Roy 27, 55
Campbell, Hugh 14
Campbell, Vincent 43
Cannizzaro, Chris 15, 143
Cano, Robinson 129
Carey, Andy 13, 177
Carey, Max 24, 43
Carlton, Steve 63, 66–67, 108, 158, 171, 174–176, 181
Carrick, "Doughnut Bill" 37
Carter, Gary 10, 25
Carter, Joe 146
Carter, Paul 12, 107
Cassidy, Scott 16, 192
Castleman, Foster 59
Chamberlain, "Ice Box" 89, 180
Chance, Dean 65
Chance, Frank 114–115, 117
Chandler, Spud 52, 57
Chaney, Larry 128
Chapman, Ben 140
Charleston, Oscar 103
Chase, Hal 134
Chesbro, Jack 117, 172
Church, Bubba 58
Cicotte, Eddie 39, 122, 192
Clarke, Fred 43, 117–118
Clarkson, John 38, 165, 180
Clay, Dain 57
Clemens, Roger 83, 181–182
Clinton, Jim 16–17
Coakley, Andy 176, 184
Cochrane, Mickey 25–27
Cockrell, Phil 106

Coffman, Dick 126
Coleman, Joe 180
Coleman, Vince 24
Collins, Ed 24, 118
Collins, Ray 122
Colon, Bartolo 182
Comiskey, Charlie 88, 93, 133
Concepcion, Davey 24
Coombs, Jack 24, 118, 159, 163, 165
Cooper, Andy 107
Cooper, Army 107
Cooper, Morton 52, 56, 192
Corbett, Sherman 180
Corbit, Claude 57
Corcoran, Larry 132
Cormier, Rheal 6
Cotter, Dan 192
Cox, Casey 181
Craft, Harry 139
Craig, Roger 145, 184
Cramer, Roger, "Doc" 25, 48
Crandall, Del 177
Crane, Cannonball 85, 90, 192
Crawford, Sam 42
Creighton, Jim 7
Crisp, Cocoa 24
Cronin, Joe 24
Cross, Monte 165
Crowder, Alvin, "Doc" 24
Crutchfield, Jimmy 103
Cueto, Bert 182
Cullop, Nick 100–101, 189
Culp, Ray 65
Cunningham, Burt 93
Cuppy, Nig 180, 188
Currie, Rube 107
Cushman, Ed 90

Daily, Hugh 36, 90–91, 147, 149, 188
Dalrymple, Abner 87
Danks, John 182
Darling, John 182
Darwin, Bobby 169
Darwin, Danny 70, 145
Davenport, Dave 101
Davis, George 121, 142
Davis, Harry 118, 120
Day, Leon 107
Dean, Charles, "Dory" 35
Dean, Jay H., "Dizzy" 48–50, 104, 174, 182, 184
Dean, Paul 48
Deane, Bill 191
DeCinces, Doug 71
De la Cruz, Fernando 6

Derrick, Claud 120
Derringer, Paul 138, 183, 189
Deshaies, Jim 145
Devlin, Jim 16–17, 34–35, 187, 192
Dickey, Bill 27
Dickson, Murray 56, 177–178
Dierker, Larry 1–2
Dinneen, Bill 122, 184, 190
Dizmukes, Dizzy 106
Dobson, Joe 193
Doby, Larry 57–58
Donahue, Bill 42
Donahue, Jiggs 120–121
Donlin, Mike 43
Dotel, Octavio 130, 148
Doyle, Dennis 168
Doyle, Larry 134
Drabek, Doug 181
Dravecky, Dave 181
Drysdale, Don 63, 65, 167, 176, 183–184, 193
Duffy, Hugh 93
Duryea, Jesse 88, 192
Dygert, Jimmy 120
Dykes, Jimmy 118
Dylan, Bob 142

Eason, Malcom, "Kid" 43
Eckersley, Dennis 144, 150, 169
Edwards, Bruce 56
Egan, Aloysius, "Wish" 188
Eller, Hod 44, 126
Ellis, Dock 180
Enatsu, Yutaka 109–110, 114
Erickson, Scott 181
Esper, Charles, "Duke" 180
Evers, John 115, 117
Ewing, Buck 25

Faatz, Jay 93
Faber, Urban, "Red" 50, 120, 160
Falkenberg, Guy 95–98, 101
Feller, Bob 52, 54, 139–141, 146, 149, 183
Ferguson, Bob 24
Ferguson, Charles 149, 192
Ferrell, Rick 137–138
Ferrell, Wes 26, 50, 137
Fidrych, Mark 69
Fielder, Cecil 9
Figueroa, Ed 68
Fingers, Rollie 69
Fisher, Cherokee 13–17, 91
Fisk, Carlton 27
Flaherty, John, "Red" 178

Name Index

Flick, Elmer 36
Force, Bill 106
Ford, E., "Whitey" 25, 56, 177, 183–184
Ford, Russ 95–97
Foreman, Frank 88, 192
Forsch, Bob 24, 181
Foster, George 123
Foster, Willie 103
Foutz, Dave 86, 88, 180, 192
Fowler, Dick 149
Fox, Nellie 23
Foxx, Jimmie 47, 118
Frey, Lonnie 53, 56
Friend, Bob 56, 184
Frisch, Frankie 47
Froemming, Bruce 94, 131
Fujimoto, Hideo 108–109
Furillo, Carl 56

Galan, Augie 56
Galarraga, Andres 128
Galvin, Jim, "Pud" 17, 36, 38, 67, 90, 92–93, 132, 149, 158, 171–172
Garces, Rich 6
Garcia, Freddy 182, 185
Garcia, Mike 56
Garciaparra, Nomar 6
Gardner, Mark 181
Garver, Ned 60
Gaston, Milt 129
Geggus, Charlie 90
Gehrig, Lou 47, 68
Geisel, Harry, "Al" 141
Gentry, Russ 185
Geronimo, Cesar 24
Gessler, Henry, "Doc" 115, 124
Getz, Gus 134
Getzien, Charles 180
Gibson, George 24
Gibson, Josh 101
Gibson, Robert, "Bob" 27, 61, 65–67, 171, 173, 176, 184–185
Glavine, Tom 82–83, 127, 181–182, 185
Gleason, Bill 24
Gola, Mark 28
Golenbeck, Peter 114
Gomez, John 2
Gooden, Dwight 25, 71, 83, 181
Goodman, Ival 138
Gorman, Tom 178
Gossage, Rich, "Goose" 61–62, 170
Gray, Pete 147
Greason, John 14

Gregg, Hal 57
Grier, Claude 107
Griffith, Clark 37, 120, 122, 136
Grimes, Burleigh 50, 161–162, 184
Groom, Bob 43, 79
Grote, Jerry 27
Grove, Robert M., "Lefty" 25–26, 47–48, 50, 118, 138, 184
Guillen, Ozzie 139
Gullett, Don 180
Gumbert, Addison 192
Gumbert, Harry 56–57
Gumbert, Randy 57
Gumbert, Ray 53

Haas, Bert 56
Haddix, Harry 56, 134, 192
Haddock, George 89, 91, 133
Hagan, Art 192
Hahn, Ed 121
Hahn, Frank 37
Haines, Jesse 47, 184
Hairston, Jerry 70
Halladay, Roy 7, 10, 83, 128, 130, 149–151, 153, 157
Hammaker, Atlee 181
Hample, Zack 75
Hampton, Mike 182
Hanson, Erik 181
Hanson, Roy, "Snipe" 192
Harden, Rich 182
Harder, Mel 50
Harper, Harry 136
Harrelson, Bud 64
Harris, Stanley, "Bucky" 136–137
Harris, Vic 103
Hartnett, Charles, "Gabby" 27, 49
Hartsel, Fred, "Topsy" 120
Hawley, Pink 37
Head, Ed 142
Heath, Jeff 54, 140
Hecker, Guy 36, 85–87
Hegan, Jim 27
Heilmann, Harry 46
Hemming, George 157
Hemsley, Rollie 140–141
Henderson, Hardie 88, 192
Henderson, Rickey 24, 127, 145–146
Hendley, Bob 154
Hendrix, Claude 24, 96, 101, 125
Hentgen, Pat 182
Hernandez, "El Duque" 181
Herr, Tom 24

Herring, Art 56–57
Hershiser, Orel 24, 77, 83
Hickman, Charlie 91
Hill, Ken 181
Hitchcock, Sterling 181
Hodges, Gil 22, 64
Hodnett, Charlie 90
Hofman, Arthur, "Solly" 115
Hogg, "Wild Bill" 155
Holloman, Alva "Bobo" 89, 141–142
Holtzman, Ken 149, 180
Honig, Donald 118
Hooper, Harry 43
Horan, Patrick 90–91
Hornsby, Rogers 46–47
Horton, Willie 65, 69
Hough, Charlie 71
Houser, Ben 120
Howard, Elston 177
Howe, Steve 78–79
Howell, Harry 155, 180
Howell, Jay 183
Hoyt, Waite 47, 159–160, 184
Hubbell, Carl, "The Meal Ticket" 47, 49–50, 162
Hudson, Johnny 49
Huggins, Miller 48
Hughes, "Long Tom" 155
Hughes, Sammy 103
Hughey, Jim, "Cold Water" 31, 192
Hunt, Ron 174
Hunter, Jim, "Catfish" 151, 153
Hurst, Bruce 185

Inao, Kazuhisa 109
Isringhausen, Jason 182

Jackowski, Bill 178
Jackson, Edwin 128, 130, 149, 181
Jackson, George 43
Jackson, Reggie 71
James, "Big Bill" 125, 184
Jenkins, Fergie 66, 168, 190
Jennings, Hugh 24
Jestadt, Garry 131
John, Tommy 63, 65–66, 70, 77, 180
Johnson, Jing 44
Johnson, Ken 149
Johnson, Walter 38, 41, 43, 47, 60, 67, 87, 104, 108, 123–126, 134–137, 149, 158–160, 165, 171–173
Johnstone, Jim 43
Jones, Andruw 128

Name Index

Jones, B.J. 181
Jones, Fielder 100, 124, 178
Jones, "Sad Sam" 182, 189
Jones, "Slim" 103–104
Joss, Addie 7, 39, 42, 124, 132, 149, 153, 155–157, 159–160, 165, 172–173

Kaat, Jim 63, 184
Kaline, Al 65
Kaneda, Masaichi 108
Kaufman, Alan 98–99
Kaufman, James 98–99
Keefe, Tim 38, 85, 91–92, 172, 180, 190
Keeler, Willie 24
Kekich, Mike 66
Keltner, Ken 140
Kennedy, Bob 140
Kennedy, MacLean 117
Kerfeld, Charles 145
Key, Jimmy 146, 181
Kilroy, Matt 86
Kincannon, Harry 103
King, Charles, "Silver" 85–86, 88, 91–94, 157, 180, 188, 192
Kinsler, Ian 81
Kirke, Jay 43
Kison, Bruce 180
Kitson, Frank 37
Klem, Bill 94
Klima, John 154
Kling, John 115
Klippstein, John 58
Knapp, Chris 181,
Knetzer, Elmer 96, 101, 157
Koenecke, Ken 46
Kolls, Lou 141
Konstanty, Jim 184
Koob, Ernie 142, 149
Koosman, Jerry 63, 65
Kopf, Larry 134
Koufax, "Sandy" 61, 63, 131, 149, 151, 153–154, 167, 173–174, 182, 184
Koyama, Masaaki 108
Kralick, Jack 150
Kramer, Jack 53
Krause, Harry 118, 120
Kubek, Tony 177–178
Kucks, John 177–178
Kuhel, Joe 140–141
Kuroda, Hiroki 182

Labine, Clem 182–183
Lackey, John 182
Lafitte, Ed 100–101
Lajoie, Larry 36, 155
Landis, Jim 23, 188

Landis, Judge K. 140
Landis, Sam 157
Langston, Mark 150
Lapp, Jack 120
Larsen, Don 7, 130, 144, 152–154, 157, 183, 190
Latos, Brad 83
Lavagetto, Harry, "Cookie" 56
Law, Vernon 183
Lazzeri, Tony 152, 162
Leach, Tommy 43, 117
Lee, "Big Bill" 48
Lee, Clifton 182
Lee, Watty 41, 188
Leever, Sam 117–118, 184, 190
LeFlore, Ron 69
Leifeld, Lefty 118, 192
Leiter, Al 24, 126, 181–182
Lemon, Bob 56, 143
Leonard, Dennis 181
Leonard, Hub 122–123
Lester, Jon 182
Lewis, Buddy 57
Lewis, Franklin 172
Lidge, Brad 130, 142, 182, 185
Lima, Jose 128, 182
Lincecum, Tim 146
Livingston, Paddy 120
Lofton, Kenny 147
Loiaza, Estaban 181
Lolich, Mickey 63
Lollar, Sherman 23
Longert, Scott 156
Lopat, Eddie 56
Lopez, Al 75, 140
Lord, Bris 120
Lowe, Derek 182
Lucas, Henry V. 89
Luff, Henry 6
Lukon, Ed 56
Lumpe, Jerry 178
Lundgren, Carl 116
Lundy, Dick 103
Lyons, Ted 47, 50, 137

Mack, Connie 25–26, 120, 136, 99–100, 118
Mack, Roy 140–141
Macullar, Jimmy 87
Maddux, Greg 27–20, 127–128, 182
Maglie, Sal 56, 190
Mails, Duster 184
Main, Alex 101
Maldonado, Candy 147
Maloney, Jim 149, 193
Manning, Jack 15
Mantle, Mickey 152, 177–179

Manush, Heinie 24
Marberry, Firpo 24
Marcum, John 48
Marichal, Juan 61, 63, 66–67, 149, 166, 171, 173–175
Marquard, Rube 43, 160, 162
Marshall, Max 53
Martina, Joe 160
Martinez, Dennis 131–132, 151, 155, 157, 181, 189
Martinez, Pedro 5–6, 80–81, 83, 128, 146, 174
Martinez, Tino 79
Martinez, Tippy 181
Mashore, Damon 79
Mathews, Bobby 8–10, 13–18, 34–36, 187, 192
Mathews, Eddie 177–179
Mathewson, Christy 25, 39, 41–42, 47, 67, 79, 123, 125–126, 134, 162–163, 149, 175–177, 184
Matlack, Jon 180
Matsui, Hideo 148
Matsuzaka, Daisuke 24, 182
Maul, Al 192
Mayberry, John 3, 160
Mays, Al 88
Mays, Carl 122–123
Mays, Willie 152, 166, 171, 176
McAllister, Lewis, "Port" 123
McAndrew, Jim 66
McAuliffe, Don 65
McBride, George 14–16, 34, 192
McCahan, John, "Sadie" 24
McCarthy, Alex 24, 43
McCarthy, Tom 90, 124
McClure, Bob 107
McCollister, John 166
McConnell, George, "Slats" 125
McCormick, Frank 138
McCormick, Harry 157
McCormick, Jim 26, 38, 90, 115, 180, 188
McCormick, Mike 180
McCovey, Willie 171
McCutcheon, Daniel 193
McDermott, Joe 14, 192
McDonald, Gil 22, 152
McDowell, Sam, "Sudden Sam" 65
McGee, Willie 24
McGinnis, George, "Jumbo" 86, 118, 133
McGinnity, Joe 36, 39, 116, 124, 157, 165, 175, 188, 190

Name Index

McGowan, Bill 141
McGraw, John 24, 114, 162, 175
McGraw, Tug 171, 181
McGregor, Scott 181
McGwire, Mark 72
McIntyre, Frank 42
McKechnie, Bill 43, 95, 138–139
McLain, Denny 65–66, 176, 185
McLaughlin, Frank 90
McMahan, John, "Sadie" 24
McNair, Eric 140
McNally, Dave 24, 65, 180, 184, 189
McQuillan, George 133, 192
McWilliams, Larry 170
Medwick, Joe, "Ducky" 57
Meekin, Jouett 88
Melillo, Oscar 26
Mendez, Jose 1105–106
Menke, Denis 2
Mercer, Win 37, 192
Mercker, Kent 149
Merkle, Fred 42, 126, 134
Merritt, George 117
Meyers, Doug 28
Milan, Felix 3
Miller, Bob 64
Miller, John 43
Miller, Wade 148
Millwood, Kevin 128, 149
Miltner, Terrence 145
Mizell, Wilmer 184
Mlicki, Dave 182
Mogridge, George 44, 160
Monbouquette, Bill 150
Moore, Jimmy 26
Moran, Pat 115
Morgan, Cy 118–120
Morgan, Dan 17
Morgan, Joe 24
Morris, Ed 86, 88, 192
Morris, Jack 185
Morrison, Mike 192
Morris, Matt 128, 182
Moseley, Earl 101
Moyer, Dennis 128
Moyer, Jamie 77
Mullin, George 176
Munro, Pete 148
Munson, Thurman 68
Murayama, Minoru 108, 110
Murphy, Danny 23, 120, 162
Murphy, John 90
Mussina, Mike 82–83, 182
Myers, Buddy 24

Nagashima, Shigeo 109
Nagy, Steve 188

Nash, Jim 65
Neagle, Denny 181
Nehf, Artie 184
Neid, David 79
Nemec, David 31, 47, 85
Newcombe, Don 55–56, 184
Newhouser, "Prince Hal" 52–54–56
Newsom, Louis, "Bobo" 52
Newton, Doc 37
Nichols, Charles, "Kid" 44, 163–165, 190, 192
Nichols, Fred, "Tricky" 15–17
Niekro, Phil 12, 77, 168, 171, 174, 176
Nixon, Willard 193
Nolan, Edward, "The Only" 90
Nolan, Gary 24
Nops, Jerry 37
Norris, Mike 181
North, Billy 69

O'Day, Hank 94
Odom, John, "Blue Moon" 180, 195
Ogden, Warren, "Curly" 160
Ogea, Chad 181
Oldring, Rube 118, 120
Olerud, John 146
O'Neill, Tip 93
Ordonez, Rey 24
Ortiz, Jose de Jesus 148
Osborne, Donovan 181
Osteen, Champ 40
Osteen, Claude 3, 170–171, 184
Oswalt, Roy 83, 130, 148
O'Toole, Jim 54
Overall, Orval 115–116
Owen, Frank 41, 121–122, 124, 155
Owens, Jesse 139

Packard, Gene 100–101
Pafko, Andy 177
Paige, Leroy, "Satchel" 102–105, 107, 141–142
Palmer, Jim 24, 61, 64–68, 169, 180, 184
Palmer, Pete 111
Papelbon, Jonathan 24
Pappas, Milt 130–131
Parent, Fred 101
Parks, Bill 17
Parnell, Red 103
Parris, Steve 182
Parrish, Lance 27
Pasculli, Len 142

Passeau, Claude 183
Patterson, Andy 103
Pedroia, Dustin 24
Peebles, Dick 1
Pena, Alejandro 149
Pennock, Herb 43, 50, 159–160
Perkins, W.G. 103
Perry, Gaylord 3, 60, 67–68, 143, 149, 171, 174
Peterson, Robert 101–102
Pettitte, Andy 185
Pfiester, Jack 41, 1116, 192
Phelps, Ed 117
Phillippe, Charles, "Deacon" 37, 118, 180
Piazza, Mike 24
Pierce, Billy 56, 182
Pierson, Dave 34
Pippen, Henry, "Cotton" 192
Plank, Eddie 24, 39, 67, 95, 99–100, 108, 120, 124, 159–160, 164–165, 172, 177, 184, 190
Podres, John 22
Politte, Cliff 129
Porter, Henry 90
Posada, Jorge 148
Posada, Leo 65
Powell, Abner 90–91
Powell, Jack 37, 90
Powell, Willie 107
Powers, Mike 165

Qualls, Chad 82
Quinn, Jack 77, 95

Radbourn, Charles, "Old Hoss" 35, 38, 89, 92, 94, 172–173, 180, 190, 192
Radcliffe, Alex 104
Rader, Benjamin 18
Ragan, Pat 43
Raines, Tim 72
Ramirez, Manny 147
Rariden, Bill 43
Raschi, Vic 184
Ray, Jim 2
Redding, Dick 106
Reese, Harold, "Pee Wee" 22, 56
Reiser, Pete 56
Remsen, Jack 24
Reulbach, Ed 39, 42, 100, 115
Reuss, Jerry 176, 180–191
Rewers, Chris 134
Reynolds, Allie 52, 56
Richards, Paul 59
Richardson, Bobby 59
Richmond, Lee 157–158

Name Index

Rickey, Branch 54
Rigler, Cy 133
Ripken, Cal 118, 152
Rivera, Mariano 129
Rixey, Eppa 50, 162
Roberts, Leon, "Bip" 80
Roberts, Robin 56, 58, 166–167
Robinson, Brooks 24, 59
Robinson, Frank 24
Robinson, Jackie 54, 102, 152
Robinson, Wilbert 24
Rodriguez, Ivan 27
Rodriguez, Nerio 5–6
Roe, Preacher 184
Rogan, Wilber, "Bullet Joe" 105, 107
Rogers, Steve 70
Rose, Pete 66
Roth, Braggo 136
Rothe, Emil 95–96
Roush, Edd 95
Rudolph, Dick 125
Ruether, Dutch 184
Ruffing, Charles, "Red" 47, 50, 189, 193
Rusie, Amos 25, 164–165
Russell, Allen 48
Ruth, Babe 43, 46–48, 57, 101, 120, 123, 139, 152, 159–160, 173
Ruthven, Dick 180
Ryan, Jimmy 93
Ryan, Nolan 16, 29, 64, 67, 77–79, 132, 145–146, 167–169, 176, 181

Saarloos, Kirk 130, 148
Sabathia, C.C. 82–83, 129
Saberhagen, Brett 183
Sain, Johnny 52, 70, 184
Salmon, Tim 126
Sambito, Joe 181
Sanchez, Jonathan 83
Sandecki, Ray 65
Sanders, Ben 157
Sanford, Jack 184
Santana, Johan 83, 182
Santiago, Jose 176
Sawamura, Eiji 108–109
Schaefer, Germany 141
Schalk, Ray 27
Schilling, Curt 24, 182
Schoendienst, Al, "Red" 177–178
Schoeneweis, Scott 193
Schourek, Pete 181
Schrecongost, Ossee 118
Schultz, Howie 56

Score, Herb 193
Scott, Ed 37
Scott, Mike 83, 145–145, 181
Seaton, Tom 96, 101, 157, 189
Seaver, Tom 64, 67, 146, 167–169, 171, 176
Sebring, Jimmy 117
Seward, Ed 86
Shantz, Bobby 59
Shaw, Bob 184
Shaw, Dupee 23, 90, 157, 188
Sheckard, Jimmy 115
Shields, Jamie 182
Shocker, Urban 50
Shore, Ernie 123
Shoun, Clyde 149
Show, Eric 181
Siebern, Norm 177
Sierra, Ruben 146
Siever, Ed 123
Simmons, Al 118
Simon, Mike 43
Singer, Bill 190
Sisler, George 159
Skowron, Bill 177–178
Slagle, Jimmy 115
Slaughter, Enos 59, 177
Smiley, John 181
Smith, Bud 142
Smith, Dan 6, 181
Smith, Eddie 141
Smith, Eugene 107
Smith, Frank 121–122, 132, 149
Smith, Harry 117
Smith, Lee 183
Smith, Sherry 184
Smith, Zane 181
Smoltz, John 80, 83, 181, 183, 185
Solters, Julius 140
Sonnenstein, Andy 82
Sosa, Sammy 72
Sothoron, Allan 48
Sowders, John 94
Spahn, Warren 52, 56, 59, 67, 149, 166–167, 174, 176–178
Spalding, Al G. 13–18, 30–31, 34–35, 157, 187, 192
Speece, Byron 160
Speier, Chris 175
Spencer, Roy 24
Stahl, Chick 164
Stahl, Larry 131
Staley, Gerry 23
Staley, Harry 94
Stanka, Joe 110
Stankey, Ed 56–57

Starfin, Victor 108
Starr, Ray 53
Start, Joe 17
Stearns, Bill 14–16, 192
Stearns, Turkey 103
Steinfeldt, Harry 115
Stellino, Vito 64
Stengel, Casey 59
Stevens, Ed 56
Stieb, Dave 83
Stivetts, Jack 85, 176, 180
Stoneman, Bill 66
Stottlemyre, Mel 65, 181
Stratton, Scott 14, 180, 192
Strong, Joe 107
Strunk, Amos 120
Sudhof, Willie 37, 41
Sullivan, Billy 121
Summers, Ed, "Chief" 176
Sundberg, Jim 127
Suppan, Jeff 182
Surkont, Max 59
Sutcliffe, Rick 181
Suttles, Mule 103
Sutton, Don 61, 67, 168–171, 174, 176, 180
Suzuki, Ichiro 2
Suzuki, Keishi 108
Sweeney, Charles 90–91
Sweeny, Bill 43, 90
Swoboda, Ron 2

Taft, Pres. William Howard 124
Tanner, Chuck 170
Taylor, Harry 89
Taylor, Jack 41, 115
Taylor, Johnny 107
Taylor, Luther, "Dummy" 44
Telgheder, Dave 78–79
Temple Family Cup 179
Terry, Adonis 86, 88, 149, 180, 192
Terry, Ralph 184
Terry, William, "Memphis Bill" 180
Thomas, Henry W. 136
Thomas, Ira 136
Thome, Jim 147
Thompson, Dan 170
Thompson, Justin 189
Thorpe, Jim 134
Throneberry, Marv 59
Tiant, Luis 65, 183
Tinker, Joe 95, 115, 125, 177
Toney, Fred 25, 134, 149
Torre, Frank 78, 167, 177
Trachsel, Steve 182
Triandos, Gus 59
Trout, Paul, "Dizzy" 56

Name Index

Trucks, Virgil 56, 142, 150
Tudor, John 181
Turley, Bob 142
Twitchell, Larry 94

Umont, Frank 178

Valenzuela, Fernando 181
Vance, Dazzy 50
Vander Meer, Johnny 56, 138–139
Van Slyke, Andy 24
Van Zelst, Louis 120
Vass, George 132
Vaughn, Irving 54
Vaughn, James, "Hippo" 125–126, 134–135
Vazquez, Javier 189
Veach, Bobby 90–91
Veale, Bob 65
Veeck, Bill 104, 141
Ventura, Robin 24, 128
Verducci, Tom 146
Volquez, Edinson 182, 190
Von der Ahe, Chris 89
Voss, Alex 90

Waddell, Rube 36–37, 39, 67, 118–119, 164–165, 156, 159, 172
Wagner, Billy 130
Wagner, Honus 24, 36, 143, 117–118, 124–125, 162
Wakabayashi, Tadashi 108
Walker, Fred, "Dixie" 55
Walsh, Ed 34, 67, 108, 115, 120–121, 124, 155, 159, 164–165, 171–173, 176
Walters, Bucky 138
Ward, John Montgomery 91–92, 151, 158, 172
Warneke, Lon 50
Warren, Mike 142
Weatherly, Roy 140

Weaver, Jeff 182
Weis, Al 2, 64, 172, 180
Welch, Mickey 36, 38, 172, 180
Wells, David 131, 157, 181–182
Wells, Willie 103
Wendell, Tim 104
Werden, Perry 90
Wertz, Vic 152
West, Max 53
Westbrook, Jake 193
Weyhing, Gus 91–92, 157, 188
White, Deacon 34
White, Devon 146
White, Guy, "Doc" 121–122, 124
White, Will 38, 55, 87–88, 188, 192
Whitworth, Dick 106
Wickman, Bob 189
Wickware, Frank 106
Wilhelm, Hoyt, 59, 77, 148, 150
Wilhelm, Irwin, 98–99
Williams, Billy, 134, 154
Williams, Claude, "Lefty" 44, 126
Williams, Dick, 59
Williams, Jimy, 7, 148
Williams, Smokey Joe, 105–106
Williams, Ted, 60
Williamson, Ned, 87, 93
Willis, Dontrelle 128
Willis, Vic, 39, 67, 163–164, 175
Willoughby, Claude, 19
Wilmington, Casey, 91
Wilmington, Murphy, 90
Wilmington, Nolan, 90–91
Wilson, Art, 134
Wilson, Brian, 83, 182

Wilson, Don, 2, 66
Wilson, Fin, 101
Wilson, Horace, 107
Wilson, John "Chief" 43
Wilson, Jud, 103–104
Wiltse, George, "Hooks" 133–134, 149
Winter, George, "Sassafras" 155
Winters, Nip 106–107
Wise, Bill 90
Wise, Rick 137
Witt, Mike 71, 150–151, 157
Witt, Peter 156
Wohlers, Mark 149
Wolters, Rynie 13
Wood, Kerry 2, 146
Wood, Smoky Joe 120
Woolner, Keith 62–63
Wright, Joanna 145
Wright, Taft 140
Wyatt, Whit 52
Wynn, Early 23, 27
Wysong, Harlan, "Biff" 192

Yastrzemski, Carl, "Yaz" 66
Yde, Emil 176, 184
Yeager, Joe 157, 188
Yokely, Laymon 107
York, Tom 24
Youkilis, Kevin 24
Young, Cy 7, 36, 39, 42–43, 67, 99, 122, 131, 145, 151, 153, 155, 162, 164–166, 176, 180

Zachary, Tom 160
Zahniser, Paul 160
Zettlein, George 14–17, 31, 34, 157
Ziegler, Brad 81
Zientara, Benny 56
Zinn, Jimmy 44

www.ingramcontent.com/pod-product-compliance
Ingram Content Group UK Ltd.
Pitfield, Milton Keynes, MK11 3LW, UK
UKHW042004140426
5217IPUK00015B/982